Urbanization in Developing Countries

Latin American Urbanization

T0382612

Urbanization in Developing Countries

edited by Kenneth Little

V. F. Costello: *Urbanization in the Middle East*
Josef Gugler and William G. Flanagan: *Urbanization and Social Change in West Africa*
Hal B. Levine: *Urbanization in Papua New Guinea*
Malcolm Cross: *Urbanization and Urban Growth in the Caribbean*
Peter Lloyd: *The 'Young Towns' of Lima: Aspects of Urbanization in Peru*
Douglas Butterworth and John K. Chance: *Latin American Urbanization*

Latin American Urbanization

DOUGLAS BUTTERWORTH
University of Illinois at Urbana-Champaign

JOHN K. CHANCE
University of Denver

CAMBRIDGE UNIVERSITY PRESS

Cambridge
London   New York   New Rochelle
Melbourne   Sydney

CAMBRIDGE UNIVERSITY PRESS
Cambridge, New York, Melbourne, Madrid, Cape Town, Singapore,
São Paulo, Delhi, Dubai, Tokyo

Cambridge University Press
The Edinburgh Building, Cambridge CB2 8RU, UK

Published in the United States of America by Cambridge University Press, New York

www.cambridge.org
Information on this title: www.cambridge.org/9780521281751

First published 1981
Re-issued in this digitally printed version 2010

A catalogue record for this publication is available from the British Library

Library of Congress Cataloguing in Publication data
Butterworth, Douglas, 1930–
Latin American urbanization.
(Urbanization in developing countries)
Bibliography: p.
Includes index.
1. Urbanization – Latin America. 2. Latin
America – Social conditions. 3. Migration, Internal –
Latin America. 4. Rural-urban migration – Latin
America. I. Chance, John K., joint author. II. Title.
HT127.5.B87 307.7′6′098 80–18486

ISBN 978-0-521-23713-0 Hardback
ISBN 978-0-521-28175-1 Paperback

Contents

Preface

Since the era of World War II the cities of Latin America have grown at an extremely rapid pace, and more people than ever before have made the decision to become urban dwellers. In this respect, Latin America conforms to the pattern found in many developing regions of the Third World, where opportunities for leading a satisfying life in traditional small villages and towns appear to many to be decreasing in direct proportion to the burgeoning development in the cities. That this continues to be true for many in the face of severe urban housing shortages, overcrowding, lack of public services, and often appalling health conditions is all the more remarkable. Rapid urban growth may be tapering off in North America and Western Europe, but in Latin America it continues unabated with no end in sight. Although Latin America's total population increased approximately 2.8 percent annually between 1960 and 1970, rural regions grew by only 1.3 percent annually. During that same decade, urban population increased from 103 million to 158 million; as a percentage of the total, urban population rose from 48.4 percent in 1960 to 55.9 percent in 1970. These trends are discussed further in Chapter 1; suffice it to say here that the most important demographic fact in contemporary Latin America well may be the mass movement of people from rural areas to urban centers (Thomas 1973: i).

City life and the social transformations promoted by the urbanization process thus constitute one of the most formidable challenges to social scientists today. But the newness of many aspects of the mushrooming metropolises of Latin America should not make us forget that the urbanization process in this region has deep historical roots, in some areas reaching back into pre-Hispanic times. With perhaps some exaggeration, Friedmann and Wulff have charged that "historical studies are antithetical to the practice of contemporary social science with its self-confident commitment to the present" (1974: 2). Taking note of culture areas that once supported flourishing civilizations that ultimately perished, those authors submit that a view of the transitoriness of cities and the life they sustained provides us with a perspective on the period of social change through which we ourselves are passing.

In this book we try to show the relevance of the history of Latin American urbanization as unearthed by archaeologists, historians, and ethnohistorians to the more immediate concerns of social anthropologists, sociologists, political scientists, economists, social psychologists, demographers, and geographers. In the most general terms, our point of reference is the broad field of urban studies, which is composed of contributions by specialists from all these disciplines. However, we wish to make clear at the outset that both of us are anthropologists. Although we draw on work done in other disciplines, this book is biased in favor of urban anthropology.

This, then, is a book about people. The reader will find that with the exceptions of the chapters on pre-Hispanic times, colonial cities, and social classes, most of the people dealt with in this work are poor. Many of them have only recently arrived from rural peasant and proletarian communities; very few of them have completely severed their ties with the country, even after many years of urban residence. While this bias toward the urban lower class has caused an unfortunate lag in studies of urban elites and the middle class, it is nonetheless readily understandable when one considers how anthropologists first became interested in urban studies.

Apart from the long-standing interest in the origins of cities and the rise of civilization, urban anthropology has been most concerned with the process of rural–urban migration and the adaptations of rural migrants to city life. This is, of course, a natural outgrowth of the long anthropological tradition of rural community studies, and one might say that anthropologists are still in the habit of seeing the city from the bottom up. In the case of Latin America, where most migrants come from peasant backgrounds and are rarely strangers to the city, urban research is often inseparable from the general field of peasant studies.[1]

Anthropological studies of urban social organization in Latin America are likewise most abundant for recently arrived mestizo and Indian migrants in the large national capitals, particularly Mexico City and Lima, Peru. The nature of the rural–urban interface and the concept of adaptation are important parts of all these studies. Neighborhoods or urban barrios and squatter settlements and shanty towns have also received much attention in Latin America. In these settings anthropologists are best able to employ their traditional methodology of participant observation and the community study approach. Underlying many of these studies are an interest in the grass-roots political organization (or lack of it) of the urban poor and a concern for the many problems they face in making a living and simply surviving in the city. Many urban research projects, therefore, have an applied aspect, and many others are designed with specific policy objectives in mind.

In general, anthropologists have been more concerned, for better or for worse, with the process of urbanization than with the nature of urbanism per se. "Urbanization" has two contrasting meanings. As used in this book, it refers to the progressive concentration of people and power in nucleated urban settlements and the attendant elaboration of city life styles. On the other hand, urbanization may also refer to the spread of these life-styles and the technology and conditions that make them possible into the rural hinterland. We will consider one facet of this process in the chapter on return migration to rural villages, but in other respects this topic lies beyond the scope of this book.

While the concept of urbanization, however it is used, always implies a process of social transformation through time, the notion of urbanism refers to a state, without regard to the time element. "Urbanization" employs a processual, diachronic perspective to analyze the process of becoming urban, while "urbanism" is structural and synchronic and refers to what it means to *be* urban. We feel that Latin American urbanism has been relatively neglected by social scientists, particularly by anthropologists. Studies of migration and migrant adaptation to Latin American cities abound, but well-informed works on aspects of urban social organization, the class structure, and urban typologies and comparisons (see Rollwagen 1975) are in short supply. This imbalance puts the cart before the horse: Without a detailed understanding of what city life in its many facets is all about, it is that much more difficult to study the process of urbanization, of becoming urban. In the chapters on colonial cities and contemporary social classes we make an effort to correct these deficiencies, insofar as the data permit, and call attention to one important aspect of Latin American urbanism – social stratification – which deserves much more attention from social scientists than it has heretofore received.

There are, on the other hand, purposeful omissions and contractions in this work brought on by considerations of space, scope, and focus. Among these we might mention exclusion of coverage of the Caribbean area. We are concerned almost exclusively with Brazil and the Spanish-speaking mainland nations.

Given these limitations, we have attempted to pull together and synthesize a large number of studies dealing with a variety of facets of the urban experience. Throughout, we seek not only to synthesize and comment on what has been done, but also to note significant questions that have been raised and to draw attention to what has not been done.

It is well to stress at the outset that at present there exists no adequate "theory" of urbanization or urbanism that can explain the Latin American (or any other) case, nor is there likely to be one for some time. Urban studies ranks as one of the youngest academic fields of study, and it is still far from attaining any sort of theoretical maturity. Social scientists interested in urban phenomena today bring to their research a large variety of theoretical interests and methodological approaches. Except for a section on migration theory, we limit ourselves to the major paradigms in the field and emphasize those used in urban anthropology.

The first formulation of urbanism as a concept in the early years of urban studies in the 1920s and 1930s was but a step removed from the still popular (and ethnocentric) stereotypes of the city as a den of iniquity that inevitably corrupts and destroys, and the rural town or village as the bastion of human virtue. This negative value placed on city life (and the corresponding positive value associated with small rural communities) has a long history in Western thought, dating at least from the time of the ancient Greeks. Traces of this bias can be found in the works of the so-called Chicago School of urban sociology, which was instrumental in launching the field of urban studies in the United States. This point of view and related matters are discussed in Chapter 5.[2]

Since the 1930s, much empirical urban research in Latin America and elsewhere has shown that, contrary to these stereotypes, urbanization does not always lead to the breakdown of traditional forms of organization, nor does it necessarily promote social instability or normlessness. Many of these findings are discussed in various chapters of this book. This rejection of some of the older notions about urbanism and urbanization, however, has left us momentarily in a kind of theoretical vacuum in which no comprehensive paradigm has yet appeared. In recent years, central place theory in geography has helped to instill an awareness that "cityness" is a relative thing and that there are probably no cross-culturally valid measures for deciding what is urban and what is not. But we are still a long way from coming to grips theoretically with the varieties of the urban experience and the reasons behind it.

In this volume we employ a broad, relativistic definition of the city, specifically rejecting formulations that rely on population size or density (see Chapter 1). This is not a book on theory, however: We are more interested in interpreting processes of change in the cities of Latin America than in putting forth any theory of urbanization. Accordingly, important concepts and definitions are introduced and defined as they become relevant in different parts of the text.

Both of us regard urban studies – urban anthropology in particular – as one of the most exciting fields in the social sciences today. It has its growing pains like any young science, but these are more than offset by the joy of discovery that only pioneering research in a relatively new field can provide. With respect to Latin American cities, it is now clear that they are not likely to repeat the stages of urban industrial development experienced in Western Europe and North America. This possibility is effectively ruled out by Latin America's extraordinarily high rate of population growth and the political and economic difficulties experienced by dependent nations vis-à-vis the dominant world powers of the United States and the Soviet Union. The future of the cities south of the Rio Grande is therefore unknown and presents a lively challenge to social scientists. Equally challenging are the human and social problems engendered by rampant urbanization where national, technological, and economic infrastructures are barely able to keep pace with the influx of bodies and demands for work. Urbanization in Latin American can be, depending on one's point of view, either highly fascinating or extremely vexing. We hope this book will serve as an introduction to the subject for people of both persuasions.

We wish to thank Joan Wells Lathrap for her assistance in many aspects of the preparation of this manuscript. She, Cheleen Mahar, and Iria d'Aquino helped with the organization of Chapter 8, "Housing, Poverty, and Politics." Johnetta Pell Bohn contributed to the section on migrant adaptation and Marcelo Naranjo helped research this and other aspects of rural-to-urban migration. Finally, Kathleen Fine was invaluable in typing and editing, in addition to offering valuable comments, particularly those about women and urbanization. Ms. Fine also prepared the index.

D.B. and J.K.C.

Principal cities in Latin America

1. The city in history

In 1519 Fernando Cortés and a band of some 200 Spaniards arrived on the Gulf coast of Mexico. After founding the city of Veracruz, Cortés and his men rounded up several thousand Indian allies and began their march inland toward the Aztec capital of Tenochtitlán. Two years later, this great city came under Spanish control and served as the center of an expanding colonial territory. Roughly a decade later, the process was repeated high in the Peruvian Andes when Francisco Pizarro and his followers marched into the Inca capital of Cuzco and declared it Spanish territory. Meanwhile, French and Portuguese explorers had touched on the coast of Brazil in search of commodities for trade, and the latter soon founded a number of port towns which would later become major urban centers.

Latin American civilization and its cities are commonly conceived of as variants of Iberian forms implanted some 450 years ago by the Spanish and Portuguese conquistadores. In some respects this is correct, for groups and individuals of Hispanic cultural background provide the driving force behind urban development in Latin America today, as they have for centuries. However, we must not forget that urbanization in Latin America did not begin with the coming of Europeans, nor does it end with them. The hundreds of thousands of rural peasant migrants who are currently swelling the cities and towns of Mexico, Guatemala, and the Andean nations bring with them cultural components with roots in pre-Hispanic civilizations that produced some spectacular urban achievements.

It is true that the territory now occupied by Brazil, Argentina, Uruguay, Paraguay, Chile, Venezuela, and other countries of northern South America never saw the indigenous development of societies that might be termed urban. But the Andean mountain chain and adjoining coastal strip in western South America, together with Mesoamerica (the area of indigenous "high culture" that covers central and southern Mexico, Guatemala, Belize, El Salvador, Honduras, and part of Costa Rica), tell a different story. These regions comprise the two cradles of New World civilization, and it was here that the first true cities in the Americas emerged.

The most vivid written testimony of the remarkable urban civilizations of the Incas, Aztecs, and other peoples encountered by the Spaniards is found in writings and chronicles of the sixteenth century, which frequently speak of these newly discovered societies in a tone bordering on awe. Few experiences of the early explorers could match that of Fernando (Hernán)

1

Cortés and his men in 1519 as they crossed a high mountain pass between snowcapped peaks and gazed down into the Valley of Mexico. The sight of the Aztec capital of Tenochtitlán, a great island city with sparkling white and multicolored pyramids, far surpassed anything they had expected. In a letter to the Spanish king soon thereafter, Cortés remarked that Tenochtitlán was as large as Seville or Córdoba, dwarfing many Castilian cities of lesser renown.

But evidence of pre-Hispanic urbanization is not limited to the Spanish chronicles, to the traces of Inca architecture that remain in modern Cuzco, Peru, or to the fascinating remains brought to light by excavations in Mexico City. As current archaeological investigations are making increasingly clear, the Inca and Aztec cities represent only the end point of many centuries of urban development. Nevertheless, pre-Hispanic urbanization is a separate topic in its own right and will not be dealt with in detail in this volume.[1] In this chapter we will touch on only a few highlights before moving on to the colonial period, for it was during the sixteenth, seventeenth, and eighteenth centuries that the social foundations of the modern cities were established, foundations which were predominantly European in character. Before proceeding, however, it is important to clarify the meaning we attach to such terms as "urban" and "civilization," for these concepts have attracted much attention and comment from archaeologists and ethnologists alike.

Cities and civilization

The late V. Gordon Childe (1950) coined the phrase "the urban revolution" to designate a development (or bundle of processes) in human history comparable in importance to the beginnings of agriculture that preceded it by several thousand years (the "food-producing" or Neolithic revolution). He listed ten criteria that he believed would be present in every truly urban society: (1) an increase in settlement size toward "urban"proportions; (2) centralized accumulation of capital through tribute or taxation; (3) monumental public works; (4) a system of writing; (5) advances toward exact and predictive sciences; (6) long-distance trade in luxuries; (7) a system of class stratification; (8) full-time craft specialization; (9) the appearance of representational (naturalistic) art; and (10) the appearance of the *state* – a politically organized society based on territorial principles rather than kinship.

In stressing these features, Childe clearly had in mind much more than a particular type of human settlement. He was addressing himself to the initial appearance of that characteristically large, complex, socially stratified, and heterogeneous kind of society that engulfs all of us today – what anthropologists commonly refer to as *civilization*. Thus, according to

Childe, the development of cities always occurs hand-in-hand with the growth of civilization as a whole – the first trait is always found in association with the remaining nine – and it is impossible to separate the two.

Soon after Childe formulated his concept (based to a great extent on his own archaeological excavations in the Middle East), it came under attack from many scholars, some of whom were puzzling over how to reconcile the high cultures of Latin America with such a scheme. To insist on writing as a criterion of civilization, for example, would eliminate the Incas from consideration. Others have questioned the significance of representational art and point out that not all of Childe's ten criteria carry equal weight (see R. Mc C. Adams 1966 for a fuller discussion). But of more immediate concern is the argument that, contrary to Childe's assertion, civilizations may exist without cities. The Mayas, who will be discussed in more detail below, are often cited as a case in point. Despite their renowned intellectual and artistic achievements, as reflected in their architecture, sculpture, and writing, the Mayas built few settlements that could be called large, permanent, or densely populated. As long as urbanism is defined primarily in terms of population size and nucleation, the Mayas and other similar cases must be classified as nonurban civilizations.

However, such an approach leaves us with the thorny question of how large and how dense a settlement must be in order to be called a city. Furthermore, how are we to control for cultural and historical differences in defining what is urban? We tend to agree with Richard Blanton (1976: 250) that it is futile to search for a set of universal criteria for defining the city and that we must avoid the notion that size and density are the most important indicators of urbanism. Instead, we define cities as *nodes of concentration* in a state society. This concentration may be reflected in large numbers of people and shelters, but this is not necessary. Of greater importance are the *nodal functions* (such as ideological, administrative, mercantile, industrial) that a given city performs vis-à-vis the society of which it is a part, functions that by definition will be absent or little developed in small towns and villages in the same society. Thinking along similar lines, Richard G. Fox (1977: 24) has defined the city as "a center of population concentration and/or a site for the performance of prestige and ceremonial functions found in a state society." Particularly in nonindustrial settings, cities may be distinguished not so much in terms of their populations or economic specializations, but in terms of their ritual status and political power.

Such was the case, we believe, with many Maya "ceremonial centers" in ancient Mesoamerica. While these centers supported few full-time residents, they nevertheless exercised important functions that served to knit together the disparate segments of this complex society. In Fox's terms, they were "regal-ritual cities" whose primary role in society was ideological. Maya urbanism was manifested primarily in the higher density of ritual and prestige functions in the ceremonial centers, traits that are difficult if not impossible to reduce to a quantitative index of urbanization.

Having thus taken a broad approach to the concept of urbanism, we find it less necessary to distinguish between urban and nonurban civilizations, for most complex, heterogeneous, and socially stratified state societies are apt to contain urban centers that will fit our definition. As we shall see, many of the first and largest cities in pre-Hispanic America took the form of city-states similar in pattern to those found in ancient Greece and Rome.

Pre-Hispanic cities in the Andes and Mesoamerica

The cities of ancient America paralleled in size and cultural importance those of antiquity in the Old World. Many centuries before the rise of the Inca Empire, for example, Peruvians were building the largest cities ever to be found in indigenous South America. Among the largest of these was Tiahuanaco, which emerged in the southern highlands around 200 B.C. at the Bolivian end of Lake Titicaca. A magnificent example of early urban planning, Tiahuanaco covered an area of at least 1½ by 1¼ kilometers and possessed a regular ground plan, massive buildings, pyramidal platforms for religious constructions, drainage canals, great stairways, and stone construction (Hardoy 1973: 330–2; Rowe 1963: 7).

Much later in northern Peru between A.D. 900 and 1463, there flourished a great urban state on the coastal desert that had as its capital at Chan Chan one of the most extensive and remarkable metropolitan centers in ancient America. This site has produced no impressive monuments or spectacular temples, but the ruins stretch over an area covering at least twenty square kilometers, including nine rectangular enclosures, some with walls over twenty-five feet high. These may have been residences of elite groups, for inside they are divided into symmetrically arranged rooms, courts, and plazas interconnected by mazelike corridors and narrow halls (Keatinge and Day 1974: 228–9; Moseley 1975: 37–40).

Curiously, the Inca Empire, which began to take shape in 1438, never attained the level of urban development manifest at Tiahuanaco or Chan Chan (the latter was conquered by the Incas in 1465 and absorbed into their empire). Cuzco, the capital city rebuilt by the emperor Pachacuti in the 1460s, was the only large metropolitan center built by the Incas in a vast empire that engulfed some six million people representing forty major linguistic groups.

At its height, the Inca capital contained an estimated population of between 100,000 and 300,000 inhabitants (Katz 1972: 279). The city was divided into two moieties – upper and lower – and into twelve sections corresponding to main provinces of the empire. Above all, Cuzco was an administrative center, and Friedrich Katz (1972: 281) and others have referred to it as a "city of bureaucrats." People could travel to and from Cuzco only on official business or with special permission from a state official. Commercial life, by comparison, was less well developed. Exchange of merchandise was in the hands of the state, and the rulers were less intent upon enriching the capital than they were on organizing their far-flung territories held together by an elaborate system of roads and some 170 administrative centers (some of them small cities in their own right) scattered throughout the realm (Morris 1972: 394).

Inca urbanism was very different from the pattern found in its contemporary, Aztec Tenochtitlán. The exaggerated enthusiasm of the Spaniards who saw the Aztec city in its glory is absent from the early Peruvian chronicles. The low stone frontages of Cuzco lacked the visual impact of Tenochtitlán, with its towering, brightly colored pyramids and platforms. These two very different cities were products of two contrasting strategies of empire building. The Incas were master organizers who redistributed state revenues throughout all parts of their empire. The Aztecs, on the other hand, enriched their capital city and left their conquered subjects to their own affairs as long as they met their tribute quotas.

While none of the Mesoamerican peoples ever put together a political empire comparable to that which dominated the Andes, it was in ancient Mexico that pre-Hispanic urbanization attained its fullest expression. As in Peru, the civilizations encountered by the Spaniards in this region were only the last of a long line of urban peoples dating back to the appearance of the Olmec culture on the Gulf coast of Mexico about 1500 B.C. The Olmec "regal-ritual" cities of La Venta and San Lorenzo, among others, functioned as political capitals and nodes of economic exchange and may thus qualify as some of the earliest urban centers in the Americas. The Olmecs were followed after the time of Christ by the Classic Maya, who made their home in the hot, humid lowlands of the Yucatan peninsula. Tikal, the largest Maya city, had an estimated population of forty-five thousand and covered a staggering 123 square kilometers at its height in A.D. 550 (Haviland 1970: 193). This was a metropolis of considerable influence, with a well-developed stratification system that included a hereditary aristocracy, substantial numbers of government functionaries and bureaucrats, priests, astronomers, clerical personnel, scholars, traders, potters, sculptors, and other specialists.

Contemporary with the Classic Maya were the great civilizations centered at Monte Albán and Teotihuacán in the Mexican highlands, where urbanization reached an unprecedented level between A.D. 200 and

700. In number of people and population density, both of these cities far surpassed the sparsely inhabited Olmec and Maya settlements (although Tikal may have rivaled Monte Albán in population). Both of these highland cities were supported by intensive cultivation techniques, and Teotihuacán, at least, appears to have been more socially complex than Tikal. René Millon (1973) has recently completed a detailed map of the entire site and believes that Teotihuacán was larger than imperial Rome, boasting a population of perhaps two hundred thousand or more in A.D. 600. "For more than half a millennium it was to Middle America what Rome, Benares or Mecca have been to the Old World: at once a religious and cultural capital and a major economic and political center" (Millon 1967: 38). In addition to 300 impressive ritual structures of various kinds, Millon has mapped more than 4,000 buildings, tightly packed in a planned fashion into an area of twenty square kilometers.

Teotihuacán was a splendid example of city planning and preindustrial engineering. Towering above the center were the great Pyramids of the Sun and Moon, the first a little over 200 feet high. The major axis of the city was the Street of the Dead, which at the north stopped at the Pyramid of the Moon and to the south ran over three kilometers beyond the city center. Not far from the pyramids were the city's two major buildings: the Great Compound and the Ciudadela. The first of these probably housed the government bureaucracy, while the second, of both political and religious importance, was most likely the home of the rulers (Millon 1976: 236–7).

The rest of the city, which was primarily residential, was laid out in grid fashion with an orderly appearance, even in areas of great crowding. There were dozens of barrios or neighborhoods containing 2,200 apartment compounds clearly designed for urban life in a crowded city. Each compound included several households that together contained an average of 100 people. At least 400 of these compounds were occupied by craftsmen, and others formed part of "ethnic enclaves" of recently arrived migrants or their descendants.

Also of note is the important role of commercial activity in the urbanization of Teotihuacán, for this was a trade center quite unlike the cities of Tikal and Cuzco, where most commercial activity was in the hands of the state. Teotihuacán housed a number of large, thriving marketplaces that must have attracted thousands of outsiders each day.

Oddly enough, this great metropolitan center was abandoned and in ruins when the Spanish arrived and had been so since A.D. 700. Monte Albán collapsed at about the same time, and Tikal and other Maya cities a few centuries later. All over Mesoamerica cities were abandoned, partially destroyed, or both. Yet urbanism never disappeared altogether in the Mexican highlands. When the Spanish came upon Aztec Tenochtitlán in

1519, what they saw was a city that had become great by imitating its many neighbors in the Valley of Mexico and beating them at their own game.

The Aztec tribe was a latecomer in the Valley of Mexico, a fertile area around the shores of five interconnecting lakes that supported many populous cities and towns that were constantly at war with one another. With the choice sites already occupied, the intruders from the north settled on an island in the lake and founded their settlement in A.D. 1325. This marshy, barren island did not seem to be a favorable site, but it possessed amazing potential, and the most highly urbanized city in the New World arose here in the short period of only two centuries.

In customary Mesoamerican fashion, the heart of Tenochtitlán contained the palaces and temples, including an imperial precinct for the residence of the emperor Moctezuma and his bureaucratic entourage. Extending outward from the center in four cardinal directions were avenues that divided the city into quarters, each with its own temple. The quarters in turn were subdivided into barrios.

Tenochtitlán was a warlike, predatory city–state that took what it could from the millions of people in central Mexico it eventually came to dominate but gave very little in return. All roads led to the capital, in which outsiders were easily accepted and integrated into urban society. There were large transient and immigrant populations that included craft groups, rulers, noblemen or warriors from subject states, and others displaced by war (Calnek 1972b: 348–9). It was not long before the island was filled to capacity, and although it was connected to the mainland by five causeways, more space was needed within the city itself. The Aztecs solved this problem by establishing new gardens and residential neighborhoods on *chinampas,* or floating gardens. By 1519, Tenochtitlán covered more than twelve square kilometers and contained perhaps as many as two hundred thousand people (Calnek 1972a: 105–9; 1972b: 348). At the time of the Spanish conquest, the Aztec capital was thus a thriving urban metropolis. It included a powerful aristocracy, a second tier of lesser nobles, a great mass of warriors, large numbers of artisans, merchants and transients, an agricultural peasantry, and the landless urban poor.

The ancient American cities varied among themselves to a much greater extent than we have been able to convey in these few pages. They arose for different reasons, occupied diverse ecological settings, and fulfilled different functions. Clearly, it would be unwise to attempt to reduce them to a single type.

In one important respect, however, all the early cities described in the preceding paragraphs were alike. Their sameness stems from the fact that they were all products of primary urbanization: each represented an extension and continuation of a particular cultural base that had its roots in the villages and towns of the hinterland. As Robert Redfield and Milton Singer (1954: 57–8) state, the cultural role of these cities was primarily orthogenetic: "It is to carry forward, develop, elaborate a long-established local culture or civilization . . . The orthogenetic city . . . is the place where religious, philosophical and literary specialists reflect, synthesize and create out of the traditional material new arrangements and developments that are felt by the people to be outgrowths of the old." This characterization applies as much to the warlike city of Tenochtitlán as it does to the sacred pilgrimage centers of the Olmecs; all were constructed, as it were, from local cultural materials.

In contrast to this type of city stands another, in which the principal urban role is to create and introduce original modes of thought, cosmologies, and social procedures into the society at large. Such cities are the result of secondary urbanization, a process carried forth by people of a different cultural background from those in the hinterland. In this setting, city ways and city ideas frequently come into conflict with those of the country folk, and such urban centers are termed "heterogenetic." Wherever this urban role is paramount, the mode of integration between city and country rests not on a common cultural consciousness but on the exercise of force or economic symbiosis. Heterogenetic cities were not absent in ancient America, for conquest and subjugation of alien populations were quite common in many times and places. But this sort of urban center is best exemplified by the expansion of the West, which brought with it great movements of people, a capitalist economy, and an exploitative colonial ideology. Almost overnight in Latin America, the orthogenetic Indian capitals were transformed into heterogenetic vehicles of Spanish colonial administration. For those who survived the experience, life would never again be quite the same.

The Iberian conquest and colonization: an urban venture

At the time of the conquest of the Americas in the sixteenth century, Spain was just beginning to acquire a national identity, symbolized by the marriage of the monarchs Ferdinand and Isabella. While commercial activity and the growth of cities were most advanced in the coastal areas of Catalonia and Valencia on the Mediterranean, the more immediate predecessors of Spanish American cities were in the heartland of Castile, the region that supplied most of the early colonists. Although the origin of cities in Castile can be traced back to Roman days (Morse 1962a: 475), urban development in this region between the eleventh and thirteenth centuries occurred hand in hand with the reconquest of Spanish territory from the Moors, who had occupied the area for several centuries. Thus, in contrast to other parts of Europe, most medieval towns and cities of Castile were founded for military reasons and did not develop from commercial activity, although the subsequent growth of many of them did stem from trade (Torres Balbás et al. 1954: 9). In Portugal, the pattern of urbanization was closer to that of northern Europe. The most important Portuguese cities in the sixteenth century were the agro-commercial, maritime towns that had developed along the coast in response to economic possibilities rather than to politico-millitary design (Morse 1965: 37).

In the strict sense, then, it is not possible to speak of a single, unitary Iberian pattern of urbanism that was imposed on the New World, for the Spanish and Portuguese programs of colonization differed substantially in this regard, especially in the early years. However, all Iberians have traditionally placed a very high value on living in compact, densely settled urban centers and the results of this cultural pattern are plainly visible in Latin America today. For the Spaniard, Portuguese, and Latin American, civilized life can best be lived in town, not among the countryfolk. Anthropologists who have studied peasant communities in the Mediterranean region have been impressed, even in the rural setting, by their compactness and density of settlement, which often create an impression of crowding to the outside observer. It is safe to say that at the time of the conquest most Iberians shared an urban ethos and a concept of urban living that set them apart from most of their neighbors in northern Europe. Spaniards especially were city-minded people, and Spain was vastly more successful than Portugal in putting its ideals into tangible form in the newly conquered lands.

Any observer acquainted with the variety and diversity of urban forms in Spain cannot fail to be impressed with the monotony of the urban landscape in traditional Spanish America. The physical and architectonic uniformity that characterizes hundreds of settlements south of the Rio Grande underscores two important aspects of the Spanish colonial experience. First, it was primarily an urban undertaking. Indian populations were subjugated and other areas colonized by the founding of cities and towns to house the Spanish population; no European peasant communities were established in Spanish America. Second, the Spanish conquest and colonization was above all a planned undertaking, directed almost from the start by the Crown and a creaking colonial bureaucracy that greatly enlarged over the years.

Nowhere is the effect of conscious planning more evident than in the physical structure of Spanish American cities, most of which are based on the twin concepts of the central plaza and the checkerboard pattern of straight streets oriented toward the four cardinal directions. Traces of this plan can be seen in Santo Domingo, the first Spanish city in America, which was established on the Island of Hispaniola (now shared by Haiti and the Dominican Republic) in 1496. In 1514 the Crown gave instructions to Pedrarías Dávila for the founding of Panama City, and in the decades to follow the same plan was repeated all over Spanish America in cities such as Mexico City, Bogotá (Colombia), Santiago (Chile), and La Paz (Bolivia), to name but a few. Royal orders for the laying out of new cities were promulgated in 1573 by Philip II (Nuttall 1922), and they are notable for their detail. They contain instructions for the selection of the site, the location and shape of the central plaza, the location of the church and government buildings, the construction of private housing, and measures for dealing with the natives.

A common feature of all early Spanish American cities was their exploitative and administrative character. They were vehicles of conquest founded for the purpose of colonial exploitation, and their political structure frequently preceded their economic base. In some cases, such as Veracruz, Mexico, for example, city governments even preceded the settlements themselves (Gibson 1969: 234). A definitive typology of colonial Spanish American cities must await the results of further research, but a few general types can be sketched here.[2]

The mining of precious metals, especially silver, was a principal goal of Spanish colonialism and the mainstay of a number of highland cities such as Potosí in the viceroyalty of Peru (see Hanke 1956) and Zacatecas, Guanajuato, and Potosí in Mexico. Large numbers of Indians, blacks, and mulattoes comprised the labor force in these settlements, which were often unstable and shared a boom town atmosphere. As Charles Gibson (1966: 122) has remarked, "The rapidly created communities housed a spendthrift, unsettled, or lawless class of colonists, a substantial number of whom were always prepared to move to other, and presumably more rewarding strikes."

Coastal cities, dedicated to oceanic commerce and military defense, were of a different character, although like the mining towns they contained large transient populations. Few of the mainland ports could match the size and importance of Santo Domingo and Havana in the Caribbean, but the cities of Veracruz in Mexico, Portobello in Panama, and Cartagena on the South American coast are well known. All of these were notable for their large fortifications, soldiers' quarters, supply houses, and commercial buildings. With the exception of Cartagena, which rivaled Havana in size, the population of most coastal cities fluctuated widely according to the rhythms of trade. Veracruz housed only a small permanent Spanish population but swelled enormously whenever the fleets arrived. In a similar fashion, Portobello mushroomed from a tiny settlement to "a huge, sprawling campsite at the time of its fair" (Gibson 1966: 124).

In a class by themselves were the highland administrative and agricultural cities founded in parts of Mesoamerica and the Andes with dense Indian populations. While not always as large or as prosperous as the mining towns during their boom periods, these more stable urban centers in many ways constituted the heart of colonial Spanish America. The Spaniards were immediately attracted by the Indian cities and the densely settled areas of peasant villages and small kingdoms. In the highland regions the Europeans found the climate and geography most to their liking, and only in these densely settled areas had Indian societies developed enough to support a large, nonproductive population. Although the first colonial capitals were erected on the ruins of Indian Tenochtitlán and Cuzco, most centers of Spanish population were founded anew, primarily for strategic reasons.

Highland towns were built with the labor of Indian workers, who were housed in separate, outlying barrios. The *traza,* or grid plan, formed the central portion of the town and was the center of all Spanish residence and all administrative and commercial activity. Normally reserved for the use of Europeans, the *traza* was theoretically off limits for nonwhite residents, although this rule was impossible to enforce. At the heart of the city lay the *plaza mayor,* flanked by the town hall (*casas de cabildo*) and other administrative offices, stores, the homes of the most prestigious families, and frequently the church. As the population grew, the city was divided into barrios or parishes, each with its own chapel. Following the practice of rigid separation of European and Indian, the indigenous population's quarters were always located at some distance from the center of the town and often constituted separate parishes. The casual, dense agglomerations of Indian huts and shelters on the edge of town stood in stark contrast to the proud, orderly Spanish center. The size and significance of the Indian barrios varied a great deal from city to city, and urban Indians will be discussed in greater detail later in this chapter. In general, all wealth and prestige was concentrated at the center of the city around the central plaza. As one moved outward toward the periphery, the buildings became smaller and less impressive and the neighborhoods became poorer and less prestigious, with increasing numbers of nonwhites among their inhabitants. This pattern of Spanish American urban ecology is still influential today in many cities, as we shall see in Chapter 6.

The two most important urban centers in Spanish America throughout the colonial period were Mexico City and Lima, both of them large political and commercial capitals. In Mexico City, Spanish and Indian urbanism merged. Although the Aztec city was almost totally destroyed, large numbers of its inhabitants remained in the outer portions of the original four indigenous quarters, now arranged around the Spanish *traza* at the center (Gibson 1964: 370). Lima, situated on the Peruvian coast at some distance from the densely populated highlands, attracted a much smaller Indian population. But it grew rapidly after it became Peru's capital city (supplanting Cuzco) and had access to the finest port on the Pacific at nearby Callao.

The contrasts in urban settlement between Spanish and Portuguese America reflect basic economic and political differences between the colonial powers. The initial goal of Portuguese colonization in Brazil was not the exploitation of large Indian populations – for the indigenous population was sparse – but individual commercial ventures. The Portuguese Crown was weak and lacked the means to plan and direct a large-scale urbanization and settlement program like its Spanish counterpart. Thus the principal Brazilian cities were modest agro-commercial settlements founded on the coast, such as Salvador (also called Bahia, Brazil's capital from 1549 to 1763), Rio de Janeiro, and São Paulo. The contrast between the Brazilian and Spanish American cities is symbolized in their physical designs. In contrast to the Spanish checkerboard and stately plaza, the Brazilian street plan was generally haphazard and contained as a central place only the *rossio,* "an unbuilt, generally communal piece of land without special architectural embellishment which is gradually absorbed into the city center as the urban limits expand" (Morse 1965: 37).

Despite their often shaky beginnings, Latin American cities remained the effective seats of power in their respective societies throughout the colonial period, as they do today. While these urban centers were parasitic in that most of their sustenance came not from within but from the hinterland, from Indian tribute and labor, mines, and landed estates, all wealth and power was funneled into the cities. Having briefly sketched the general nature of the urban landscape, we turn to a consideration of important features of social structure. Urban social history as a field is just beginning to emerge for Latin America, and as yet there are few studies that deal directly with social life. Consequently, the remainder of this chapter will emphasize the highland Spanish cities of Mexico City and Oaxaca and the Peruvian coastal capital of Lima, for they have received closest attention from historians and anthropologists.

Europeans, Indians, and blacks

The social system that began to take shape in the early colonial cities exhibited some of the characteristics of the old social estate system of feudal Europe, in which strata were defined by law and granted distinctive rights and privileges. In Spanish American cities, the equivalent of the three-fold European system of noble, clergy, and commoner was represented by the three ethnic groups of Spaniards, blacks, and Indians. In Brazil, where Indians were much fewer in number and never a significant component of urban society, the principal division in the early years was simply between black slaves and free whites. As we shall see however, this clear-cut pattern of ethnic stratification did not survive the sixteenth century.

Spanish emigrants to the New World came from all parts of Spain, and many of the first urban settlers were men of low social status (many of them artisans and small proprietors) who participated directly in the conquest of Indian groups and pacification of the areas in which they settled. These settlers soon were forced to rise above their different regional backgrounds and to forge a new kind of social system tailored to the colonial situation. Those with the most status and power in the sixteenth century were the *encomenderos,* holders of grants of Indians awarded them by the Crown for their participation in the conquest. Subsequently, many of these and others received titles of *hidalguía,* thus confirming the principle of seniority. To be able to trace one's descent from an original conquistador, encomendero, or city founder carried considerable prestige in colonial society, as it continues to do today in some countries.

As time went on and the colonial cities developed more complex power and occupational structures, the European population itself became more highly differentiated. As in Spain, it was important to be able to demonstrate one's *limpieza de sangre* (purity of blood) in order to lay claim to the highest positions in the social system. Any traces of non-Spanish or non-Catholic elements in one's ancestry were looked upon with disparagement if they became publically known. In time, the *peninsulares,* or Spaniards born in Spain, came to be distinguished from the *criollos,* or creoles, whites born of putative Spanish parentage in the New World. While the peninsular population of most cities remained small throughout the colonial era (for example, in 1792 peninsulares comprised less than three percent of the population of the Mexican cities of Oaxaca and Guanajuato [see Chance 1978 and Brading 1971]), the creole population grew rapidly and eventually comprised the largest racial segment in many cities.

Creoles eventually became the proprietors of many great haciendas and controlled the municipal governments (*cabildos*) in most cities, but the colonial bureaucracy, commerce, and mining, in Mexico at least, were dominated by peninsulares. Although landowning was certainly an important mark of status in colonial times, the great fortunes were more often amassed by peninsular merchants, and high-level political power remained in their hands as well.

Peninsulares and creoles alike in the early period, however, showed little interest in landholding and commerce, especially in the densely populated areas of Mesoamerica and the Andes. Here the immediate goal was the exploitation of the Indian population, either directly, through encomienda grants and tribute, or indirectly, through forced labor in mines and in the cities. In sixteenth-century Mexico, the whites in the cities made lavish use of Indian labor, and even the poorest colonist was relieved of domestic tasks. In the words of Woodrow Borah (1951: 19):

Manual labor and even many of the skilled crafts were held to be beneath the dignity of Europeans so that for the service provided for the relatively small number of white artisans and Negro slaves, the white townsfolk ate food raised by Indians, clothed themselves in materials produced by Indians and in most instances worked into cloth by them, lived in houses built by Indians and largely furnished by them, and remitted to Europe specie mined and processed largely by Indians.

Many of the early urban settlers depended on their encomiendas for sustenance, despite the fact that their Indians were sometimes located at a distance from the Spanish towns. Gradually, however, this institution was converted into a right to collect a specific head tax on a certain number of Indians, and in the seventeenth century a system of rotating labor known as the *repartimiento* emerged to meet Spanish demands for manpower and personal service (Indian slavery in the strict legal sense did not survive the early sixteenth century). On any given day in the highland Spanish towns there were hundreds of Indian peons from a variety of indigenous communities. Many of them had had to travel great distances on foot over difficult terrain to reach the city and after a week's time would depart to make way for the next contingent. By law, all workers were to be paid for their services, but in fact most were not, at least not adequately. Some of them lived in makeshift quarters at the homes of their masters, while others involved in church construction or public works projects were probably housed in labor camps set aside for them. Since repartimiento personnel changed every week, there was little opportunity for permanent relationships of the patron–client or master–slave type to develop between the peons and the city whites. It appears that the system did not contribute significantly to the processes of urbanization, acculturation, or assimilation of the Indian population. Repartimiento was the chief means by which many cities were built, but it had no lasting impact on the urban social structure.

Another source of urban (as well as rural) labor was the West African slave trade, and black Africans were brought to Latin American cities from the early sixteenth century. Blacks in Latin America have always been more numerous in the coastal areas, where they were used most extensively as plantation laborers. Europeans found that Africans worked better in the hot, humid, tropical environment than did imported Indians from the highlands, and of course there was less need for slave labor in the more thickly inhabited mountain districts. Indian mortality was also an important factor. On the Peruvian coast, for example, the Indian population succumbed to European diseases at a higher rate than in the highlands, and consequently Lima came to rely heavily on black labor. By 1636 Lima had a population of 27,394, over half of which was composed of blacks and mulattoes. In contrast, Mexico City, a larger urban center, had numerically more people of color, but proportionally fewer blacks and many more Indians because of its location (Bowser 1975: 335).

In Brazil, a large proportion of black slaves was put to work on the sugar plantations of the northeast coast. The cities of Salvador (Bahia) and Recife were the centers of the slave trade until mining in Minas Gerais attracted many slaveholders to Rio de Janeiro. Today, African cultural influence and the Negroid physical type are stronger in the northeast coast, especially in Salvador, than in any other region of Brazil. "In fact the mulatto has been called the regional type of the Northeast; certainly, a few aristocratic families have preserved their European lineages and appearance, but the vast majority of the people of the region are to some degree racially mixed" (Wagley 1971: 33). Other Spanish port cities such as Cartagena and Veracruz also contained significant numbers of blacks and mulattoes. As the colonial period wore on, increasing numbers of slaves were freed and more of them entered a variety of skilled and semiskilled occupations. Urban blacks and mulattoes were at an advantage compared to their rural counterparts and were absorbed more quickly into Spanish colonial society.

Urban Indians in colonial Spanish America

Writing about sixteenth-century Peru, James Lockhart (1968: 207–8) notes that

At any time from the early 1540s on, the Spanish cities were surrounded by a forest of huts which contained three different kinds of Indians making up a single continuum: organized tribute parties, individual migrants seeking temporary or permanent work, and permanent personal servants of the Spaniards.

In Lima, the largest indigenous section, El Cercado, was located outside of the city walls (Spalding 1970: 646), but a significant number of urban Indians lived in Spanish homes, especially the servants and concubines. Highland Cuzco, the old Inca capital, presented a different situation. Here there was both *rancho* living (on the edge of town) and living with Spaniards, but many Indian servants also lived in substantial private dwellings on lots they owned themselves (Lockhart 1968: 217).

Virtually all the Spanish cities in Mexico also possessed outlying Indian barrios. The small provincial city of Oaxaca, for example, was surrounded by Indian settlements on three sides, and in a dispute with the conquistador Fernando Cortés, the Spanish residents complained that he had ordered the Indians to crowd the city until it was uncomfortable for whites to enter and leave it (Chance 1978: 38). It is safe to say that no other Spanish town in the Americas surpassed Mexico City in the size of its Indian sector. In addition to the Mexican capital's four indigenous barrios, there were also the fringe settlements of San Juan Tenochtitlán and Santiago Tlatelolco, each of which had its own Indian municipal government (Gibson 1964: 371). Particularly in Mexico City, it appears that the Indian barrios were undesirable places to live. Charles Gibson (1964: 383–4) has documented the Spanish neglect of the urban Indian population of the Mexican capital:

In the eighteenth century the number of homicides was reported to have increased, and the Spanish government specified severe punishment for Indians who carried arms. Spaniards spoke repeatedly in late colonial times of the vile, vicious, fetid, homeless, and unclothed population of the city, living in filth and disease and drunkenness. Humboldt estimated in the first years of the nineteenth century that ten or fifteen thousand of the city's inhabitants were sleeping in the open. The extreme urban squalor aroused repeated comment, in conjunction with observations on the depressed state of Indians and mestizos. It is clear from the accounts that urban poverty in the seventeenth and eighteenth centuries had a special character, distinct from that of the towns and countryside, and that large portions of the late colonial city were slums.

We do not wish to exaggerate the significance of this side of urban Indian life, but it is clear that like their modern counterparts, Mexico City and other colonial urban centers were not without a number of pressing social problems.

Certainly one of the most extreme hardships that the colonial Indian population was forced to endure was disease. Lacking resistance to the new diseases introduced by blacks and Europeans, millions of Indians perished in the Americas during the sixteenth and seventeenth centuries. Although there is reason to believe that the urban Indian populations may have been less vulnerable to epidemics than the rural masses, this was not universally true. In Lima in the 1540s, for example, one contemporary observer estimated that disease and starvation caused the deaths of two or three thousand Indians each year (Lockhart 1968: 217). By 1614, the city's Indian population consisted of only 1,978 persons, despite continued immigration from the countryside (Spalding 1970: 646).

Thanks to the painstaking analysis of Charles Gibson (1964: 377–81), Mexico City is again our best-documented case, and here the decline in Indian population was steep. From a total of between 250,000 and 400,000 in 1519, by 1560 the city's Indian population had dropped to about 80,000. The decline continued until the mid-seventeenth century: In 1550 there were 22,000 recorded Indian tributaries in the city (a figure that would include only household heads and single adults), but by 1650 the number had fallen to slightly less than 8,000. These figures are all the more significant when we take into account Mexico City's steady growth in white population, which reached 70,000 by the end of the colonial period. Gibson (1964: 380) concludes that "the Indian population of the city outnumbered the Spanish by ten to one in the middle sixteenth century, that whites outnumbered Indians by more than two to one in the late eighteenth century, and that Indians approximately equaled the intermediate classes [i.e., mixed bloods who were neither Indian nor Spanish] at the end of colonial times." Mexico City was a unique urban center in many ways, however, and certainly not representative of Spanish towns in general. A contrasting situation is found in the city of Oaxaca, some 500 kilometers to the south, which by 1792 contained only eighteen thousand inhabitants. Here there is little evidence of population decline among the urban Indians. In-migration from the hinterland steadily increased the proportion of Indians in the city throughout the colonial period, and the sources rarely mention disease or epidemics, though they were quite common in the rural areas (Chance 1976: 617; Taylor 1972: 27–34).

Although large numbers or urban Indians worked at construction, public works, and menial chores as servants of the Spanish, many were independent. Many became artisans in Spanish crafts, and Indian weavers, tailors, shoemakers, bakers, and butchers were commonplace by the mid-sixteenth century (Chance 1976: 614; Lockhart 1968: 218). In Mexico City there were also Indian swordmakers, glovemakers, glassworkers, saddlers, bellmakers, blacksmiths, and tailors, the latter turning out such items as Spanish doublets, waistcoats, and breeches (Gibson 1964: 398). Indian artisans in Mexico were also regularly incorporated as journeymen in any number of craft guilds along with Spaniards and the mixed bloods (Chance 1976: 622; Gibson 1964: 400–1).

Although we can say that Indians were an integral part of the social and economic structure of Spanish colonial cities, it must not be forgotten that the whites considered them to be of low social status. They were part of an oppressed urban proletariat of manual workers and lived in segregated neighborhoods. Beyond this, we know too little about them to advance firm generalizations about their rate of assimilation to Spanish urban ways. The little data we now possess indicate that Indian assimilation and acculturation probably varied a great deal from city to city. In the highland Mexican cities, for example, descendants of pre-Hispanic Indian noble families quickly adopted European dress and customs as well as the Spanish language. They were accorded some of the rights and privileges of Spanish hidalgos and appear to have cast their lot with Hispanic urban society to the extent they could afford it. On the other hand, Lockhart (1968: 213–15) found that in Lima, three decades after the conquest, few Indian nobles spoke or wrote Spanish and many of them actively resisted Spanish influence. He believes that lower-class Indian servants and mistresses were more rapidly acculturated, since they were thrown into daily household contact with Spaniards: "By 1560 some former Indian concubines had become emancipated in a fashion, wearing Spanish clothes, living by themselves, and operating houses of prostitution" (Lockhart 1968: 216). Urban Indian acculturation in Peru seems to have been more rapid in the coastal cities, especially in Lima, where Spanish impact was strongest and the fragmentation of the displaced highland Indians was greatest. The pace of change moved considerably more slowly in Cuzco, where "a relatively intact Indian world . . . existed right within the Spanish city and made the Indians much more resistant to Spanish influence" (Lockhart 1968: 217).

It appears that the indigenous portion of Lima had been radically transformed by the late colonial period. Karen Spalding (1970: 647–8) argues that by this time at least some urban Indians had become virtually indistinguishable from the Spaniards. They dressed in European clothes, participated fully in the money economy and invested in urban property, purchased the same prestige items as their Spanish contemporaries, and even owned Negro slaves. Some of the Indian nobles were far wealthier than many Spaniards, thanks to inherited lands and other assets.

Despite the extensive acculturation, however, the bulk of the urban Indians never merged socially with the creole or peninsular segment in any colonial city. The Indians for the most part remained a distinct group in a decidedly inferior position, no matter how much Spanish culture they were able to absorb. This is well illustrated in Oaxaca, where even by the late eighteenth century almost two-thirds of the Indian commoner bridegrooms were still taking Indian women as wives. In contrast, only 11 percent married white creole women (Chance 1976: 627). Future research may well show that population proportions and other demographic factors were crucial determinants of the rate of Indian absorption in the colonial cities. The larger the indigenous population, the longer the process seems to have taken. Thus Oaxaca, a very "Indian" city, can be contrasted with the north Mexican city of León, located in a region in which the Indian population was much more sparse. The intermarriage between urban Indians and mulattoes in León was so great by the close of the colonial period that the two groups were on the point of coalescence and the Indians were fast losing their separate ethnic identity (Brading and Wu 1973: 36). This underscores the importance of race mixture as a component of the social system of the colonial Latin American city. We turn now to a case study of Oaxaca.

Colonial social stratification in Oaxaca, Mexico

Social stratification arises as a mechanism for the distribution of scarce resources in societies with productive capacities above the subsistence level. It is manifested in three basic sorts of inequality, which characterize all large, complex societies: inequality in material wealth, in power, and in prestige. Inequality in wealth occurs in situations in which certain social segments gain privileged access to basic resources and the tools and techniques of production, thereby restricting the access to these elements of other segments. Max Weber (1958: 181) calls such segments "classes," and we shall follow his usage. Power refers to the ability of individuals, groups, or social segments to influence or control the behavior of other such units. Finally, prestige (or in Weber's term, "social honor") refers to the social estimation in which an individual, group, or social segment is held by others. Unlike the class and power dimensions of stratification, the prestige axis rests wholly on subjective judgments made by people themselves and is therefore more difficult to measure.

Although these three hierarchies of stratification must be kept analytically separate, two or more of them may empirically influence one another or sometimes even coincide. In one society, for example, great wealth (high class status) may be a mark of prestige, while in another one's social honor may depend more on noneconomic factors such as family background or religious orthodoxy. Some societies may grant substantial power in the form of political office to their wealthiest citizens, while others may distrust such individuals and attempt to limit their influence in the public arena. In some cases, all three hierarchies may coincide – as they tend to do in relatively static societies with rigid class structures and little social mobility – but more frequently, they do not.

We will apply these concepts to the stratification system of one colonial Spanish American city that has been studied in detail (Chance 1978; Chance and Taylor 1977). We wish to answer such questions as: How were differences in class, power, and prestige expressed in the colonial urban setting? To what degree did the three hierarchies coincide or operate independently of one another? Was any one of the factors more important than the others in determining the general shape of the stratification system? And finally, how did the system change during the three centuries of colonial rule? The city in question is Oaxaca, a small provincial capital in the southern highlands of Mexico, which today has nearly two hundred thousand inhabitants. We do not yet know to what degree colonial Oaxaca's social structure was similar to that of other cities of its size, for there are few comparable studies. But Oaxaca did share a number of general features with other highland towns in Spanish America: (1) it was established in a heavily populated indigenous area and contained a permanent core of urban Indians; (2) it was an important administrative center with well-developed government and church bureaucracies; (3) its economic base rested primarily on landholding and trade, mining being of little importance; and (4) it was the only urban center of any significance between Puebla to the north and Guatemala City to the south in which virtually all segments of colonial society came together – Europeans, Indians, Negroes, the mixed bloods or castas, the rich and the poor, the slaves and the free.

Oaxaca was founded in 1521 by a small band of Spanish conquistadores on the site of an Aztec garrison that had been charged with collecting tribute from the many Zapotec and Mixtec town–states in the Valley of Oaxaca and surrounding areas. This multiethnic Indian population subdued, Oaxaca (or Antequera, as it was known in colonial times) began to grow, but only slowly. By 1600 it contained only about 2,500 people, and a century later about 6,000. A detailed census count in 1792 listed 18,008 inhabitants. During most of its colonial history, Oaxaca was a small, rather isolated urban center that based its existence at first on the exploitation of the region's large Indian population, and later on Spanish-owned haciendas and trade. Soon after its founding, Oaxaca became a focal point of interethnic relations and race mixture. Indian migration to the city began almost at once, and although black slaves were never numerous in this part of Mexico, they were imported to work as personal servants and help build the city.

Students of colonial Latin American society have customarily stressed the prestige dimension of the stratification system, arguing that ethnic and racial factors were the most important criteria of rank and that differences in wealth were of only secondary significance (cf. McAlister 1963, Mörner 1967). In Oaxaca, as elsewhere, the initial estatelike system of Europeans, blacks, and Indians was soon complicated by the appearance of individuals who did not fit neatly into any category. The Spanish conquest was carried out largely in the absence of European women, and the resulting ethnic mixture (referred to as *mestizaje* in Spanish) produced a racial pattern very different from that in North America. In Latin America, it was (and remains today in many regions) not a simple matter of being black, white, or something else; rather, a whole gradient of fine distinctions based on phenotype, ancestry, and other criteria was employed. The lack of white women during the early years was of course only one of many factors that combined to make the Latin American racial system distinctive. The multiracial heritage of the Iberian peninsula itself, the ambivalent attitudes of the Spanish and Portuguese toward racial differences, the prevalence of female concubinage and a double standard for sexual activity, the nature of the Indian societies encountered, as well as a number of demographic factors, all produced a system of race relations that is much more subtle and complex than that found in the United States and Canada.

In the first postconquest generation in Oaxaca, most individuals of mixed racial parentage (most of them with Spanish fathers and Indian

mothers) were simply absorbed into the group of one of their parents. But
during the latter half of the sixteenth century the boundaries separating
the three principal ethnic groups began to erode as the frequency of
interracial sexual unions kept pace with the growth of the city. The "mixed
bloods" soon emerged as identifiable pariah groups, categorically defined
as illegitimate (as most of them were) and inferior persons. The terms
mestizo and *mulato* (from *mulo* or mule), and the generic term *casta*
(literally, "caste," but not to be confused with the kind found in India)
came into general use to describe what was thought to be their inherent
moral and biological nature. In Lyle McAlister's words, "Their existence
was deplored. They really were not supposed to exist. In the eyes of most of
the white population they were lazy, vicious, irresponsible, and a threat to
social and political stability" (1963: 357–8).

This growing miscegenated population could not remain in social limbo
for long, however. By the middle seventeenth century the castas had
become too numerous to ignore and too necessary to the city's economic
functions to be excluded; they were thus accorded a place in urban society,
ranking in prestige between the whites and the black and Indian proletariat. The result was the *sistema de castas* in its classic form, a prestige
ranking of the entire population created by Spanish law and the white elite.
The strata in this status hierarchy were as follows:

     Peninsular Spaniard (defined as white and Spanish)
     Creole (defined as white and Spanish)
     Castizo (creole + mestizo)
     Mestizo (white + Indian)
     Mulatto (anyone with visible Negro ancestry)
     Negro
     Indian (if not *caciques*, or Indian nobles)

With minor modifications, this system represented the most important
aspect of social prestige in Oaxaca and many other cities during much of
the colonial period. The *sistema de castas*, as it was called, had both
cognitive and legal significance. It represented the most common conception among the ruling elite of how their society was stratified, and people
lower down on the hierarchy (and darker in color) thus had to contend with
it, even if they did not share the same outlook themselves. Furthermore,
the *sistema de castas* soon received legitimation in Spanish law, the
emerging mestizo and mulatto groups becoming the target of a number of
decrees from the Crown and the viceroys that attempted to limit their
social and economic mobility and permanently exclude them from positions of power and authority.

Race was certainly not the only factor that served to differentiate the
population, however, despite the inordinate amount of attention it has
received from historians. We need to look next at evidence of socioeco-

nomic criteria of rank and try to measure the significance of class differences. An understanding of this dimension of stratification will also help us to comprehend better the significance of the racial hierarchy and how the factors of race and class influenced each other. A major obstacle that must be noted at the outset is the lack of data on income and personal and family wealth in Oaxaca. Some material is available on the property of a few creole landowners and the fortunes amassed by a handful of peninsular merchants, but for most of the population direct information is simply nonexistent. There are other ways of attacking the problem, however, such as through the analysis of overall population proportions, marriage patterns, and the distribution of occupations.

If the class hierarchy in Oaxaca were subordinated to, or aligned with, the prestige hierarchy embodied in the *sistema de castas,* then we would expect the choice of marriage partners and occupations to be patterned along racial and ethnic lines. We would also expect that the numbers of people in the higher layers of the system would be small, for in preindustrial urban centers of this sort elites rarely average more than five to ten percent of the population. If the findings deviate significantly from these expectations, however, it would be reasonable to interpret them as evidence of a developing system of economic classes that at some points may have overlapped, yet did not merge, with the racially based prestige hierarchy.

That such was indeed the case in Oaxaca as early as the late seventeenth century is hinted at by statistics on the relative sizes of the mestizo and mulatto groups. Contrary to expectations, between 1700 and 1792 the proportional representation of the creole group rose from 31 percent to 37 percent of the urban population, while that of the mestizo sector remained stabilized at about 15 percent. The proportion of mulattoes actually declined, from 22 percent to 13 percent. These figures suggest two conclusions. First, it is doubtful that all the creoles occupied as high a place in the class system as they did in the prestige hierarchy, for there were simply too many of them, proportionately, for this to be so. Second, the figures call our attention to an obvious discrepancy between the biological facts of race mixture and the evolving system of racial categorization. Since other sources indicate that miscegenation was going on at an ever-increasing rate and that few castas were leaving Oaxaca, the decline in representation of the mestizos and mulattoes seems puzzling – unless, however, many such individuals were "passing" as white creoles and successfully concealing or minimizing the black and Indian elements in their backgrounds. This hypothesis seems more likely when we look at the racial classifications of marriage partners in the record books of the Oaxaca cathedral, sampled for the years 1693–1700 and 1793–7.

Intermarriage among strata in the *sistema de castas* was strikingly high in Oaxaca, averaging over 40 percent at the end of the seventeenth century and increasing slightly during the eighteenth. Due to the lack of European women, most peninsular bridegrooms married creoles, although such unions were not numerous because of the small size of the peninsular population. Most interesting, however, is that although roughly two-thirds to three-quarters of the creole and Indian males married within their respective groups, less than half of the mestizos and mulattoes followed this pattern. Indeed, the eighteenth-century figures show that 28 percent of the mulatto grooms married white creole women. Since it is safe to assume that most people choose marriage partners with whom they have something in common, it is clear that other factors besides race were operant in the stratification system. With substantial numbers of castas marrying into the creole group, we can also begin to understand how "passing" or racial mobility was achieved. If a mulatto did not have sufficient wealth or social connections to pass for white, for example, by marrying a creole he increased the likelihood that his children could.

One further indicator of the discrepancies between race and class in Oaxaca is found in the distribution of occupations. A detailed 1792 census shows that the stereotype of all the whites living a life of colonial leisure supported by slaves and Indian workers must be discarded. This is best seen in the fact that as many as 40 percent of the city's 2,058 non-Indian low-status artisans were creoles. Assuming that occupations may serve as a rough indicator of class position, the pattern seems clear: the tiny group of peninsulars were at the top of the economic hierarchy and had a firm hold on trade. The creoles in turn dominated the ranks of the wealthy landowners, but such people were few in Oaxaca and only a small proportion of the creoles (8 percent) were members of the city's elite. Fully one-half of the male creole labor force worked alongside mestizos, mulattoes, and Indians in a large variety of lower-status manual occupations.

The foregoing analysis, along with other considerations too numerous to mention in this brief account, leads to some concluding observations about social stratification in colonial Oaxaca. First, as a system of status ranking, the *sistema de castas* was not as rigid as it appears at face value. A degree of racial mobility was part of the system from its inception, and some individuals were able to change their racial identities (or those of their children) through strategic marriage alliances or accumulation of wealth. Class rank had a definite effect on racial status in that the more wealth an individual of color possessed, the better his chances were of passing as a creole and marrying into a white family. Racial categories in Oaxaca were surprisingly fluid and to a large degree situationally determined. This is the only plausible explanation for the continued growth of the city's white creole group, despite the small size of the peninsular sector. While theoretically all creoles were of pure Spanish heritage, by the eighteenth century it is doubtful whether there were any at all in Oaxaca who did not have some trace of Indian or black ancestry. The background of the following individual is probably typical of many social climbers who managed to enter the creole group, although not many of them had to resort to the courts to achieve their ends:

An interesting case in point is that of Manuel Yllanes, a master blacksmith who was born in Antequera [Oaxaca] and lived in the town of Zimatlán in 1791. In that year Yllanes was compelled to go before the authorities to verify his status as an *español* [creole] in order to avoid having his name listed on the mulatto tribute roll. He presented four witnesses, all of whom testified that he was of pure Spanish ancestry, of Old Christian stock, and free of any Indian, Negro, Moorish, or Jewish blood. Soon thereafter his status was confirmed by the city's procurador mayor [city attorney]. The following year, however, the official in charge of tribute collection in Zimatlán became suspicious and had the curate check the marriage certificate of the blacksmith's daughter and the record of his father-in-law's death. According to the church documents, both Yllanes and his wife were pardos [light-skinned mulattoes], and it was also learned that the blacksmith had intentionally falsified his wife's surname in the 1791 limpieza de sangre proceedings in an effort to conceal her mulatto heritage. In keeping with the ambiguity surrounding mulatto-español status in this period, even with this information the tribute collector was unable to make a decision and solicited the advice of the intendente in Antequera. [Chance 1978: 177–8]

Second, while the ultimate fate of the blacksmith is unknown, this rather fluid, racially based status hierarchy was crosscut by a system of economic classes that developed along with the *sistema de castas* during the seventeenth and eighteenth centuries. By the late colonial period, the distribution of property was out of kilter with the prestige hierarchy. All of the wealthy were white, but the middle and lower sectors of the class structure contained many creoles as well.

Third, upward racial mobility on the part of many castas would not have been as common if it were not for the downward economic mobility of many creole families. No doubt these conditions were behind many of the marriages between mulatto men and creole women. Oaxaca's elite was far from stable throughout the colonial period, and as merchants and land-owners periodically failed or fragmented their estates through partible inheritance, they increased the mobility chances of those below them.

Looking at this urban stratification system as a whole as it unfolded over the course of three centuries, it is possible to trace the changing emphasis on the three criteria of rank. In the sixteenth century, especially the first half, the power dimension was paramount, as one would expect in a conquest situation. The picture was relatively clear-cut: Spaniards were in control and power was categorically denied to all others. Power continued to be apportioned in this binary fashion until the end of colonial times, although the line between whites and nonwhites became blurred. The seventeenth century ushered in a preoccupation with racial pride as the *sistema de castas* emerged as the pivot of the stratification system. But it was also during this period that the internal contradictions of the system became evident, for we also discern the beginnings of a class system that crosscut several of the racial categories. Finally, by late colonial times, the system had evolved to the point at which the class structure rivaled the prestige hierarchy in importance. The growth of the urban economy and a boost in commercial activity placed more wealth in circulation, and many individuals were able to use their class position to improve their rank on the prestige scale. Modern-day Brazilians use the phrase "money whitens" to describe this process, as we shall see in Chapter 6.

The changing Latin American city

In most parts of Latin America, the colonial era ended as the boundaries of today's modern nations took shape during the first decades of the nineteenth century. During the late colonial period and the nineteenth century, Latin America's population began to increase "at a rate that has accelerated ever since" (Morse 1965: 38). Demographic changes, coupled with the liberalization of trade restrictions with the rest of the world, brought a period of economic development and urban growth to many regions. Almost everywhere, the roles of merchants, traders, and middlemen of all sorts became more prominent, and urban elites became more diversified. The elites did not change significantly with the coming of independence, however, for in most places this meant only a change in personnel, as creole nationals replaced peninsular Spaniards.

The nineteenth century thus brought with it an increasing emphasis on the accumulation of wealth. Gradually, money became more important than race. Slavery was abolished and the *sistema de castas* was done away with by the new national governments, although it is clear that it had already become obsolete. In many cities race mixture had made it exceedingly difficult to distinguish mestizos from creoles or mulattoes from mestizos. Large numbers of blacks, mestizos, mulattoes, and Indians melted into a general urban population that today simply regards itself as mestizo or *café con leche* (coffee with milk). This process was perhaps most advanced in the highland cities of Mexico, were today there are virtually no visible signs of the once-large mulatto populations; the only urban Indians today are recently arrived migrants, and there are no longer any criollos or "whites": there are only Mexicans, most of whom are regarded as mestizos. Prestige in most Latin American cities therefore no longer rests primarily on racial and ethnic affiliation, but is now determined by a host of factors, race being only one of them, that will be discussed in more detail in Chapter 6.

Various attempts have been made to classify cities and construct typologies of urban systems in order to throw light on how they have changed over time, either on a worldwide basis or on a more restricted national plane. In concluding this chapter we shall consider some of these and point out their relevance to the Latin American context.[3]

Richard Morse, one of the leading students of Latin American urban history, has distinguished two broad stages of urbanism for the entire region. The initial centrifugal phase began with the Iberian conquest and was characterized primarily by a flow of colonists and power outward from the newly founded European cities as they staked out and developed their hinterlands (Morse 1962a: 480). Later, during the nineteenth century, the scale began to tip, as urban development, rural population growth, and a general loosening of latifundiary ties greatly stepped up the rate of rural–urban migration. "The urban centrifugalism of colonial times has become centripetal. The Latin American city now reaps as it once sowed. The rural settlement patterns which it long ago created now give their stamp to the process by which millions are drifting and regrouping across the land" (Morse 1965: 41). Using the terminology of Redfield and Singer (1954), we might say that the trajectory of change has proceeded from a heterogenetic urban base to a more orthogenetic one. The colonial city was implanted from without and established sharp discontinuities between city and country, but today these differences are subject to constant erosion as large numbers of migrants from the hinterland transform the face of the urban landscape and form a bridge between the rural and urban settings.

This general shift over time must not be stated too simplistically, however. At best, the transformation from heterogenetic to orthogenetic (or centrifugal development to centripetal development) represents only a change in central tendencies, for both sorts of roles have always coexisted with varying degrees of intensity. We have seen, for example, that rural–urban migration was certainly not absent during the colonial period, and it would be fallacious to ignore the substantial influence of rural colonial Indian societies on the European cities founded in their midst. Likewise, inasmuch as the migration rate today has accelerated greatly, we cannot ignore the fact that the loci of technological and economic change are still in the urban centers and tend to spread outward from them. At any point in time in any urban society the relationship of the city to its hinterland will always be reciprocal and characterized by various sorts of give and take. The task of the social scientist is to find out what kinds of things are being exchanged and to study the functions of a given city in relation to its hinterland and the wider society to which it belongs.

This brings us to one final holistic classificatory scheme that we wish to examine. Many discussions of social change employ a basic distinction between preindustrial and industrial forms of society, and Gideon Sjoberg (1960) has made this the basis for his twofold typology of urban social systems. He claims that social scientists have been so preoccupied with the study of modern industrial cities that they have tended to ignore the preindustrial cities, all of which, past and present, exhibit some common features. Briefly, the preindustrial urban type, according to Sjoberg, is embedded within a feudal state apparatus with a rigid class system in which a small, urban-based elite exploits a large, subservient peasant population (Sjoberg 1952: 232–3). Cities serve as political, religious, and trading centers; they are characterized by a rigid, dual-class system of elite and commoners in which social mobility is at a minimum; members of the elite are primarily concerned with political and religious matters and shun all forms of economic activity as degrading and beneath their status; the city itself is divided into cohesive ethnic quarters; its economic structure is dominated by craft guilds that foster a high degree of occupational specialization (Sjoberg 1960: 323–8).

It is evident that some of these traits apply to colonial Latin American cities as we have described them and others do not. We do not wish to detail the shortcomings Sjoberg's model has for studying Latin America, because others have done this (see Chance 1975, Morse 1975), and Sjoberg himself explicitly excludes this region from his analysis (1960: 63). But because the temptation to think in dichotomous preindustrial–industrial or "traditional" versus "modern" terms is so widespread, we wish to enter a note of caution for the Latin American case.[4]

Although colonial Latin America surely was preindustrial in its level of technology, not all areas were characterized by a "feudal" social system as Sjoberg's preindustrial city model would assume (cf. Sjoberg 1952). While the notion of a feudal society resting on well-defined social estates and personalistic ties between landlord and peasant may have some validity for some of the rural areas, it does not hold up well for the colonial cities. Morse (1964: 144–5) has argued that classical feudalism based on a manorial system never existed in either Spain or Spanish America because of the strong urban tradition and the subjugation of culturally and ethnically distinct colonized populations. In both places, he points out, there was considerable latitude for the achievement of status and material wealth that was largely absent in the classical feudal societies of Northern Europe.

The case of colonial Oaxaca, which we have discussed in some detail, cannot be understood in the context of feudalism or in terms of Sjoberg's model of static, rigid, two-class social system. To the contrary, economic goals and activities frankly capitalistic in nature seem to have been the driving forces behind the changing class structure in Oaxaca.[5] The city's initial reliance on forced labor and head taxes gradually gave way in the latter half of the sixteenth century to a system of commercial capitalism operating through an open marketplace and cash nexus (Chance and Taylor 1977: 485). It was this crucial transition that made possible the racial and economic mobility, both upward and downward, that characterized this city throughout much of its colonial history. The system was surely not without its contradictions, for the Spanish elite continued to conceive of their society as essentially a feudal hierarchy of estates defined in racial terms: the *sistema de castas*. Nonetheless, this world view was consistently contradicted by the behavior of an increasing number of individuals as the class system gradually increased in strength. Although the timing differed from region to region and city to city, we suspect that these socioeconomic changes in Oaxaca had their counterparts in other areas of Latin America.

It does not seem to us that technological elements are necessarily the key variables behind the changes in social structure in Latin American cities over the past few centuries. We agree with Aidan Southall's (1973: 93–5) observation that many of Sjoberg's preindustrial urban characteristics are equally manifest in modern industrial cities and that the continuities between his two types appear to outweigh the discontinuities. Conversely, in colonial, preindustrial Oaxaca we have noted several features that have a decidedly "modern" look: a developing capitalist economy, an unstable elite, achieved statuses of various kinds, and a significant degree of social mobility.

In the final analysis, then, how are we to conceptualize the relationship between the colonial and the modern Latin American city and their attendant social systems? A definitive answer to this question has yet to be formulated, but it is clear that we must go well outside the city itself and examine other dimensions besides the industrial one. In constructing his typology of cities, Richard G. Fox (1977) places special emphasis on the nature and extent of the power of the state and how it affects the cities within its borders, and also on the degree of urban economic independence from the hinterland. For the time being, too much emphasis should not be placed on the differences between colonial and modern cities. The roots of modern city life in Latin America lie not so much in the adoption of industrial technology in the nineteenth and twentieth centuries, but rather in the Iberian conquest itself and the spread of a supranational economy based on the capitalist mode of production. The industrial development that followed in a number of key cities simply built upon the social and economic foundation established in colonial times.

The growth of cities

The expanding population of mainland Latin America from late colonial times to the present has been in large part the result of natural growth. However, urbanization in continental nations was associated with other, more complex, phenomena. Morse and his colleagues (1973) outlined population figures for eight countries and sixty-one cities in Latin America during the period from 1750 to 1920. The nations included were Argentina, Brazil, Colombia, Cuba, Chile, Mexico, Peru, and Venezuela.

Morse notes in his introduction to the national case studies that three tendencies appear to be particularly associated with urbanization: economic and demographic growth in the late Bourbon period; national independence and the tendency at the end of the nineteenth century to increase exports and foreign investments; and national unification. By the middle of the nineteenth century the total population of Latin America began to grow from perhaps 10 to 12 million people, at which level it had stagnated for a century or more, to around 22 to 23 million in the age of independence (1973: 12).[6] The population of Mexico, for example, increased from about 5 million in 1793 to 9 million in 1880 to over 15 million by 1910. For those same years, Mexico City grew from approximately 130,000 to 250,000 to some 470,000. Argentina's population expanded from only 300,000 in 1797 to 1,700,000 in 1869 to almost 8 million in 1914. Its capital had corresponding increases of from 24,000 to 178,000 to a million and a half. Brazil grew from a little less than 2 million in 1776 to 8 million in 1850 to over 17 million in 1900. Rio de Janeiro's population increased from 43,000 at the turn of the nineteenth century to perhaps 250,000 by the middle of that century to 800,000 shortly after the beginning of this century (Boyer and Davies 1973: 5–33).[7]

It will be noted that the percentage of people living in what eventually would become known as "primate cities," as compared to the total population of these nations, never exceeded 8 percent until the twentieth century.[8] Furthermore, the relationship of the cities to national growth was not always consistent. Rio de Janeiro, for example, had more than quadrupled its 1779 population by 1865. This number, in turn, nearly tripled by 1890 and by 1906 had more than quadrupled again: The 1906 population was nearly twenty times larger than that of 1799. At every stage, cities grew proportionately more rapidly than the nation as a whole. On the other hand, Buenos Aires increased its population by a factor of 4.5 in the period 1801 to 1869, but this rapid rate of growth was less than the national increase of 5.6 for the same period. From about 1855 on, the city's rate of growth accelerated so that the population of 1869 had increased nearly fourfold by 1895 and ninefold by 1914. National rates increased by factors of 2.3 and 4.5 for the same intervals (Boyer and Davies 1973: 7, 24).

Urban and national growth continued to accelerate during the first half of the twentieth century. Using the same nations for illustration, Argentina had over 16 million, Mexico 25 million, and Brazil 50 million inhabitants by mid-century (United Nations 1963: 152). Their primate cities had populations of 4.7 million, 3.4 million, and 3.0 million respectively (R. W. Fox 1975: 7; United Nations 1952: 203–6).[9] In 1950, 39 percent of the Latin American population, or 61 million people, lived in urban centers of more than two thousand inhabitants, while 61 percent, or 95 million people, lived in rural areas (Morse 1965: 42).[10]

The population of the primate cities of Latin America has, in general, been growing faster than that of the next largest cities. Rates of growth for cities of twenty thousand or more inhabitants have been, with few exceptions, very high. Average annual increases of 5 percent or more are frequent (Beyer 1967: 93; United Nations 1961: 100). By the 1970s, the cities proper (excluding the metropolitan areas) of Santiago de Chile and Rio de Janeiro had over 3 and 4 million people respectively. Buenos Aires contained about 3 million inhabitants within city limits and 8.5 million in the urban conglomeration; Mexico City proper equalled that 8.5 million and had about 12 million in the agglomeration area (United Nations 1976: 235–8).

R. W. Fox observes that there are two strong demographic trends in Latin America today: a continuing rapid rate of population growth and a great exodus of people from rural areas to the city. These forces, he states, are reshaping the economic and social fabric of each nation in the region, particularly in the medium-sized and large cities. The urban expansion (or, perhaps more properly, explosion) began in the 1950s and has since become increasingly strong because of two mutually reinforcing factors: sharply declining mortality rates combined with high birth rates, and the steady influx of rural residents (R. W. Fox 1975: 1).

Urban growth has outstripped national growth rates, Fox notes, so that in some cases (particularly Argentina and Chile) there is a question about the size of absolute population losses in the rural sector. Six countries – Argentina, Brazil, Chile, Mexico, Peru, and Venezuela – comprise 73 percent of the Latin American population and contain 639 of the approximately 800 cities of twenty thousand or more people in the region (Fox 1975: 2). In the early 1970s, some 55 percent of Peruvians, 58 percent of Brazilians, 61 percent of Mexicans, and 76 percent of Chileans lived in cities (United Nations 1974: 112–13).

It was projected that by 1980 all but eight of twenty mainland Latin American countries would have over half their populations living in urban agglomerations containing twenty thousand or more inhabitants, with Argentina having 83 percent of its people residing in cities (J. Wilkie 1976: 81). Projections made by the United Nations indicate that three-fourths of the 652 million Latin Americans would reside in urban areas by that date.

Yet it is still not clear which of the two factors – high fertility or migration – is more responsible for the urban explosion. Many students of the demographic situation in Latin America believe that half or more of urban growth stems from rural-to-urban migration (Beyer 1967: 95; see Morse 1965 for citation of authorities). However, the available data do not allow us to generalize, particularly since there are obvious extreme cases that complicate attempts at such generalizations. A United Nations report covering intercensal periods from the 1930s to the 1950s for selected countries discloses some of these extremes. In the 1941–50 period, Venezuela's urban growth was the result of an approximate 29 percent natural increase and 71 percent migration to cities. On the other hand, the same study indicated that over about the same period (1940–50) the population growth of Mexico's cities was attributable more to natural increase than to migration – 58 percent to 42 percent (United Nations 1961: 110).

A more recent investigation of three Latin American nations (Chile, Venezuela, and Mexico), using data from the 1960 censuses, showed that the growth of cities in those countries was due principally to natural growth (Arriaga 1968: 242). On the surface, the situation appears to be anomalous. Browning (1967: 86-7) states that fertility is one of the most problematic aspects of demographic change in Latin America. Until recently, most scholars considered urban fertility as a positive force in the modernization process. That is, from the available evidence, urban fertility rates were demonstrably lower than fertility rates in rural areas. This led to the expectation that as countries became more urbanized, fertility rates would decline. Because evidence indicated that this process occurred in the development of Europe and the United States, there seemed to be little reason to doubt that the same process would repeat itself in Latin America. Recently, however, this assumption has been called into question. Browning states:

Although the trend is not universal in Latin America and the data for recent years are still incomplete, an unexpected pattern seems to be emerging. Fertility has not been low and declining in urban areas; on the contrary, it has been rising. While urban fertility rates still remain lower than those in rural areas, the difference between urban and rural rates is being narrowed, but in such a manner that urban rates are rising toward the rural rates rather than the reverse or anticipated movement. [1967: 87]

In a study of female migrants to Guayaquil, Ecuador, Susan Scrimshaw (1975) examined the relationship between urbanization and fertility. Migrants go to Guayaquil from villages and towns in the sierra and on the coast and tend to be young. Sixty-five percent of the women are single when they migrate. Contrary to the assumption that migrants would have a higher fertility rate due to lower educational levels, Scrimshaw shows that not only does the average migrant woman have the same fertility (pregnancy history) as the long-term urban dweller (seven pregnancies, as compared with an average rate of nine pregnancies among rural dwellers), but they are, on the average, older when they enter into their first *compromiso* (engagement or trial marriage) or legal marriage (19.6 years as opposed to 18.4 for urban-born women).

Because the average number of pregnancies decreases by two within the same generation as rural women move to urban areas, fertility behavior has apparently been altered by the migration process. This may be related to the desire and ability of migrants to keep the number of children at a number they can afford to educate. It is also evident that migrant women have sought out contraceptive knowledge and utilized it effectively. Scrimshaw concludes that "migrants are an aspiring group who see the potential for the realization of some of their aspirations in urban values as probably related to comparatively low fertility" (1975: 325).

Finally, although modern developed countries have reduced both mortality and fertility in the process of industrialization, the situation in the presently developing countries (such as those in Latin America) is quite different. The decline in mortality does not appear to be closely related to economic and technological development. Mortality rates in Latin America have declined much more rapidly than the economies have developed (Arriaga 1970: 5).

2. Why people move

Definitions and concepts in migration

Migration is one of the three major components of population change; the others are births (fertility, natality) and deaths (mortality). Like being born and dying, the phenomenon of population movement is as old as mankind itself, yet it is the least understood of these processes. Difficulties of definition and conceptualization, and lack of a general theory, have, at least until recently, left migration analysis to those who are mainly interested in compiling tables of figures. Such tables, while impressive in quantity, usually tell us little about migration as a process.

In his presidential address to the Population Association twenty years ago, Dudley Kirk observed:

The study of internal migration is the stepchild of demography. Too little attention has been given by the leadership of our profession to the theory and measurement of migration, despite its role as the chief determinant of differences in population change and structure among local populations... In the words of one leading authority in this field, the majority of recent migration studies are "planlessly empirical and trivial in content." [Kirk 1960: 30]

P. A. Morrison notes that prior to about 1960 "studies of migration did little more than describe net migration patterns." For analytical purposes, these net figures were, he adds, little more than statistical fictions: "There are not 'net migrants'; there are, rather, people who are arriving at places or leaving them. Why they are doing so is central to understanding the dynamics of urban growth and decline" (Morrison 1977: 61).

Even a cursory examination of the literature on migration soon indicates why this situation arose: Migration is a complex phenomenon embracing aspects of many disciplines:

Migration is a demographic problem: it influences sizes of populations at origin and destination; it is an economic problem: a majority of shifts in population are due to economic imbalances between areas; it may be a political problem: this is particularly so in international migrations where restrictions and conditions apply to those wishing to cross a political boundary; it involves social psychology insofar as the migrant is involved in a process of decision making before moving and that his personality may play an important role in the success with which he integrates into the host society; it is also a sociological problem since the social structure and cultural system both of places of origin and of destination are affected by migration and in turn affect the migrant. [Jansen 1969: 60]

Migration is often a major symptom of basic social change. Demographer Donald Bogue maintains that every region and every nation that has undergone extensive industrial development has simultaneously undergone redistribution of its population (Bogue 1959: 486). Nevertheless, as Arriaga has noted, the reverse is not necessarily true. In less urbanized Latin American countries such as the Central American nations, urbanization is occurring without any industrialization (Arriaga 1968: 241).

It has been said, facetiously no doubt, that middle-class people move but lower-class people migrate. There are some subtle implications behind this aphorism. Most microstudies of movements of people in Latin America, particularly from rural to urban areas, have dealt with the poorer elements of society. Perhaps linked to this is an unconscious value judgment: "moving" implies a degree of permanency; "migrating" may suggest a kind of shiftlessness or temporary change of residence.

Population movements may be permanent or temporary, they may occur over long distances or short, and they may involve individuals or groups of various socioeconomic levels. Some writers consider any movement of populations, no matter what the distance or time involved, to be migration. Probably what most of us have in mind when we think of migration, however, is what Petersen (1975: 41) defined as "the permanent movement of persons or groups over a significant distance. But Petersen admits that this definition is ambiguous. Does "permanent" mean forever, or just for a long time? How many miles or border crossings make a movement "significant?" "We know whether someone has been born or died, but who shall say whether someone has migrated?" (1975: 41).

Other scholars would include in their definition of migration not only geographical mobility of slight distance and duration but also social mobility:

If geographical mobility is taken to refer to the movement of people in space, and if we are interested in assessing its social and cultural concomitants, then our model [of migration] must be expanded to include social variables, such as social mobility, and micro-movements, such as visiting and hosting, for it is during these latter activities that information about geographic mobility is exchanged. [Weaver and Downing 1976: 11]

These authors concede, however, that most sociologists would exclude social mobility and microtemporal and microspatial moves such as visiting from a definition of migration. "Social mobility," they acknowledge, "in the sociological and anthropological sense, does not generally refer to physical movement, but rather to social movement: a person moves from a lower socioeconomic class to a higher or from a higher to a lower class. The physical movement of people is migration: the social movement of people is social mobility" (1976: 11). Petersen, however, concurs with Lacroix's assessment that since "no objective, natural criterion exists on the basis of which migrants distinguish themselves from travellers . . . one should not expect to arrive at a unique criterion or definition of migration" (Lacroix 1949: 73; Petersen 1975: 41).

However true that may be, we shall adopt in these chapters an operational definition of migration – whatever the ambiguities and short-comings of such a course – based upon a composite of definitions set forth by Lee (1966) and Mangalam (1968). We will define migration as a permanent or semipermanent change of residence of individuals, families, or larger collectivities from one geographical location to another that results in changes in the interactional systems of the migrants. As Man-galam states, migration involves an implicit or explicit decision-making process carried on by the migrants on the basis of a set of values, presumably arranged hierarchically; and, as in Lee's definition, no restric-tion is placed on the distance of the move or upon the voluntary nature of the act and no distinction is made between external and internal migration, although visiting, migratory labor, and habitual nomadism are excluded (Lee 1966: 49, Mangalam 1968: 8).

General theory and methods

Mangalam and Schwartzweller have observed that scholars from various disciplines agree that progress in migration studies is hampered by serious inadequacies in theories about migration: migration theory tends to be time-bound, culture-bound, and discipline-bound; and migration cannot be understood without a comprehensive grasp of the interplay among demo-graphic, economic, social, psychological, and other relevant factors that converge in the process of migration (Mangalam and Schwartzweller 1969: 4).

It is generally recognized that the first systematic attempt to generate "laws" of migration was made by E. G. Ravenstein in a paper presented before the Royal Statistical Society in 1885. The original paper, based upon an analysis of the British census of 1881, was expanded in 1889 to include data from other nations. Both papers bore the title "The Laws of Migration." Their conclusions may be briefly summarized: (1) Most migrants move only a short distance and the number of migrants from any one place decreases in proportion to distance. Migrants going long distances generally move to large centers of industry and commerce. (2) Consequently, there occurs "a universal shifting or displacement of the population," producing "currents of migration" in the direction of these centers. The inhabitants of the countryside surrounding a town of rapid growth flock into it; the gaps thus left in the rural population are filled up by migrants from more remote districts. Thus there is a step-by-step migratory process whose influence emanates from the largest cities. (3) Each main stream of migration produces a compensating counter-stream.

(4) The natives of towns or cities are less migratory than those of the rural areas (Ravenstein 1885: 198–9). (5) Females predominate among short-journey migrants. (6) Technological development stimulates migration. (7) "Bad or oppressive laws, heavy taxation, an unattractive climate, uncongenial social surroundings, and even compulsion . . . are still producing currents of migration, but none of these currents can compare in volume with that which arises from the desire inherent in most men to 'better' themselves in material respects" (Ravenstein 1889: 286–8).

Everett S. Lee (1966: 48), reviewing Ravenstein's work some eighty years after its original publication, observed that this century has brought no comparable excursion into migration theory. The various historical and behavioral sciences have attempted to develop their own theories and models to explain, predict, and understand human migration. The demographic approach describes the data via historical or cross-sectional associations. Both demographers and economists employ statistical models to describe relationships between variables. There are also formal quantitative models based on those developed in physics and mathematics, such as the "gravity model," multiple regression models, and computer simulation models. A discussion of these is beyond the scope of this work, but a few words should be said about the most influential of these attempts, the so-called equilibrium model.

Lee has commented that "with the development of equilibrium analysis, economists abandoned the study of population, and most sociologists and historians are reluctant to deal with masses of statistical data. A crew of demographers has sprung up, but they have been largely content with empirical findings and unwilling to generalize" (Lee 1966: 48). The major components of the equilibrium model have been stated by Bogue (1959: 487):

Migration is a necessary element of normal population adjustment and equilibrium. . . By siphoning off excess population into areas of greater opportunity, internal migration becomes a mechanism of personal adjustment for the citizen. For the nation it is a device for maintaining a social and economic balance among communities; if migration were suddenly to be stopped, only a very short time would be required for population to "pile up" in areas of rapid growth but of low opportunity for earning a livelihood. Thus, migration is a process for preserving an existing system. Migration is an arrangement for making maximum use of persons with special qualifications. The special abilities of a particular person are useful to the nation only at certain sites, and persons who possess or acquire special abilities are not necessarily born or educated at the site where their talents are needed. Migration moves these specialized persons to the communities where their services can be used effectively.

We see here a strong tendency, perhaps inherent in the model itself, to view migration as a force independent of people. The model approaches human migration "as one would approach the study of migration of birds or the dispersion of insects from a common source" (Bogue 1959: 348; Mangalam and Schwarzweller 1969: 12–13; Goldscheider 1971: 2746). Individuals, families, and other groups are, in fact, the ultimate locus of the decision to move or not to move. Equilibrium theory tends to be static and mechanistic, while decision-making models can and ought to be dynamic, considering process and meaning, contexts, linkages between micro- and macrolevels of analysis, and the integration of migration with other cultural phenomena (Guillet and Uzzell 1976).

Decision-making processes

Unless a person or group is forced to move to a certain place at a specified time under stated circumstances, migration must involve some kind of decision on the part of the individuals who go from one place to another: when, where, and why to go; perhaps how long and with whom. It is wise to keep in mind that it is people who move and people who make the decisions. Goldscheider (1971: 2747) reminds us that whether migration is conceived of as sociodemographic behavior or sociodemographic process, we must account not only for decisions to move but also for decisions not to move; not only for rates of population movement but also for the general stability of populations.

The problem of population stability has been addressed by demographers, sociologists, and geographers, many of whom rely on statistics of net change rather than gross movement. This has led to what Jackson has referred to as one of the myths or underlying assumptions regarding the human condition and the decision-making process that studies of population movements quite unconsciously constructed (Jackson 1969: 3). One such myth is the idea that migration is usually a "once and only" phenomenon, a notion that grew out of the emphasis on net population change. The most obvious of these assumptions, however, is the myth of the static society. This implies, by calling up the idea of a preexisting rural utopia, "that the natural condition of man is sedentary, that movement away from the natal place is a deviant activity associated with disorganization and a threat to the established harmony of *Gemeinschaft* relationships which are implied by a life lived within a fixed social framework."

We return to this subject in a different context in Chapter 5. This seemingly Rousseauistic view of a once-upon-a-time paradise in which harmony prevailed among people intimately involved in face-to-face relationships was in reality an ideal point on a theoretical folk–urban continuum postulated by Robert Redfield a generation ago (1947: 293–308). This ideal folk society was isolated and its members were conceived of as remaining always within the small territory they occupied. Members were bound by religion and kinship ties and the motive of commercial gain did not exist. There was neither money nor any common measure of value. The distribution of goods and services was part of the conventional and personal status relationships that made up the structure of the society: goods were exchanged as expressions of good will and largely as incidents of ceremonial and ritual activities. Quoting Raymond Firth, Redfield concludes, "On the whole, then, the compulsion to work, to save, and to expend is given not so much by a rational appreciation of the [material] benefits to be received as by the desire for social recognition through such behavior" (Redfield 1947: 305–6).

However, as cities came into being, tribal peoples lost their isolation and, according to this line of reasoning, new relationships developed and the relations between peasant and town or city were expressed in part through financial institutions: "Gain is calculated; some crop or other product is sold, in the village or elsewhere, to a buyer of a more urbanized community who pays money" (Redfield 1953: 31–2). The source of money – the city – acts as a magnet and the quest for Mammon drives people from village to metropolis, from one region to another. "Thus the expansion of civilization results in vast and complex migrations of peoples" (Redfield 1953: 46).

Assuming that Redfield's analysis represents a rough approximation of what occurred on the advent of cities and civilizations, we might expect that individuals and groups would have had to decide where, when, and if to move and that these decision-making processes would have repeated themselves through the millennia. But the imponderables – the human errors of judgment, faulty assessments, intervening variables that go into a determination of whether or not to move – went relatively unheeded by migration analysts. With economists in the fore, the equilibrium model became the standard explanation of population movements.

An economic analysis of the causes of internal migration begins with the basic hypothesis or assumption that "the redistribution of people is a purposeful way in which a population responds to its perception of changing economic opportunities" (Carvajal and Geithman 1974: 105). The most influential model attempting to cast rural–urban migration motivations in an economic straitjacket was published by Todaro in 1969, in which he underlined "the fundamental role played by job opportunities and probabilities of employment in the actual migration decision-making process" (1969: 140). In Todaro's model, the decision to migrate from rural to urban areas is functionally related to two principal variables: the rural–urban real income differential and the probability of obtaining an urban job (1969: 139). This way of looking at decision making, at "man, the rational economic creature," perforce ignores such variables as individual tastes, habits, prejudices, loves, and hates – in short, all those non-economic factors that influence the day-to-day decisions of our lives.

Even when economic factors are an overriding consideration, as in many land-poor villages in Latin America, the decision to migrate may be less important than determinations that must be made in the wake of that decision. In their investigation of San Jerónimo, an impoverished community in the Mixteca region of Oaxaca, Mexico, Stuart and Kearney (n.d.: 7) state that "in the absence of other viable alternatives, it is meaningless to talk of a household's decision whether or not to send some of its members outside the community to work. The focus of decisions is where to go, who to send, and when to send them; decisions that must be made each year by most households."

In summary, however interesting decision-making processes on the individual, family, or household level may be, scholars are becoming more convinced of the far greater need to examine external constraints and structural relationships in general as the main determinants of migration behavior.

Repulsion and attraction: the push and the pull

Clifford Jansen (1969: 65) observes that perhaps the question most asked and least understood about migration is "Why do people move?" He believes – and our experience and that of many other researchers confirm that belief – that in most cases the migrants themselves do not know the answer to this question. When asked, they usually give vague and general reasons, such as "work," "family reasons," "education," which help little in the study of the processes involved in the decision to migrate or in the construction of a general theory of the decision-making process. Jansen also commented that one attempt to cover all moves under a general heading is the so-called push–pull hypothesis (Jansen 1969: 65). As we have already noted, it suggests that migration occurs due to socioeconomic imbalances between regions, certain factors "pulling" migrants to the area of destination, others "pushing" them out of the region of origin.

The push–pull hypothesis is only one aspect of the great dichotomy that has pervaded the literature on migration. Guillet and Uzzell suggest that it is to a large extent part of the legacy of the Redfieldian continuum and the sociological tradition of Durkheim, Tönnies, and earlier European scholars. The terms rural–urban, Gemeinschaft–Gesellschaft, and others color our understanding by introducing an unnecessary and misleading polarization of what is essentially a continual interaction over time and space within particular contexts (Guillet and Uzzell 1976: 3).

In short, the polar view of migration considered as a simple push–pull mechanism is "at best confusing, at worst misleading, and in need of considerable revision in light of current research" (Guillet and Uzzell: 4). Nevertheless, most writers concerned with migration, including the most vociferous disclaimers of the bipolar view, continue to utilize it. The reason for this is clear. Simplistic as the push–pull view may be, it is a convenient tool for organizing and analyzing data. We use the push–pull scheme in this book for that reason. It is one, but only one, of the ways of looking at forces causing people to move, and we do not limit ourselves to this kind of analysis. We are aware that there is almost always a combination of factors involved; therefore, we use the push–pull model as one of our main tools for analyzing the masses of data on migration in Latin America.

The push

Most studies of internal migration (mostly rural to urban) have something to say about the forces that work upon a given population to encourage its movement from the country to the city. The most commonly mentioned push factors are lack of sufficient or productive land; alternative economic opportunities; absence of sanitation and medical services; poor educational facilities; and, in some places, lack of security and natural disasters.

Insufficient and poor land and lack of economic alternatives are usually cited as primary reasons for out-migration from rural communities.[1] In general, evidence supports the contention that growth of the rural population and decreasing fertility of the land, combined with fragmentation of plots by inheritance practices, create an imbalance between the population and its available economic resources. The result is an increasing shift of population from its traditional agricultural base to an urban economic foundation. This process is attested to throughout Latin America in various degrees of importance and is one of the salient demographic facts of our time. Unfortunately, some of the inferences drawn from this movement are hasty and based on insufficient and outdated information.

Many current notions are based upon ideas put forth almost a generation ago. For instance, Corrado (1955: 356) reported that people who tend to migrate are those who feel most strongly the disequilibrium between population and economic resources. "Consequently, it is the poor, rather than those who enjoy a certain welfare, who leave." Similarly, Eder (1965: 27) concluded that the raquitic economic situation of the small farmer in Latin America "has caused thousands to flee to the cities." Benítez (1962: 697) maintained that "in general, it can be said that rural–urban migration is the result of abandonment of the land because of the impossibility of subsisting on it." This rather simplistic relationship between rural poverty and migration to cities was summed up by George Hill and his colleagues: Faced with the depressed standard of living in the countryside, and "... desperately seeking better opportunities for them and their children, *the rural populations feel forced to migrate* . . . Better conditions *would undoubtedly induce* many of the young men to stay with their agricultural pursuits and to attract others [to the rural areas]" (quoted in Poblete

Troncoso 1962: 44, his emphasis). More recent studies by Martínez (1968) in Peru and by Diéguez (1970) and Martine (1975) in Colombia tend to reinforce this opinion.

Certainly there is no question but that rural poverty has resulted in mass population movements out of the country to the city, and that the poorest sector of the rural population is well represented in the migrant group. Nevertheless, it is clear that there is no mechanical cause-and-effect relationship between poverty and migration.

Perlman (1976: 11) cites evidence that when rural areas of Brazil are divided into zones of varying degrees of poverty and economic/climatic depression, the rates of out-migration are fairly constant from each. No greater migration is evident from areas where push factors should be strongest. She notes that there may be land pressure without migration and there may be rapid urban growth without land pressure (Perlman: 67).

In Chile, Herrick (1965: 70) found little variation in migration to Santiago accompanying fluctuations in unemployment rates; in Costa Rica, Carvajal and Geithman (1974: 118) show that unemployment rates in towns and cities in that nation are not an important factor in migration. Germani (1969: 15–48) observed that although job opportunities for migrants are often related to urban industrial development, in many developing nations massive population movements to cities come about even when new and better employment opportunities are scarce or absent. In such cases there is a combination of forces in which the weight of the pull factors to urban areas is greater than the expulsive factors from rural zones. Analogous mechanisms can be used to describe not only the existence and intensity of rural–urban migration, but its absence as well.

Germani (1965: 74) contends that under desperately bad conditions people do not emigrate. On the other hand, in the face of rather acceptable situations people do leave. What happens is that so-called objective factors are filtered through attitudes and decisions of individuals. Impersonal decisions do not decide migration. Decisions are personal and conditioned by the attitudes of individuals. Furthermore, it is fruitless to contend that the push off the land is more important than the pull of the city, and that the attraction of the city would not exist but for the difficulties of rural life. There is a continual interaction between the rural pole and the urban pole, and there is no clearly definable boundary between some locality labeled "urban" and a rural hinterland.

Perlman (1976: 63) and others have spoken of "poles of attraction." To reintroduce the regrettable but virtually unavoidable use of labels, there is not only rural–urban migration, but urban–rural, rural–rural, and urban–urban migration as well. We repeat, however, that until very recently most research has been concerned with the first.

Earlier studies in the emerging field of urban anthropology generally took the "peasant in the city" as their central concern, focusing upon adjustment to the urban milieu and assuming, often without empirical evidence, that the push off the land was the reason the migrant had moved to the metropolis. Personal decisions were (and still are) stressed in explanations of the migration experience.

Here we are confronted with several problems. By studying the migrant in the city, the anthropologist was largely dependent upon the informant's recall of the socioeconomic, political, and personal situation in his place of origin prior to departure. Few of these earlier studies worked both ends of the continuum – the folk and the urban. As we have said, individuals and families – and perhaps other small groups – are the ultimate locus of the decision-making process concerning migration. But these decisions are made within the structural constraints of village, state, and nation. In their study of a community in Colombia, Romero and Flinn (1976) indicated that the chief underlying postulate of their investigation was that the commercialization of the agricultural sector of Colombia, resulting in changes in the socioeconomic structure of the countryside, had brought about migration, as one response by the peasantry of the community, which was impoverished in all its resources except labor (p. 37). They continue:

Based on this premise it is hypothesized that structural variables – relationship to the means of production – will be significantly related to migration and will be better predictors of migration than the personal characteristics of the migrants. It is also hypothesized that in economically declining communities migration will be forced rather than "pulled" or self-selective as reflected in the objective measures of the relationship to the means of production. [Romero and Flinn 1976: 37]

In general, these hypotheses were confirmed. On the other hand, it was found that individual characteristics were also important in predicting migration (1976: 57). Thus structural and personal or individual factors are, except for analytical purposes, never entirely separable. For example, uneconomical exploitation of resources is widespread throughout Latin America and is frequently named as an agent in out-migration from rural areas. But is this a structural or personal factor? Consider the mechanization of agriculture. This may be based on personal decisions at some level and result in structural changes in a region or nation. Usandizaga and Havens (1966: 27) note that manpower displaced by mechanization of agriculture in Colombia has found its way to cities in that nation (and we might add to other countries, including the United States). Similar findings have been reported throughout much of Latin America.

Camargo (1960: 65–94, 115) found a relationship in Brazil among technical advances in agriculture (including better means of transportation), natural increase in rural population, and out-migration. He considers them interdependent phenomena, the first two bringing about the last. National industrialization, he believes, is the preponderant cause of the rural exodus and "deruralization" of Brazil. Referring to Comargo's analysis, Ianni (1970: 32) states that the relative retardation in the agrarian sector should not be considered indicative of the absence of progress or even of significant changes. The rural exodus, he believes, is not a unilateral fact arising from the attraction of the city and its industries, but is also related to the changes in the technical and social conditions of production in several of the agricultural regions.

Roberts (1978: 98–9) has examined some structural considerations in population movements. He refers to the work of Douglas Graham (1970), which contrasted patterns of internal migration in Brazil in the period 1940–50 with the period of 1950–60. In the earlier period, despite the poverty of the northeastern region of that nation, fewer migrants left this region than left Minas Gerais, which, while poorer than the southern area to which the migrants went in search of work, was wealthier than the northeast. It is only in the period 1950–60 that outmigration from the northeast became greater in volume than outmigration from Minas Gerais.

Graham explained the change in migration patterns between the two periods by the greater rate of economic growth in the later period, with industrialization proceeding faster than the expansion of agricultural production. He also pointed out the improvements in road networks and in transport that facilitated long-distance migration.

Graham's analysis suggests that in the first stages of urban-industrial expansion it is not necessarily the poorest areas in a nation which have the most substantial outmigration rates but those areas close to the expanding economic centers. The costs of transport and the risks of seeking work far from home counter the attraction of substantially higher incomes. Studies in Chile, Colombia and Mexico show that most migrants come from the areas close to the expanding centers (Herrick 1965; Simmons and Cardona 1972; Balán, Browning and Jelin 1973). This migration pattern is similar to that of England during her industrialization where, also, there was little long-distance migration of poor farmers from the south to the north of England. [Roberts 1978: 99][2]

Paradoxically, two apparently opposed types of land holding in Latin America – *latifundios* (large, sometimes corporate estates) and *minifundios* (small, usually family-owned plots) – have each been considered "structural determinants" of migration of almost equal importance. Latifundios generally absorb little manpower if they are efficient or mechanized, and minifundios, even where there is high productivity, cannot employ all available manpower (Muñoz et al. 1974: 18).[3]

Another structural factor in migration is the existence of external markets. In varying degrees of importance, these impose conditions on the kind of production a nation or region puts out. They may require an expansion, a decrease, or even a substitution of crops. Migration from rural areas increases when international prices or market conditions stimulate a

Table 1. *Structural and individual forces in migration*

Force	Structural	Individual
Push	Type of land holding (latifundio, mini-fundio)	Lack of skills
	Insufficient or poor land; uneconomical exploitation of resources	Boredom, loneliness
	Lack of alternative employment	
	Absence of sanitation and medical facilities	
	Lack of transportation improvements	
	Violence	
	Poor educational facilities	
	Rudimentary communications	
	Mechanization and commercialization of agriculture	
	External markets	
	Poverty	
Pull	Employment opportunities	Chance of advancement
	Health and medical services	Presence of relatives
	Transportation	
	Educational facilities	
	Bright lights and adventure	
	Rising expectations (all categories)	

type of production that requires little manpower (see, for example, Muñoz *et al.* 1974; Margulis 1967; Margulis 1968; Riverola 1967; Diéguez 1970; Martínez 1968; Martínez 1969).

Table 1 gives a brief overview of some of the push–pull, structural–individual forces in migration. Although these structural causes of migration often point out factors crucial to the migration process, they do little to explain the existence of these causes; such things must be explained in terms of particular national and regional contexts. Migration in Venezuela, for example, has been largely influenced by the demands of the petroleum industry (Dipolo and Suárez 1974: 184), and population movements in Argentina are related to the role of that nation as a supplier of beef and agricultural products (Testa 1970: 99).

These national and regional contexts are in large part a consequence of historical antecedents: Countries in different phases of development and with different types of economic development will have dissimilar forces acting to bring about internal (or international) migration. For example, the latifundios, minifundios, and feudal structure of the rural economy described by Mejía (1963: 184–6) as of primary importance in out-migration from Peruvian villages in the 1950s and early 1960s are largely absent in, say, contemporary Mexico, but similar phenomena exist in other countries such as Ecuador, and even in such economically more advanced nations as Argentina (Viale 1960: 110).

Political factors, particularly civil wars and revolutions, have stimulated large-scale population movements in Latin America. This was the case, for example, during the Mexican Revolution of 1910–21. Oscar Lewis (1951) mentioned that large numbers of people fled Tepoztlán during the Zapatista movements and subsequent battles, and doubtless the same thing occurred in many other Mexican villages. Rivarola (1967: 4–5) recalls the mobile atmosphere created in Paraguay by the Chaco War (1932–5), giving peasants more opportunities to make contact with urban life and creating new attitudes and forms of behavior among the peasantry. Similarly, the revolution of 1936 and the civil war of 1947 in Paraguay stirred significant population movements. The effects of natural disasters, such as the 1966 earthquake in Guatemala, on population redistribution are obvious. Wars and natural disasters may be considered examples of "forced" migration.

Rural insecurity is endemic in large areas of Latin America. *La violencia* (killing and other forms of violence by marauding bands) in the countryside of Colombia has resulted in important population movements, not only from country to city but from village to village. Flinn and Cartano made a comparison of the migration process to an urban barrio and to a rural community in that nation. They reported that 44 percent of the immigrants to Granada (a rural community) listed *la violencia* as a motivating factor in their decision to migrate, while only 13 percent of the residents of El Carmen (a shantytown) gave it as a reason for their move to the city (1970: 38–9).

Michael Whiteford (1976b: 17) wrote that only a few migrants in barrio Tulcán gave *la violencia* as a cause for movement. "In fact, in most cases migrants came from areas not badly affected by the violence." He cites a report by McGreevey (1968: 213–14) stating that although it is often mentioned as one of the principal causes of rural–urban migration, rural violence has with few exceptions not played a significant role in interdepartmental movement of people.

It is not only such well-publicized sanguinary violence that may create sufficient insecurity to cause people to leave their villages and small towns. The aura of distrust and fear that pervades numerous rural communities has, at least until recent years, received but scant attention from social scientists investigating migration motivations. One apparent reason for this is the continued vitality of the folk model of social relations, in which the presumed idyllic nature of rustic existence is corrupted through contact with the urban way of life. In his study of La Rioja, Argentina, Margulis

(1967: 78–93) describes how the economic life and belief system of the villagers were compatible until influences of the city created conflict. Roberts (1973) relates some of his experiences with informants in two neighborhoods in Guatemala City:

The one aspect of provincial life that migrants constantly refer to more than any other, favorably and unfavorably, is the slow tempo of life in the villages and small towns from which they come. In responding to a survey question about the possibility of returning to the provinces, the reason most frequently cited in favor of returning was the peace and quiet of the countryside. It is . . . a longing that is a constant theme of their conversations, and it affects their recreational activities. To go to the countryside with the family is the preferred recreation of this sample. Many choose to take vacations there, fishing or visiting relatives, as well as going on shorter day trips from the capital. In the tape-recorded life histories, the respondents were most nostalgic about the leisure activities of rural life, about the picnics, the fishing, playing by the rivers, or dancing to a small band on the balcony of the village hall. There is an evocation of tranquility and relaxation that undoubtedly does not reflect the reality of every rural day, but which is an evocation that brings up common memories among a group of men and women chatting in the street of a city neighborhood. [Roberts 1973: 50–1]

There is, then, an obvious discrepancy between people's ideals and the reality of the countryside.

As for the "reality of every rural day," we can no more generalize about that than we can about the average day in an urban metropolis. There are, to be sure, serene, antiviolent communities (see Paddock 1975), but there is abundant evidence that rural life in Latin America is often characterized by inter- and intracommunity strife, familial tension, and personal isolation. Viale (1960: 94) observed that far from enjoying intimate social contacts, the Argentinian peasant suffers from isolation from his fellow human beings and that this isolation is cause for innumerable cases of out-migration from rural areas. Margulis (1967: 93–4) described the people who remained in the village that he studied in Argentina as passive, skeptical, and resigned. Lewis (1951), Friedrich (1962), G. Foster (1967), Maccoby (1967), Butterworth (1969), and Romanucci-Ross (1973) have noted that suspicion, distrust, and uncooperativeness are characteristic of Mexican villagers.

Caciquismo (rule by a political boss or bosses) is common in much of Latin America. In Tilantongo, the community in Mexico studied by Butterworth, *caciquismo* takes the form of terrorism by one or more individuals who are not necessarily in recognized positions of authority, although they may hold political office. By virtue of their brutality and unscrupulous dealings through bribery and deceit, they may not only keep the ordinary citizen in a state of trepidation but also intimidate the authorities into inertia. An illustration from Butterworth's fieldwork is the career of Amadeo Sánchez (a pseudonym).

Always a ruthless opportunist with a notable lack of scruples, Amadeo arrogated the presidency of Tilantongo and lost little time in establishing his personal *cacicazgo* (rule by a *cacique*) in the community. Fines were leveled at the citizenry for minor or nonexistent infractions of the law and complaints were answered by incarceration, physical beatings, and even assassination. No one is certain how many murders can be attributed to Amadeo Sánchez, but there are at least four cases where sufficient testimony is available to indict Amadeo. While he was president, he openly preempted all fines and municipal income for his personal use, stole cattle, and abused women.

Amadeo eventually was stabbed and killed in the plaza of the community. During his reign as *cacique* (political boss), however, Amadeo had caused numerous individuals and families to leave their village in search of a more secure environment – another village or an urban center. The push factor here is obvious. The pull is not so clear. Why do some people go to another rural village while others choose the city?

The pull

The conditions that draw members of rural communities to urban centers – the attractive or pull factors – are for the most part the complements of the conditions that obtain in the countryside. Employment and educational opportunities are generally ranked foremost among urban attractions, followed by the presence of health and recreational facilities and the excitement of urban living. Nowadays the presence of relatives in the city may be a prime factor in migration. This will be discussed in the next chapter.

The "bright city lights" explanation of migration motivations has been heavily criticized of late, but there is sufficient evidence that it is indeed a contributing (although certainly not usually a decisive) factor in rural–urban migration. Butterworth (1975b: 195–6), Usandizaga and Havens (1966: 42), and Michael Whiteford (1976b: 15) are among those who have mentioned the lack of *ambiente* (atmosphere) reported by informants about their place of origin and the *movimiento* (movement, "life") in the city. In discussing the residents of Tulcán, a barrio in the southwest corner of the city of Popayán, Whiteford (1976b: 15) relates that often the economic situation of the peasants before they moved to the city was not desperate. Many moved to the city because they saw it as an opportunity for a better life rather than because such a move was the only possible solution to a problem. Such peasants generally are young men and women without families, who have less at stake than family men who have been pushed off their land. In the city, the former group hopes to find high-paying jobs that will bring them closer to obtaining the good life.

Thus, although few studies of migration to urban centers in Latin

America (or to other regions) fail to mention the pull of employment opportunities, both researchers and informants differ about the relative weight to give to the economic pull. Usandizaga and Havens (1976: 42) list the usual reasons given by informants for going to the the city: work, education, health care. But a number of reasons are less concrete: "*más ambiente,*" friends and relatives in the city, and similar noneconomic motivations. In such cases, "the wish to move refers more to an adventurous spirit than to a criticism of the situation in which the migrant finds himself" (Usandizaga and Havens: 42).

Jobs in the city are of course limited, and the influx of unskilled laborers into the urban complex often creates strains upon the national and municipal economies. Nevertheless, many Latin American countries have shown a remarkable flexibility in handling the migrant masses. Unskilled or semiskilled labor is still very much in demand in many parts of Latin America. Second, many migrants display an admirable ingenuity in carving out an economic niche for themselves. Third, the very presence of a multitude of new city dwellers expands the economic opportunities by generating its own needs, including housing, transportation, services, entertainment, and consumer goods.

The desire for education – for oneself, or, more commonly, for one's children – ranks high among the motivations for migration to urban centers. In his landmark study, Oscar Lewis (1952: 32–3) noted that even prior to the Mexican revolution young men were leaving Tepoztlán to get a higher education, a motivation still active today. Butterworth (1962: 267), Kemper (1977: 91–3) and Browning and Feindt (1971: 50) have also commented upon the importance of educational goals in attracting peasants and their families to urban centers in Mexico. Simmons and Cardona (1968: 10) and M. Whiteford (1976b: 15) have done the same for Colombia, and Elizaga (1966: 353) for Chile. Elizaga points out that although the principal motive given for moving to Greater Santiago was work, education was the second most commonly cited reason. Among those coming from rural and semiurban places, an overwhelming majority claimed work to be the principal motive, while those coming from urban settings were more inclined to report education as the prime motivating force.

Browing and Feindt (1971: 50) report that older family men give education very high priority for moving, but the authors observe that this clearly is education not for the respondents but for their children. Métraux (1956: 402) related how Aymara Indian families in Peru often place their children as servents in urban homes, asking in return only that the patron family send the children to school. In Colombia, M. Whiteford (1976b: 15) tells us that Tulcaneses regard education as an important way to obtain the better life. Some individuals are able to combine the desires of educating children and maintaining life in the country. They keep their landholdings but move the family into town, and the husband divides his time between city and country.

When asked for a list or ranking of motives for moving to the city, informants almost invariably list medical facilities or other reasons involving health. The medical facilities available in urban centers are absent in villages, although migrants often mention the salubrious climate of the countryside. M. Whiteford (1976b: 16) mentions that some informants migrated to Popayán because they feel that the latter has a "healthier" climate than their previous home.

While the broad outlines of what motivates peasants to abandon their rural birthplace for urban settings are fairly well understood, the relative importance of the various motivating factors is difficult to measure. A generation ago, investigators were more sanguine about the possibility of weighing the why's of migration than are their more skeptical counterparts today. Studies such as those of Matos Mar (1961), which used Peruvian census data to break down reasons for migration of household heads to Lima, attempted to give precision to this aspect of demography, yet to state that 61.05 percent of families migrate for economic reasons, another 22.85 percent for social reasons, and so forth, presents an artificial view. Even so, investigators continue to utilize these kinds of statistics to analyze push–pull motives (see Cardona 1968: 63). Such studies do provide some idea of the weight given to various factors in the move away from the countryside, and the economic factors appear to be foremost. However, as Perlman (1976: 67–8) wrote:

According to migrants themselves, economic considerations are not the only factor in their decisions. Less than half (46 percent) mention an economic concern as the reason for their move. We found most migrants unable to describe their decision to migrate with any precision. It was clear that specific decisions involved complex factors.[4]

A word of caution may be added. Educational, health, and recreational facilities have always been negligible in most villages in Latin America, and rural poverty is by no means a modern phenomenon. However, only in relatively recent times have these been put forth as important reasons for the rural exodus. One reason for this seems to lie in the rising expectations of ruralities – a result of increased national prosperity and availabiltiy of modern conveniences in urban areas, plus better communications between the city and its hinterlands. Roads, television sets, telephones, and schools help make the peasant realize that there is a better world beyond his village, thereby adding impetus to migratory flows.

It is therefore presumptuous to assume that improving rural conditions would, at least at first, limit out-migration. To be sure, the problem is a complicated one, involving the interplay of local and national priorities. Dovring (1968: 25) comments that many people concerned with economic development seem convinced that one of the foremost requisites for underdeveloped countries is a reduction in the agricultural sector of the population. This proposition contains two elements: first, reducing the *relative* role of agriculture in the industrial or occupational structure of a country, which is the direct corollary of increasing the role of other industries that are evolving. Second, and most important, the plan consists of trying to achieve an *absolute* reduction in agricultural workers as one of the conditions to raise the productivity of those who remain on the land as well as that of the community as a whole.

Looking at the problem from the urban point of view, Benítez (1962: 97) contends that in spite of the difficulties industry has in absorbing unskilled laborers, the cities still attract ruralities, because of government policy of putting more schools, better doctors, and so forth in cities rather than in the country. The chances of eliminating migration depend on the creation of similar conditions in the countryside, including adequate employment.

Todaro (1969: 147) thinks that the most significant policy implication emerging from his model of rural–urban income differentials is the great difficulty in substantially reducing the size of the urban traditional sector without a concentrated effort at making life more attractive:

Instead of allocating scarce capital funds to urban low cost housing projects which would effectively raise urban real incomes and might therefore lead to a worsening of the housing problem, governments in less developed countries might do better if they devoted these funds to the improvement of rural amenities. In effect, the net benefit of bringing "city lights" to the countryside might greatly exceed whatever net benefit might be derived from luring more peasants to the city by increasing the attractiveness of urban living conditions. [Todaro 1969: 147]

There are obvious difficulties, not to say inconsistencies, in trying to reduce the number of agricultural workers and at the same time attempting to induce the peasant to stay on the land. The solution proposed by most national planners in Latin America is diversification and decentralization of industry – moving the factories to the fields. Most of these plans remain on the drawing boards. When they have been implemented, the results, as Miller (1973) has shown for a new town in Mexico, are not always what was intended. One of the problems is the selective nature of who remains at home, who goes to a new town, and who becomes a city dweller.

3. Who moves from where: selectivity and migration

The push–pull factors discussed in the preceding chapter do not operate mechanically upon an undifferentiated mass, but upon men and women of differing ages, skills, educational achievements, geographical origins, and degrees of sophistication. Migration is selective, involving differentials of a biosocial nature. Some individuals and groups respond to the social, economic, and psychological forces impinging upon them by leaving their rural environment for another milieu; others do not. The social, psychological, and economic characteristics of the migrant population are obviously of paramount importance for determining and predicting demographic movements and have been receiving increasing attention by social scientists working in Latin America.[1]

Until the mid-1950s, most inferences regarding selective forces were based upon data gathered in the United States and Europe. The state of knowledge on this subject was summarized in a United Nations report on the world social situation in 1957:

The migratory process is not simply a movement of peasants and farm labourers from a completely rural setting to the big cities, and the migrants are not, in the main, the poorest or least able to make a living in their places of origin (although such persons are well represented). The migrants include representatives of various social strata from the small towns as well as the countryside, and many of the people of rural origin who ultimately go to the cities first spend some time in the small towns, or migrate to work in mines or plantations. A considerable number gain some experience of urban ways of life, and often learn to read and write, during their term of compulsory military service. Many of the migrants are artisans or semi-skilled workers (particularly masons or other building trades workers). Some of them are young people who have gone through secondary school and hope to continue their education at a city university, or obtain bureaucratic or white collar jobs. This is probably a rough self-selecting process. The small-town or rural non-agricultural worker or artisan is more likely to migrate than the cultivator who possesses no skill usable in the city. The literate or semi-literate are more likely to migrate than the illiterate. The man with relatives or acquaintances in the city is more likely to migrate than the man with none. [United Nations 1957: 79]

This summary analysis compares migrants with nonmigrants. However, a study of differential migration should include other comparisons; for example, differences within the migrant population, differences among migrants coming from different regions, and differences between migrants and natives of the point of destination. Donald Bogue states: "Evidence of

51

differential migration exists with respect to a given category whenever a disproportionately greater or smaller percentage of migrants falls into that category than is found in the base population with which they are compared" (Bogue 1963: 405).[2] The base population, then, may be that of the place of origin or the place of destination, or perhaps the total population of a region or nation, or any segment of these categories. In this chapter we are mainly concerned with differences among people who leave their place of origin and move to urban centers. Differences between migrants and natives of the place of destination are discussed later.

The usual theoretical framework employed in analyzing selectivity of migration is a modified decision-making model that emphasizes the structural constraints within which individual decisions are exercised (Graves and Graves 1974: 122). As in the "push–pull" model, determinants of decisions to migrate can be divided into two broad categories: structural, and psychological or personal. Structural variables can be further separated into those that reflect the potential migrant's position within the opportunity system of both urban and rural communities, and those that bear on his network of social relationships (Graves and Graves: 122).

The relationship between general structural or causal factors in migration and individual decisions by people who choose to migrate on their own brings about some of the greatest difficulties in presenting a theory of selectivity of migration. Lourdes Arizpe (1978: 38) maintains that it has not yet been possible to utilize analytical concepts that clarify the relationship between historical/structural and individual phenomena. In other words, there are factors beyond the control of individuals that may force, or at least influence, their choices of if, when, or where to move.

If we are seeking universals concerning selective factors in migration processes, it may be argued that we have not progressed far beyond what Bogue and the United Nations reported about these universals: that it is the young and flexible who predominate in migration streams. Indeed, Bogue (1963: 410) insisted that "as yet demographers have not succeeded in establishing any other 'universal' migration differential [than that of the flexible young] ... *Further differentials do not exist and should not be expected to exist*" (his emphasis).

Selectivity by age

Among migrants arriving in urban centers, the only selective factor operating nearly universally seems to be that of age. It is the young adults who desert their native homes, leaving the middle-aged and elderly behind.[3] This is reported for every country in Latin America for which reliable data on migration are available, although there are exceptions reported within some countries. As we shall see, stages or phases of development of a family, community, region, or nation influence selectivity of all kinds, including the "universal" of age.

In one of the earlier studies of selectivity in migration in Latin America, Gino Germani (1963: 322) reported that 60 percent of internal migrant residents in Greater Buenos Aires in 1947 were between 20 and 59 years of age. By far the highest rate of selection was from the 15 to 34 age group. In the years since then, virtually every investigation on migration in Latin America that has touched upon the subject of selectivity has confirmed the overwhelmingly positive selectivity for the young and able.[4] Probably the only shortcomings in our data in this are studies that take the time factor into account. More attention needs to be paid to the life and domestic cycle of migrants and their families.

These cycles are, of course, related in complex ways to such variables as economics and education. Kemper (1977: 60) found that the great majority of migrants leaving the village of Tzintzuntzan, Mexico, were below the age of thirty. But the largest increase in migration in recent years has occurred in the 0 to 15 age cohort. Kemper believes that this change is due to the exodus of whole families stimulated to migrate because of increased competition for limited local resources within the traditional occupational categories of pottery-making and agriculture. In addition, the newly affluent families are using wealth gained from storekeeping, pottery wholesaling, and sales to tourists to send their older children away to secondary and vocational schools. Butterworth's data from Tilantongo (1969; 1970) further illustrate the cyclical nature of age differentials in migration. Thus, selectivity by age may in the long run be a time- and culture-bound universal. Corollary to the proposition that it is generally the youthful sector of a population that migrates to cities is that these are single individuals, married or unmarried (usually the latter), who come to urban centers by themselves. Predominance of unmarried young adults in migration to Latin American cities has been reported for São Paulo (Brandão Lopes 1961: 237), Lima and Santiago (Elizaga 1970, 1972a, 1972b), Bogotá (Flinn 1966: 32–4), Buenos Aires (Margulis 1968: 144), Mexico City (Butterworth 1975a: 278), and Monterrey, Mexico (Balán, Browning, and Jelin 1973: 157). However, as the pattern of age and sex differentials changes over time and place, so do the marital and parental statuses of migrants and potential migrants.

The characteristics of the specific sample population influence the generalities made. For example, in William Flinn's investigation of two barrios in Bogotá, he found that in one (El Carmen), about 51 percent of household heads migrated as single, unmarried adults, while approximately 41 percent migrated with their families or brought them later. The other eight percent of household heads migrated to Bogotá as children in their family of orientation (Flinn 1966: 34). Household heads are a frequently used sample, but not always a reliable one.

But Flinn acknowledges that a barrio study skews results, because most people who live in these areas live in family units. Single migrants may live in rooming houses in other areas of the city. Also, a high percentage of single women migrants are domestic servants who reside in the houses of their employers in middle- or upper-class neighborhoods. Flinn adds that studies in rural areas are also skewed, because if a whole family moves from the community, no family members are left to report the migration. If only one or two children migrate, this change is more easily detected by an ex post facto study (Flinn: 32–4).

In a landmark migration study, the Monterrey Mobility Project, Harley Browning and his associates attempted to put some flesh on the bones of demographic data. The central problem they addressed was "how and why men move geographically and occupationally within the context of a developing society" (Balán, Browning, and Jelin 1973: xiii). Selectivity in migration was one of their concerns, particularly the relationship between marital status and the family life cycle. The authors concluded from their data that

Migration, in the perspective of familial units, is best seen as a continuous process not limited to the number of days an individual, with or without companions, needs to make the journey to another place. A sizable part of the migration to Monterrey involves family groups that take months and years to complete the transfer. It is a relatively stable pattern, for there are no great differences when the migrants are examined by time-of-arrival cohorts. This fact implies that for any specific time we can confidently predict for Monterrey, or other places with substantial inmigration, a fair volume of subsequent migration, simply as a consequence of the split-migration pattern. In other words, migration to Monterrey generates its own momentum and becomes, even if to a limited extent, somewhat independent of economic opportunity. [Balán, Browning, and Jelin 1973: 159]

Selectivity by sex

Sex is another of the bio-demographical facts upon which migration theory is built. Although it has generally been held that males are more migratory than females (more adventurous, less confined by tradition, and so forth), current research indicates that not only is sex less selective in migration than age, but that it is less uniform over time and space (Shaw 1975: 20).

Cardona Gutiérrez (1968: 64) feels that the preponderance of females moving to urban centers is closely related to the desire for independence by women, who, one way or another, manage to find work in capital cities of Latin America. In Guatemala, Roberts (1973: 67–8) states, there are few alternatives to migration open to women in the provinces. They cannot find employment as itinerant laborers or plantation workers to the extent that males can, so for women the city is the surest and most available source of employment. Margulis (1968: 144) also argues that the factors that stimulate migration sometimes operate most intensely on women. Women in their home communities, he states, have fewer opportunities of recreation and almost no possibility of work.

Women, work, and migration

Traditionally, women in rural Latin America have had a great deal of control of household finances and input into subsistence and marketing activities. However, studies of these women have shown that the advent of industrialization or modernization brought by "factories in the field" and the like have often weakened women's positions (see, for example, Rubbo 1975 on rural proletarian women in Colombia). Changes in position are related to political aspects of family life and distribution of power and authority within the family. In studying women's strategies, Lamphere (1973: 111–12) distinguishes between societies in which the domestic and political spheres are integrated and those in which they are separate. In many tribal societies, such as the Bushman, Eskimo, or Navajo, domestic and political arenas are integrated, in that men and women share a certain amount of authority and have similar strategies for recruiting aid into the local group. In these societies, women's strategies focus on cooperation with one another and are basically economic in nature (Lamphere 1973: 100–1). Although men are still dominant in these societies, crucial decisions are made in the domestic arena and women serve to mediate effectively between men.

In peasant communities and in some tribal communities within state societies, however, there is greater separation of the political and domestic arenas. The authority structure of the domestic group is affected by the state society and is hierarchical, with power usually held by males. Many Latin American groups – especially those in such places as the highlands of Mexico and Peru – follow this dominance pattern, in which men hold the positions of *caciques* and *alcaldes*. Although women are usually active in some aspects of trading and selling, they rarely control power and influence at the community level.

Lamphere distinguishes a third conceptual level of domestic organization, one that seems to characterize many of the black communities in Latin American areas where plantations have dominated, or people who rely on wage labor in situations where industrialization is breaking down patterns of self-subsistence. This level is found in modern industrial societies and includes groups in both rural and urban areas. Among such groups as urban working-class families or rural proletariats, a paradox exists: Although women may exert much authority in situations that involve "matrifocal" households (S. E. Brown 1975: 322–32; N. Gonzalez

1969: 128–42; Rubbo 1975: 333–57; Stack 1974: 113–28), the domestic sphere is so completely separate from the political that neither men nor women have much real power or authority. An ideology of male dominance may exist, but women have access to importance economic resources and their interests are shared with those of other women in extended community networks and kindred groups (Stack 1974: 127–8; Whitten 1974: 146–73).

Family relations change not only as a result of imposed alterations caused by industrialization, but because of migration as well. A great amount of material has been written on the nature of male migration, but little is known about how large-scale semipermanent or permanent movements of men affect the women who remain at home in rural areas. A study by Jon Olson (1977: 73–88) reports the emerging pattern of "matrifocal" households in a north Mexican town resulting from migratory wage labor of a sizeable proportion of the town's male population. Poor women in this town were able to join together as a group to work actively for political change, even getting one of their group elected as mayor, a rare occurrence in Mexico.

Sidney Mintz (1971: 253) has pointed out that justification for modernization has often rested on the assumption that economic development will increase individual opportunities and eliminate many sorts of "traditional inequalities." He emphasizes, however, that certain kinds of modernization may have an opposite result:

Implicit here is the suggestion, of course, that a gradual increase in the number of females who can become nurses, say, or elementary-school teachers may be counterbalanced by a decline in the number of women traders whose particular position in society depends in some part on their economic independence from their husbands. The point here has to do with what happens to sex roles as society changes. Even should economic opportunities for women expand, there is no assurance that they will be able to maintain the stakes associated with female sex roles if growth in other sectors of the economy come to dwarf their activities or to forestall traditional opportunities for reinvestment when they are successful. [Mintz 1971: 253–4]

The evidence from Latin America indicates that modern urban industry and trade favors the employment of men over women. In rural areas it has been men who have been taught new agricultural techniques and who have been recruited for modern activities, while women remain in the declining home industries (Boserup 1970: 139). Speaking of developing countries in general, Boserup remarks: "The inferior position of women in urban development is exacerbated by the strong preference for recruiting men to the clerical and administrative jobs" (1970: 139). Women are usually hired for unskilled, low-wage jobs, thus widening the gap between the productivity and earnings of men and women.

One reason that it is difficult to obtain accurate figures on women's participation in the labor force is that a large percentage of women go into domestic service. Young unmarried rural women may be sent by their families to the city temporarily to find domestic employment and send money back home, or married women may seek what they feel is the only available and acceptable employment. Lourdes Arizpe notes that domestic work may be an "economic safeguard" for migrant and poor urban women because of its continued availability (1977: 33). For poor women, domestic service may be the best way to obtain food and lodging for themselves and their children. However, the pay for these jobs is generally very low and the women may be taking a risk. Urban domestic servants are usually denied contracts, because the job is rarely seen as a formal one (and hence is usually not represented in labor statistics). Domestic servants are therefore subject to abrupt firing and may be relieved from duty when a younger worker is desired. This puts middle- and advanced-aged women in a precarious position and they often must resort to petty trade or the sale of food in the street (Arizpe 1977: 34).

Compared to other developing regions of the world, the number of domestic servants is particularly high in Latin America. Boserup (1970: 103) attributes this to Latin America's situation at an intermediate stage of economic development, a stage at which many domestic services "become commercialized outside the household by men or women specializing in one or other of these service activities" (restaurants, bars, cafeterias, laundries, house- and office-cleaning services, and so forth). Table 2 shows a representative sample of percentages of women in private

Table 2. *Women in private domestic service in Latin America*

Country	Women in private domestic service[a] as % of		
	All adult women	All women in nonagricultural occupation	Total labor force in private domestic service
El Salvador	5	26	97
Costa Rica	6	34	100
Colombia	7	37	94
Chile	8	35	92
Venezuela	5	26	94
Dominican Republic	4	22	92
Puerto Rico	3	13	94

[a] Includes domestic servants – occupations in private households, but excludes personnel in domestic service establishments.
Source: Boserup 1970: 102.

domestic service, indicating that this kind of service is an almost totally feminine phenomenon in Latin America.

One reason for the high female participation in the domestic sector is, as Elizabeth Jelin suggests, that in Latin America women perform a wide range of activities in their place of origin that can usually be reproduced in the towns and cities (Jelin 1977: 135). Women can perform many tasks for cash, such as mending, ironing, cleaning, taking care of children, that they normally perform in the course of their everyday duties. As Jelin states, "the fluidity of the informal labor market for domestic servants allows for the existence of a number of women who can enter or leave part-time paid employment as a simple extension of their domestic subsistence tasks" (Jelin 1977: 136).

It may be seen that urbanization does not necessarily improve women's social status. Although movement to cities may bring better job opportunities, these are still fewer than those available to men and often are in the informal sector where pay is comparatively low. Women's roles may change upon movement to an urban area as they work publicly to find jobs and establish networks, but as Harkess (1973: 232) suggests, once a woman is economically secure she may return to old patterns of conservatism. Michael Whiteford gives an indication of the difficulties facing poor women who come to urban areas:

As bleak as the labor situation appears for men in Tulcán, it is even gloomier for working women. Widowed, abandoned, or otherwise single women have very few job opportunities. Largely unskilled and more poorly educated than men, they must make a living for themselves, often while supporting a large brood of children. Some receive aid from kinsmen or have offspring who are old enough to make financial contributions, but these instances are more the exception than the rule. Because of financial difficulties, most of them share homes with other families, often having only a single room into which they must crowd with their children. They generally take in laundry or sell arepas, *masamora* (a corn and sugar broth), and other cooked foods. Some make their living bringing wood down from the hills and selling it to barrio stores. Others manage to keep going by picking raspberries and cutting flowers which they sell in the markets and on the streets in Popayán. Most do a combination of these things and send their children to beg in Popayán. Some turn to prostitution.

Margarita Chávez is single, and although she is only twenty-nine years old, she looks forty. Life has not been easy for her. At the age of fifteen, unmarried, she had her first child. Now, fourteen years later, she has eleven children living with her. They survive on what the children bring home from begging and what she makes washing clothes and as a prostitute. Luz Benavides is eighteen years old and unmarried. She lives with her two daughters, ages four and two, and four half-brothers and half-sisters, ranging in age from thirteen to six, in a one-room, dirt-floored hovel. Luz and her thirteen-year-old half-sister make tamales and in this manner earn approximately 150 pesos a month. The other children beg. The plight of the urban poor is thus accentuated in the case of women. [M. Whiteford 1976b: 38–9]

Education and selectivity

Despite ambiguous, sometimes contradictory reports, evidence strongly suggests the existence of a positive relationship between migration and formal educational achievement. Writing in 1975, Paul Shaw stated that "over the last decade, the findings of a considerable number of studies add support to the proposition that while controlling for a wide range of socioeconomic factors, migration is highly selective with respect to education. The rationale is simply that the higher an individual's level of educational attainment, the more likely he will be aware of differential opportunities, amenities, etc. to be had at alternative places of residence" (Shaw 1975: 22). However, the situation is, unfortunately, not quite so clear-cut. Bouvier and his colleagues recognize that educational attainment can mean different things at different times and different places. They ask, "What does educational attainment mean when 70–80 percent of the population is illiterate?" And they point out that the quality of education should be considered, especially between rural and urban areas. "Does it contribute to the development of a degree of 'innovativeness' on the part of the students; or is it merely traditional in content?" (Bouvier, Macisco, and Zárate 1974: 26).

These authors propose a tentative hypothesis regarding migration and education differentials: (1) The relative educational quality depends on the type of society and the economic development at both place of origin and destination. (2) The less advanced a society, the more likely migrants will be educationally inferior to nonmigrants. (3) The more advanced a society, the more likely migrants will be superior to both "stayers" (people not migrating from places of origin) and "natives" (people who are original residents of the place of destination (Bouvier, Macisco, and Zárate: 31).

Latin America does not conform closely to this theoretical framework. Herrick (1971: 74–5) has remarked that regardless of the relation between education attainments of urban migrants and urban natives, there seems no doubt about migrants' educational superiority to the population groups from which they come (Butterworth 1975a; Carvajal and Geithman 1974; Herrick 1965; McGreevey 1968; Margulis 1968; Moots 1976: 830; Roberts 1973; Scrimshaw 1975; and Simmons and Cardona 1972a, 1972b). Herrick continues:

These findings shed additional light on the degree of rationality present in the migration process. Economic folklore sometimes attributes a large degree of irrationality to the process of urban migration, owing to alleged higher unemployment in the biggest cities, the more taxing pace of urban life, etc. It is hard to reconcile, however, the relatively high levels of education of migrants with allegations of their irrational decisions to migrate, the more so since migration has continued and perhaps even increased in strength during the entire post-World War II period. [Herrick 1971: 74–5]

There are, to be sure, exceptions to the educational superiority of migrants, some of which relate to the time factor. Ducoff (1962: 131) wrote that within the metropolitan area of San Salvador there was a much higher frequency of illiteracy among the migrant than among the nonmigrant population. However, the migrants who arrived in the decade 1950–9 had, in general, a higher educational attainment than those who came to the San Salvador area in the years before 1950. Ducoff noted that the educational differential existed at both ends of the scale. That is, there was a higher concentration among migrants of persons with very little schooling as well as of persons with a high educational attainment.

Roberts (1973: 63–5) observed that migrants to Guatemala City are better educated than the provincial population that does not migrate but have less education than the city born; the difference between the migrants and the stay-at-homes is quite considerable. However, Roberts admits that drawing upon the migrant population in the city may be false or misleading, because some of the differences between migrants and stay-at-homes are produced by migrants receiving an education in the city. Obviously, the investigator must control for place of formal schooling.

In Mexico, Kemper (1977: 63) reported that Tzintzuntzeños who migrated prior to 1960 came from homes with somewhat higher than average levels of literacy, but in recent years differences between migrant and nonmigrant households have disappeared or at least somewhat narrowed the gap (the author is ambiguous on this point).

Balán and his colleagues (1973: 144–6) relate that migrants to Monterrey are positively selected by educational level, but this general statement masks the important variations present among the five socioeconomic categories they distinguish and the change that occurred between 1940 and 1960. Between those two census dates there was in Mexico as a whole an increase in educational levels: the percentage with six or more years of schooling rose from 12 to 21, and the proportion of the population engaged in nonagricultural activities rose from 31 to 41 percent. However, among migrants to Monterrey the trend was exactly the opposite. Between the early (pre-1941) and late (1951–60) times of arrival, those with six or more years of formal schooling decreased from 43 to 34 percent, and those with nonagricultural employment from 71 to 50 percent. Thus, migrant selectivity as measured by these two indicators has decreased.

Migration differentials in employment, occupation, and social class

As is to be expected, differential migration with respect to education is generally correlated with employment, occupation, and social class in Latin America. These characteristics may in turn be related to the stage of development and industrialization of a country or region. Simmons and

Cardona (1972a: 177–8) state that studies in various Latin American nations suggest that the social stratum of the metropolis into which the majority of migrants enter is determined in great part by the pattern of economic development of the nation, particularly the pattern of rural–urban social and economic differences. Thus, at this level we are dealing with structural rather than individual characteristics (Balán 1969: 23; see also Shaw 1975: 24–5; Richmond 1969: 271–81).

In less-developed countries, in which the process of urbanization has just begun and there are as yet relatively few urban opportunities for less skilled ruralites, migration to the city may be highly selective of rural elites and their children. In this situation, rural-born migrants and the native urban population may differ little in occupational characteristics (Simmons and Cardona 1972a: 177). Balán (1969: 21–4) cites studies by Ducoff and the United Nations in San Salvador and Guatemala City that support this argument.

Simmons and Cardona (1972a: 177) contend that in nations with greater socioeconomic and urban development there may be intermediate towns and small cities with rather sizeable skilled strata (artisans, factory workers, businessmen) from which rural migrants may come. In such nations even heavy streams of migrants may differ little from the urban-born men with regard to occupational skills. For example, migrants to Santiago, Chile, come heavily from such intermediate towns and cities, and their occupational characteristics do not differ greatly from those of the native urban-born population (see Elizaga 1966 and other CELADE studies). However, in'nations in which rural stagnation and rapid urban growth are combined, migrants may be relatively unskilled compared to the urban-born population.

Simmons and Cardona refer to the Monterrey Mobility Project to illustrate the change of selectivity over time and its relationship to national development. Simmons and Cardona (1972a: 170–1; 1972b: 630) found that migrants who arrive in Bogotá, Colombia, are a heterogeneous group who come from all sizes of communities and from all social levels. Migrants from small villages tend to enter the lowest strata in Bogotá, but migrants from the largest communities enter at medium or high levels. Migrants from both large and small communities tend to be a select group with reference to their community of origin, in terms of father's status and their own status and education. This selectivity, however, has undergone reduction in the last forty years.

This last finding is congruent with that of Browning and his colleagues. Browning and Feindt (1971: 51) found that agricultural employment was the most important pursuit of migrants prior to their move to Monterrey, but the city is becoming increasingly attractive to those who come directly from an agricultural background. Roberts (1973: 62–3) noted that migrants to Guatemala City were drawn predominantly from nonagricultural occupations. Even those employed in agriculture came from those groups least tied to the land–agricultural laborers and workers on family farms.

Migration and the "dynamic personality"

Economist Simon Kuznets, relying mainly on North American data, has suggested that migration is highly selective of dynamic, venturesome individuals "capable of adjusting to a variety of circumstances and . . . responsive to economic opportunities and attractions . . ." (Kuznets 1964: xxxii). Studies of migrants in Latin America have, on the whole, strengthened Kuznets' contention. Browning (1971), Butterworth (1969), Carvajal and Geithman (1974), Kemper (1977), and Perlman (1976) are among those who have discussed the "risktakers" and "innovators" who are sorted out from their fellow villagers for out-migration. Butterworth (1969; 340–1) summed up his observations as follows:

I have indicated that there are psychological variables as well which are associated with out-migration from Tilantongo. Those attributes found more often in migrants than in non-migrants may be called sophistication, cosmopolitanism, and adventurousness. These are harder to define, measure, and evaluate objectively than the characteristics already considered [age, sex, education, etc.], and my data on these variables are less quantitative and quantifiable than the others. To some extent they are impressionistic, noted during conversations and interviews with migrants and non-migrants. I did not design tests or questionnaires to identify these traits. I did, however, systematically prod my informants for knowledge of other ways and places, and the extent to which they have experienced, even vicariously, exotic customs. These indices of nonprovincialism I have termed cosmopolitanism. By adventurousness I mean simply the lack of trepidation which permits a man or a woman to undertake a new venture without being shackled by fear and apprehension.

Sophistication is a bit more difficult to pin down neatly, but is the term I use to describe a series of behavior traits and outlooks which readily distinguish people from one another, no matter how difficult to define. Most importantly, I think, is the ability to play more than one role, to interact with individuals on several levels, depending upon the company, time, and circumstance. It is a sensitivity to situations, a plasticity which allows one to adapt to situations, and a sense of appropriateness. It involves the ability to express oneself differently and effectively on varied occasions, and, perhaps, to manipulate people and situations.

Ethnicity and differential migration

Although there has been a long tradition in the United States of social scientists studying the relationship between ethnicity and internal migration, particularly among the white and nonwhite population, little work of this type has been done in Latin America. A review of the literature on racial, ethnic, and language differentials in migration indicates that the significance of these factors is particularly bound by time and place (Shaw 1975: 32).

As we might expect, the slim amount of work done on this subject in Latin America has taken place in countries with heavily indigenous populations, such as Guatemala and Mexico. Investigations in other nations that have sizeable contingents of blacks and Europeans have dealt largely with race and cultural relations rather than with migration differentials. In Guatemala, Arias (1967: 10–13) found a tendency among the Indian population to migrate less than the non-Indian or Ladino; the Indian population also tended to move shorter distances (to adjoining *departamentos*) than the non-Indian. Migration movements of the Indian population were "more varied" than those of the Ladino. The main reason seems to be that a high percentage of the indigenous group works in agriculture, an activity more widely dispersed throughout the country than nonagricultural activities; the latter are practiced more frequently by non-Indians.

Roberts (1973: 60–1) agrees that Guatemala's urban population is overwhelmingly Ladino. In a national population that was classified as 43.3 percent Indian in the 1964 census, Indians comprised an estimated 5.4 percent of migrants living in the city. "When an Indian leaves his village, he is . . . leaving a location to which he has strong social ties and entering a world in which he is potentially exposed to hostility and exploitation." Thus, Roberts concludes, although Indians are likely to migrate to supplement their subsistence agriculture, their migration is likely to be short-term and circulatory, involving a return to their home village. Mestizos from the Mazahua region usually migrate to better their economic and social positions. Indians, who are the poorest and most marginal group, migrate to improve their position in the village. Thus their migration tends to be temporary and seasonal (Arizpe 1978: 238).

This occurs in Mexico as well. Butterworth (1969, passim) shows how the mestizo segment of the population – numbering perhaps one in four – is leaving the village of Tilantongo for urban centers in increasing numbers. This has not only to do with wealth and education differences (the mestizo generally being positively selected, the Indian negatively), but also political machinations. "Although *envidia* (envy) and blood feuds occur among the Indians, they reach their apex among the wealthier mestizos. Discretion, in the form of migration, is frequently the better part of valor. Since the mestizo is more likely to be involved than the Indian, it is the mestizo family that suffers most profoundly from the heavy out-migration that is severely eroding the strength of the extended family" (Butterworth 1970: 8). This aspect of migration will be discussed further in Chapter 4.

Origins, routes, and destinations

For migration to occur there must be both a starting point and a place of destination. The point of departure need not, of course, be the place of birth, nor must study be restricted to members of a single generation. Similarly, the place of destination need not be a final stop. It is a reflection of the immature status of our understanding of migration processes that most studies of these phenomena tell us, in so many words, "This is where they came from (usually a rural birthplace) and this is where they ended up (usually a large city)." Longitudinal studies covering two or more generations are rare; few studies pinpoint lengths of stay in various types and sizes of conglomerations. The reasons for this are clear: Migration to large urban centers did not assume awesome proportions in Latin America until the 1940s, and urban anthropologists took as their own point of scholastic departure the peasant in the city.

However many types of migration we care to distinguish (rural–urban, urban–urban, and so forth), the trend in Latin America is overwhelmingly rural to urban.[5] The degree of precision demographers can apply to this trend is limited by lack of agreement about what is urban and what is rural. Given the rural-to-urban demographic trend, it should be emphasized that migratory streams originate in many disparate parts of Latin American nations and are not necessarily composed of *campesinos* (peasants, countrymen). These migrants are frequently natives of towns and cities and come from various socioeconomic strata, including the landed gentry of rural areas. For example, Elizaga (1966: 353) reported that two-thirds of the in-migrants to Santiago, Chile, came from places of 5,000 or more inhabitants. Richard Morse has commented:

Given the fact that in much of Latin America, two-thirds or more of the migrants to large cities come from towns and small cities, one wonders why the contemporary social scientists pay them little attention, or why the small-town studies of the 1940s and 1950s by such anthropologists as Foster, Gillin, Harris, Hutchinson, Lewis, Pierson, Redfield, Wagley, and Willems are so neglected in urbanization research. A survey-analysis of such studies which related them to processes of change at the national level would be a service at this point. [Morse 1971: 25]

A. M. Conning (1972: 148) observed that empirical surveys of rural–urban migration in Latin America have often tended to treat all rural communities of origin as identical. Systematic distinctions among rural communities have not often been made. Butterworth (1969: 50–1) noted that there are vast differences in degree of urbanization of "rural" communities. These differences include not only size and density, but the presence or absence of communications, transportation, and recreational facilities; the degree of sophistication and cosmopolitanism; and the extent to which rural dwellers regularly visit town markets, shrines, fiestas, and the like. An isolated municipio in the sierra is entirely different from a commercial community on an international highway, although both may be classified as rural (or urban) by census officials. In contrast to the municipio, the commercial community has various communication media at its disposal that afford plentiful information on the urban situation and a ready means of transportation to the city.

Conning hypothesized that the ratio of rural–urban migrants to all migrants from a given community is directly related to the level of differentiation of that community. In other words, the more differentiated the community, the greater the proportion of migrants that goes to the city. Conning expanded:

> The underlying dimension, termed "community differentiation," will be viewed here as the degree to which a community is coupled with the national system via national institutions such as those involved in the educational, economic and religious subsystems. The more closely bound a community is to the national system, the more roles or artifactions representing the national institutions will be found in the community. Low differentiation communities are those usually designated as "rural" and high differentiation communities are those designated "urban." [1972: 50]

Conning surveyed seven rural communities in Chile. He found that out-migration from the most rural (the least differentiated) communities to places with ten thousand or more inhabitants was much less than that from the least rural. Conning felt that this was not accounted for by the distance between the communities and urban areas, but appeared to be partially explained by the level of differentiation of the communities (Conning, 1972: 152–6).

We thus once again return to the important distinction – not opposition – between structural and personal (individual) characteristics of migrants and, in this case, their places of origin. Balán (1969: 23) has emphasized that although the literature dealing with internal migration has dealt extensively with the characteristics of migrants, such as their motivations and adaptation to the urban environment, it has seldom paid attention to the structural conditions attending migration; that is, the characteristics of the communities of origin (and destination), should be studied, in addition to those of individuals.

Herrick (1965: 51–2) found two pieces of evidence that the pattern of English internal migration experienced during the Industrial Revolution has been repeated in Chile. One compares the responses given in two sample surveys in Greater Santiago: an employment survey of the University of Chile's Institute of Economics (IE), and a separate CELADE survey. In the IE survey, 63 percent of the migrants replied that they had been born in towns later identified as having more than ten thousand people. Preliminary findings of the CELADE study showed that 65 percent lived in towns of more than five thousand immediately before coming to Santiago. Herrick points out that "if we had observed a pattern of migrants with repeated moves from smaller towns to larger, the percentage *born in towns* would have to be far smaller than the percentage *living in towns* immediately before coming to Santiago" (p. 52).

The second piece of evidence comes from a sample survey by Herrick done in cooperation with the IE and CELADE. The results of the survey of economically active recent migrants to Santiago were surprisingly similar to the earlier surveys, which had covered all migrants. Two-thirds of the economically active migrants had been born in places of more than ten thousand inhabitants. Only about one-seventh claimed places of birth with fewer than one thousand inhabitants – "places which could be classified as clearly rural" (1965: 52).[6]

Herrick felt that he had established an important part of the Ravenstein-Redford migration pattern: that the migrants to the biggest city came largely from smaller cities rather than from the countryside. Obviously, however, it is unsafe to generalize from a single case, no matter how thorough the documentation; and, at this point, Herrick had failed to account for fill-in or step migration.

Choice of destination

In Chapter 2 we observed that, unless it is forced, migration must involve some kind of decision or decisions on the part of the individuals and families who go from one place to another. Here we shall take a brief look at some of the choices of destination made by people once they have decided to move.

We reemphasize that by no means all migrants from villages and small towns choose – or are in one way or another coerced – to move to an urban center. In discussing migration in Andean America, Preston (1969: 281–3) indicated that movement to major population centers in the region is complemented by movements to new agricultural areas. Mestizos from small towns with some financial resources frequently go to "frontier areas" to bring virgin land under cultivation; others go to marginal agricultural areas where subsistence cultivation is possible or necessary. Such movements are apparently rather common in Colombia, Ecuador, and Peru.[7]

Aside from seasonal labor, however, most migrants from rural areas head for larger centers, even if by plan or accident they make one or more stopovers on the way. Methodological problems we touched upon earlier also face us here. One is the hindsight of informants when asked about their choice of destination. For example, Browning and Feindt (1971: 53–4) reported that 89 percent of their respondents in Monterrey did not consider other destinations before making their choice. For the other 11 percent it was preponderantly a large urban place. Rural or small urban centers hold very little attraction for the migrants. However, it seems incredible that nine of ten migrants never even thought of going somewhere else, particularly when, in an earlier phase of the study, the authors revealed that Monterrey has not had a monopoly of access to the "reservoirs" of potential migrants in the region, because several other cities in northeastern Mexico, especially those on or near the United States border, also have had very rapid growth (Browning and Feindt 1969: 356).

Then there is the problem of trying to decide when a migrant becomes a migrant. An infant who is taken by his parents to a city for several years and is still a child when his parents decide to return to their village is, from one point of view, a migrant who went home after several years in the city. But his is obviously a different case from that of his father, who, let us suppose, went and returned of his own volition. And in the case of a man whose seasonal labor becomes permanent migration over the course of years, it is difficult to determine at what point he has become a migrant.

Consider the case of Vicente Montesinos[8] from Tilantongo, Mexico. When Vicente was a boy he used to accompany his mother to Taltepec, a neighboring community in the Mixteca Alta region of Oaxaca, where his mother sold palms and dates. On one trip a woman in Taltepec offered him a job as a *mozo* (errand boy, house boy), which he accepted, but he sneaked back home when he became homesick. Not long afterwards, he and his mother moved to Villa de Etla, in the Valley of Oaxaca. They both obtained employment there; later Vicente moved around other places in the Valley, including the state capital of Oaxaca de Juárez. His mother went back to Tilantongo and Vicente returned there after a time. Discouraged by the lack of opportunities at home, Vicente returned to Oaxaca City with his mother when he was still a youth.

Vicente then took a notion to sign up for the sugar-cane harvest in Veracruz state. He worked here and there in the states of Oaxaca and Veracruz for a number of years, including eight years in Córdoba, a medium-sized city in the latter state. Then once again he returned to Tilantongo, where he took a bride. Although his wife's family had sufficient land and cattle for Vicente and his bride to live comfortably, Vicente had problems with his in-laws, so he and his wife left for Mexico City, where they have lived for twenty years.

At what point, we may ask, did Vicente become a migrant? When he spent a week in Taltepec? When he and his mother went to Villa de Etla? When they went to the city of Oaxaca after a respite in Tilantongo? Or when he finally left autonomously? Further, at what point can we attribute motivations, decisions, or choices, to Vicente's actions? Migration motivations imply at least some degree of autonomous decision making, which Vicente did not have until he left his mother, and his choices of destination seemed almost limitless. Many cases, like Vicente's, have to be determined in an arbitrary way.

Vicente is literally one of millions who have migrated to the Federal

District of Mexico. It is by far the greatest magnet in that nation. In view of the projection that the metropolitan area may reach thirty-two million persons by the year 2000, Robert Van Kemper asks: "What continues to attract migrants to the capital? Why do Tzintzuntzeños [natives of Tzintzuntzan in the state of Michoacan] and thousands of other Mexican villagers and city dwellers keep coming to an urban agglomeration with shortages of water, adequate housing, and municipal services? What makes the struggle for survival in Mexico City more easily endured than in the migrant's home community? (Kemper 1977: 77).

Kemper's answer is simple: Despite its population problems, the rapid industrialization of Mexico City has – at least until recently – provided sufficient employment opportunities for semiskilled, skilled, and technical workers so that most migrants and natives have been able to find work. Residents of Mexico City almost always experience a standard of living superior to that in other places in Mexico (Kemper: 79–81).

Plans for decentralization of industry offer some hope for dispersal of the migrant population, but James Wilkie (1974: 76) believes that rural workers seem to be increasingly hopeful of finding "redemption from peasant poverty through escape to the big city." This is as true, says Kemper, for the people of Tzintzuntzan as for those in thousands of other Mexican villages and towns (Kemper 1977: 95).

This does not, however, hold true throughout Latin America. Michael Whiteford has made a most interesting analysis of why many migrants from the Colombian countryside select a barrio in the small city of Popayán as a final destination. Whiteford (1976b: 17–18) writes:

It is surprising that individuals choose to migrate to Popayán, a city with very little industry and hence little to offer in the way of employment. Cali, a city of a million inhabitants, second largest and one of the most industrial cities in Colombia, is located only 150 kilometers from Popayán and would seem to be a more natural choice. Yet there are a number of plausible explanations as to why Popayán is selected instead, which may throw some light on the general processes and problems of migration in Colombia.

Among these explanations are that many of the inhabitants of Tulcán barrio either are natives of the area just south of Popayán or had lived in that area just before coming to the city. Proximity is the key here. Others spend several years in Popayán and then move to Cali or other large cities. These people represent the "step migrants." Whiteford notes that with Cali only two hours away by bus, proximity to Popayán as a reason for its choice may seem unconvincing as the determining factor in the stage progression. Nevertheless, he writes, for poor rural families, any uprooting is a financial hardship of considerable proportions. Popayán may thus be seen as a place where they can add to their resources before continuing the journey (Whiteford: 18).

Another reason for choosing Popayán reflects the serious unemployment problem in Colombia. A number of people from Tulcán barrio have lived in Cali and Bogotá, but finding no work there, come to Popayán:

These people express the peculiar truism that it is less costly to be un- or underemployed in Popayán than in Bogotá or Cali. Those who have lived in either or these large cities also say that they prefer Popayán because it is a safe, quiet city, without most of the problems of crime they experienced in the larger cities. Thus, many Tulcaneses present a new twist on the standard theories of migration, in which the individual ends up living in the large industrial centers. Data from Tulcán indicate that some people go to the large city and then, for one reason or another, reject it and seek a smaller and economically less attractive city in which to live. [Whiteford 1976b: 19]

Finally, another explanation for settling in Popayán is that many people have friends or relatives already living there. They hear about life in Popayán from them; then, when they decide to move, they choose Popayán because they have an idea of what to expect and know someone who can help them find housing and a job (Whiteford 1976b: 18–19). It is untrue, however, that the *decision* to move is brought about by the very existence of kin and friends in a place.

Distance and migration

One of the major interests in migration theory has been the effects of distance and choice of destination on migration patterns. In their review of evidence from village studies in various parts of the world, Connell et al. (1976: 72) claim that from this interest "has evolved one of the few 'laws' in behavioural science that have been thoroughly tested and found, in the great majority of cases, to be true; that distance deters migration, first proposed in 1885 by Ravenstein." Among Ravenstein's propositions was the statement that migrants proceed only short distances; migrants proceeding long distances generally go to one of the great centers of commerce and industry. Consequently, there occurs the "universal shifting" of population we alluded to in Chapter 2. The inhabitants of the countryside immediately surrounding a town of rapid growth flock into it; the gaps left in the rural population are filled by migrants from more remote distances.

Stage migration

The idea of "step" versus "nonstep" (or "stage" versus "direct") migration is another false dichotomy. The routes migrants take to reach a so-called final destination have to do with sex, friends and kin, distance, and time. Chen (1968: 155) holds the traditional view that, in Venezuela, the migrants move first to municipal capitals, state capitals, and other important cities. Then they go to the largest cities of the nation in accordance with pull factors and kin and friendship ties. Usandizaga and Havens

(1966: 39) reported that half of their barrio informants lived in a place other than that of their birth before settling in Barranquilla, Colombia. In Peru, Valdivia Ponce (1970: 171) suggests that step migration may be the rule, perhaps giving the migrants progressively more security as they move to ever larger centers, until they arrive in the city. These studies are, however, poorly controlled for the variables mentioned.

Richard Morse (1971: 23) observed that on the whole, "regional and national migration studies show refreshing agreement on the proportion of stage to direct migration to large cities." Germani (1963: 321) estimated that some one-third of the migrants to Buenos Aires made one or more intermediate stops en route to "final" destination. In two barrios in Bogotá, Cardona (1968: 68–9) reported that 73 percent from one barrio and 41 percent from the other went directly to the capital, and 12 percent from the first and almost 40 percent from the second made only one stopover before arriving in Bogotá. In other words, over half the respondents had migrated in one or more stages from their place of birth. However, the stopovers were often brief; two-thirds of the informants had completed their trip in less than one year and another seventh did so in from one to five years. Cardona's study is one of the few that controlled the time factor in single-generation mobility.

In two other barrios in Bogotá, Flinn (1968: 61; 1971: 83–4) had similar findings. In both cases, the majority of migrants moved directly to Bogotá without intermediate stops. On the other hand, at least 30 percent of both samples made intermediate stops of widely varying lengths.

Using 1960 census data from Chile, Herrick showed that none of the fifty-nine cities of more than ten thousand people had undergone a decline in population between the 1952 and 1960 censuses, and some cities smaller than Santiago had experienced dramatic population growth. While the urban population was growing at an annual rate of almost 4 percent, the rural population increased by only 0.7 percent. "Migration was plainly stripping people from the agricultural parts of the country. We have already seen that these rural people, in general, were not those found in Santiago. They must therefore have gone to the smaller towns" (Herrick 1965: 53). The conclusion is that Ravenstein and Redford were right in their "laws" of step migration and fill-in.

Morse apparently agrees. While taking into account regional discrepancies, he argues that one can plausibly generalize that (1) only a quarter to a third of migration to large cities occurs in stages, and (2) direct migration from rural and semirural places to large cities, although not unusual, cannot account for the balance of the migratory movement (Morse 1971: 23). The inference is that this balance comes from semiurban and urban places.

Morse's second conclusion is supported, he claims, by "a frequent finding that migrants to large cities are 'urbanized' beyond national averages by indices of educational and occupational skill and that they are not severely disadvantaged in the urban job market with respect to native urbanites" (Morse 1971: 23). However, in the Monterrey Mobility Project we find contradictory or at least mitigating evidence. Although Browning and his colleagues established the fact that migrants tended to leave their community of origin at an early age, the researchers did not know how much time had passed between their departure and their first arrival in Monterrey. The investigators theorized that migrants might have spent a considerable amount of time in other, usually smaller, communities that would serve as "anticipatory socialization" for life in Monterrey. But this was not often the case. Some 63 percent of all migrants moved directly from their community of origin to Monterrey; 17 percent took up to ten years and the rest more than a decade until they arrived in the city. The researchers think it noteworthy that, when size of community of origin was considered, 59 percent of those of rural origin came directly to Monterrey. "Thus, for the majority of these kinds of migrants, there is no possibility of advance socialization to metropolitan Monterrey by way of residence in some smaller urban place" (Balán et al. 1973: 150).

They point out that this finding is contrary to the expectations of the stage or step migration model, explaining that the fit of that model to Monterrey is a poor one for a number of reasons:

The stage-migration model assumes a population distribution pattern whereby all parts of a given territory are equally habitable, with a geometric arrangement of different size communities such that any person randomly selected within the territory (excluding the perimeter areas) would be located the same distance from communities of different sizes as any other person. But in Mexico, and particularly in areas providing the bulk of migrants to Monterrey, the population distribution is very uneven because of geographical and historical factors, and the urban hierarchy itself has many "holes," that is communities of the expected size are lacking. Consequently, for some migrants the proper community is difficult to "find." The model also presumes a well-developed transportation system linking all communities of the size hierarchy. It further assumes that urban places are not greatly different in their economic attractiveness to prospective migrants. But, of course, many small and medium-size places are bypassed for the very good reason that there are few jobs available to migrants. Finally, the model entirely ignores the social context of migration, especially the fact that most people migrate to places where they have relatives or friends awaiting them. [Balán et al. 1973: 151]

In summary, our current state of knowledge concerning origins, routes and destinations of migrants in Latin America is as follows:

1. All migrants are not campesinos. Many migrants who go to large urban centers come from towns and small cities.

2. There are important differences among rural communities, particularly in their structural characteristics.

3. In analyzing places of origin and destination, we must distinguish between structural and individual characteristics of migrants and the places they come from and go to.

4. The choice of destination and routes taken is often heavily influenced by the presence of friends and relatives.

5. Men usually migrate first, followed by women. This pattern may be either inter- or intragenerational.

6. Men generally move longer distances in one step than women do.

7. Stage or step migration is not a universal. Generalizations about stage versus direct migration must be phrased in terms of time and context.

8. Previous mobility may be related to distance traveled and place of origin.

9. The influence of prior urban experience – direct or indirect – on choice of destination and routes followed is as yet undetermined.

4. Return migration, brokerage, and effects on the community

The aspect of migration that has been least amenable to quantification is return migration. Very few village or other surveys record the proportions of migrants who return to their native villages – information on who they are, why they return, and the impact they have on the village economy and social structure (Connell et al. 1976: 121). Feindt and Browning (1972: 158) maintain that return migration always has been "one of the more shadowy features of the migration process." They add that "the nets cast out in national censuses to obtain data on migration allow return migration to slip through. Reliance upon state of birth or state of residence 'x' years ago versus state of current residence, the customary census procedures, are unsuited to get at the incidence of return migration."

These authors suggest that the most reliable way to obtain information on return migration is through the use of migration life histories. This technique was used to interview informants in Monterrey and in Cedral, a small agriculturally oriented community in the state of San Luis Potosí, Mexico. Among other things, the questionnaires contained a life-history form that systematically listed all changes in residence lasting six months duration or longer. Any return to a former residence for this period of time within the lifetime of the respondent was considered return migration. In the Cedral study there was also a series of questions probing the reasons for return migration to Cedral and the social context of the return.

Butterworth (1969) used similar techniques in his investigations of migration from Tilantongo, Oaxaca, Mexico. In addition, he recorded extensive genealogies, which enabled him to trace migration patterns back to the middle of the nineteenth century. Butterworth's recording of life histories differed from that used in the Cedral study in several respects. First, changes of residence in Butterworth's work were not limited to six months or longer: Shorter stays were also recorded. Further, "return migration" in Butterworth's study meant a return to Tilantongo, not any return to a former residence. This is less confusing than it is to analyze return migration from the point of view of a person who has moved from his natal place to city A, back to place of birth, then to city B, back home again, to city C, once more to city A, and so forth.

Consider the case of Mauro Rojas. He was born in Tilantongo in 1885 and lived the first decade of his life in La Labor, one of the outlying ranchos of the municipio. He spent the following ten years in nearby

Nochixtlán, the district capital, where he attended school and worked as a *mozo* (house boy). In 1905 he returned to Tilantongo and assisted his father with farming chores for seven years.

In 1912 he left for the city of Oaxaca to try his luck as a *comerciante* (a trader), but having little success, he headed for the state of Veracruz, where he worked at odd jobs for several years. In traditional stepwise fashion, Mauro then went to Mexico City to try his luck in a small business venture, but he was forced to return to Tilantongo because of the death of his sister. During this stay, Mauro married and began to raise a family.

In 1917, at the age of thirty-two, Mauro joined the Zapatista forces (followers of Emiliano Zapata) in the Mexican Revolution. He achieved the rank of captain but left the service after a year when the Zapatistas began to fall into disarray.[1] He made a brief visit to Tilantongo to look after his land and family and then went back to Mexico City, where he worked as a shopkeeper's assistant.

Mauro sent for his wife and young son, spending six years in the nation's capital before he was recalled once more to Tilantongo, this time to serve as president of the municipio, a one-year tenure post which he held on two occasions. At the end of his brief but influential political career, Mauro went back to Mexico City to work as a clerk. However, concern about his land holdings and political manipulations resulted in his return once again to Tilantongo, this time for a period of five years. In 1933, he left with his growing family to take a job in Mexico City as a concierge and part-time entrepreneur. He made his final return to Tilantongo in 1936, where he was killed in a vendetta. It is a most baffling task to place Mauro in some kind of migrant category.

Michael Whiteford (1976b: 20) used the Feindt and Browning approach to defining return migration, reporting that many people from the Tulcán barrio of Popayán are "return migrants": In other words, they have moved from the country to Popayán, then on to another city or back to the country before eventually returning to Popayán. Whiteford reports that 26 percent of migrant household heads in Tulcán previously had lived in Popayán and then moved away. However, we prefer not to use the term "return migration" in this sense.

Whiteford also noted that there are people who stay in Popayán but would prefer to move elsewhere. Many would like to return to the country and resume previous ways of life, but they remember that they left the countryside in the first place because they were unable to make an adequate living tilling the soil. Only a few return to rural areas (Whiteford 1976b: 20).

Because return migration is but one aspect of migratory movements, we should expect to be able to differentiate patterns of in-migration similar to those for out-migration. Thus we could distinguish among seasonal return, repeated return, and permanent return (see Connell et al. 1976: 121). Probably all three patterns occur in most rural communities in Latin America, involving different families or persons, or perhaps one individual over time in a kind of progression. Vicente Montesinos, the informant from Tilantongo discussed in the previous chapter, is an example of the latter.

In Chapter 3 we asked at what point a migrant becomes a migrant. Here we can pose a similar question: When does a returned migrant become a permanent returnee? Take the case of Genaro Landa. He left Tilantongo in 1921, when he was seventeen years of age, to fight in the last months of the Mexican Revolution. He stayed in the army until 1938. Following his discharge, he joined the Oaxaca police force and was stationed in the capital of that state. After twelve years as a policeman, he returned to Tilantongo where he purchased land and built two small adobe houses, one of which he converted into a small store, and sold such miscellaneous items as matches, cigarettes, beer, and *aguardiente* (an alcoholic beverage distilled from sugar cane). When interviewed in 1967, Genaro had lived in Tilantongo for the previous sixteen years and stated his intention of staying there until his death. Unfortunately, the sale of *aguardiente* proved to be his undoing. He had no license for the sale of alcoholic beverages (liquor laws are usually honored in the breach in the region), and in one of the unsavory political machinations that have marked the history of Tilantongo, he was fined, his property was threatened with confiscation, and, in fear of the authorities, he fled the community. When heard from, he was living in the city of Oaxaca. Thus, no matter how permanent their intention, return migrants may again leave their villages.

The incidence of return migration (of whatever duration) is largely unknown. Herrick (1965: 55) reports return migration in Chile to be rare, at least according to survey data of migrants who came to Santiago in the ten years preceding his study. The reason may be that because Chilean migrants have proceeded to Santiago mostly from cities and towns instead of directly from agricultural districts, they have few rural ties: therefore, return or back-and-forth migration is uncommon.

There are no overall figures on return migration in Mexico, but several village studies give at least a hint of the fact. Return migration to Tilantongo is cyclical. Prior to World War II it was common, it declined during the economic boom years of the 1940s to the middle or late 1960s, and since then has increased steadily as the national economy has sagged and fewer urban employment opportunities have existed. However, ties to the community remain strong no matter where the migrants go or how long they live away from their *tierra*.

Kemper and Foster report for Tzintzuntzan (1975: 57) that, in earlier years, return migrants were uncommon. Now there is a much higher incidence of returnees. The investigators admit that it is difficult to predict which of these returnees will leave the community again. They hold that the recent increase in the number of return migrants is a result of declining selectivity within the expanding migrant population. Cedral, Mexico, may be statistically typical. Feindt and Browning (1972: 159) calculated that about 30 percent of the male village population were return migrants, but the figures are complicated by their definition of return migration as any return to a former residence lasting longer than six months.

In discussing return migration we must once again weigh personal variables against structural ones. Both are complementary and each is related to the time factor. For example, personal success or failure in an urban venture is of obvious importance. Unlike in Africa, "target" migration – in which the migrant's goal is to build up a preplanned amount of capital over a targeted period of time – is relatively uncommon in Latin America, where it is more common for a man and his wife to return to their natal community to retire. This individual or personal decision is related to the level of economic and social opportunities available in the native village or the ability of the returnee to create opportunities there. This decision is, in turn, closely related to the availability of particular kinds of jobs in the village. Thus in many communities with high man–land ratios, the probability of return migration is low, unless the migrant has saved up a reasonably large sum of money (Connell et al. 1976: 124–6).

In cases where land can be acquired rather easily and at a cheap price, relatively small amounts of cash enable a migrant to make investments that can place him in a dominant economic or social position in the community (Connell et al. 1976: 124–6). Simmons and Cardona (1972a: 179) reported that in the rural highland communities in Colombia they surveyed, between one-fifth and one-third of the men in any given community had lived for some time in a large city, usually Bogotá. Some of these return migrants may have been rejected by the city; but the generally high social background, higher education, and easier entry into the urban labor force of these migrants indicated that they are members of the middle and upper social strata who return to take advantage of rural opportunities not available to men with lesser skills and fewer resources.[2]

There are also the cultural and economic "brokers," who have one foot in each world, the urban and the rural (the latter usually but not necessarily their home community). These will be discussed later in this chapter. Here, however, we shall discuss an example of one such type from Tilantongo to illustrate a subtype of return migrant. This man, whom we shall call Miguel Lara, owns some of the best land in the village. He maintains a house there and rents or sharecrops his land while he spends most of his time at his home in the city of Oaxaca. Miguel is a comerciante who travels from Oaxaca to isolated communities buying and selling merchandise, particularly foodstuffs such as maize. His favorite market is

Tilantongo, where he has contacts and influence. He purchases maize there at a reduced price during and immediately after the harvest in late fall and then returns to sell it and other foodstuffs during the late summer and early fall when supplies in the municipio have dwindled. For a small-time entrepreneur, his profits can be impressive: he buys cheap and sells dear. Miguel is roundly disliked in Tilantongo for his profiteering and political maneuvers (he was the person who denounced Genaro Landa for selling illicit aguardiente), but he is a powerful figure and many people count on him to pull them through shortages by futures buying and other similar activities.

There are also migrants who might have made a success of their urban undertaking, but who return for a miscellany of reasons. In addition to inability to find work, Margulis (1968: 114) found that among the Argentinian migrants he studied, reasons given for returning were health, family, and homesickness. Illness of family members is a common reason for at least a short return visit (and not infrequently is an excuse to leave urban employment for a while). Death or incapacitation of kin may cause an otherwise well-adjusted migrant in the city to return home for extended periods of time, perhaps permanantly, to take care of family affairs.

Then there are the failures, the migrants who could not make it in the city. There are at least three types of unsuccessful migrants: those who return after being unable to find employment elsewhere, those whose work outside the village ends after a limited period, and those who return because they are unable to adapt to the social and cultural life outside the village. In their review of the literature on out-migration from villages, Connell and his associates (1976: 128) concluded that return migration seems more likely to signify failure than success, although the determinants of success or failure are not always in the hands of the migrants.

In other words, external constraints must be considered. An important consideration is the landholding system of rural communities, which may be based on local, regional, or national law or custom. This is quite apart from, or may be viewed as complementary to, the ability of individuals to hold or acquire real estate in the sense discussed above. Roberts (1973: 67–8) has this to say about landholdings:

One of the major reasons for differences between countries appears to be the ease with which rural systems of landholding accommodate returning migrants and single females by giving absent people rights to which they can return and which females can "protect" for them. In Guatemala, there are, however, few alternative possibilities open to women in the provinces; they cannot find employment as itinerant laborers or plantation workers to the extent that male migrants can. For women, the city is the surest and most available source of employment. Also, the considerable male outmigration from villages and towns creates a potentially difficult marriage market. Males often do not return to their home villages, and rarely is there communal property in which they are interested in retaining rights.

So . . . women in Guatemalan villages have little economic or social inducement to await the return of males, and, once in a city, they have few claims on their home village that make their return worthwhile.

We are not certain to what extent we can accept Roberts's generalizations about Guatemalan villages and their women nor his use of the term "communal property." Land that is communally owned or worked is not typical of Guatemalan communities, nor, for that matter, is it typical of Mexico. The *ejido* program, often thought to involve communal ownership or labor, is a system whereby land is granted to a village (or municipio) and distributed to individual families for their use. Little of the land is communally worked.

Retention of property rights by individuals who leave the village is, however, apparently widely practiced in Mexico. In Tilantongo, perhaps a third of the migrants still own land in the community. Many migrants return to fetch brides, and some remain in the municipio after marriage to work their land or that of their bride. The custom of land retention by migrants often operates to the disadvantage of the community, but it offers security and inducement to return to migrant males.

National policies may have a strong impact on migration practices. Guillet and Whiteford, for example, looked at the effect of the Peruvian agrarian reform of 1969 on migration patterns in that country. They noted that the agrarian reform was successful in eliminating indirect usufruct and noncultivation of land located in peasant communities and, because out-migrants had used these means to maintain control over land, the reform forced them to reassess their situation in the city in relation to a rural, land-based life style. In a community that Guillet studied (Rumipata, a pseudonym), his data indicated that a substantial number of migrants had returned to the village because of the threat to their land. They feared that their plots would be taken. However, the reforms in Peru had also fostered return migration because of the better economic circumstances of Rumipata (Guillet 1976: 301; Guillet and S. Whiteford 1974: 230).

As part of one of the best-publicized attempts at directed culture change in the annals of anthropology – the Peru-Cornell Project in Vicos, Peru – Mario Vásquez and his colleagues undertook a study to determine the factors that had motivated the return of former Vicos residents to their natal community since 1954.[3] The unusual incidence of return migration to Vicos, situated in the Callejón de Huaylas, some 3,000 to 4,500 meters above sea level, was of particular interest, because at that time, most Andean migrants established more-or-less permanent residence at places where they could find better living conditions, preferably on the coast.

The conclusions reached by Vásquez were that the return of migrants to Vicos was not directly related to any single factor such as the abolition of the hacienda system or the work of the "promoters" (culture change agents) of the Peru-Cornell Project, but was determined by the concurrence of other economic, social, and psychological factors. Vásquez reported that migrants returned to their community if they were offered better economic opportunities and security in the form of land, credit, technical assistance, and education, which might guarantee them new social position within the regional structure. Another conclusion was that return migrants are less conservative than those who have had little or no contact with people outside their natal place; they are also more receptive to innovations (Vásquez 1963: 93–102). As such, they may act as cultural brokers or mediators between the urban and rural sectors or the national and local systems.

Brokers and mediation

The close connection between rural and urban sectors has a number of interesting facets that have only recently begun to capture the attention of anthropologists and other social scientists. One of these is the role of brokers or mediators in relating the community to the nation. This area is an example of the increasing concern of anthropology with problems at the national level and of the articulation between village and supracommunity organizations.

Eric Wolf's writings have been primary influences in moving anthropological interests in this direction. His article "Aspects of Group Relations in a Complex Society" (1956) focused upon the web of relations that exists between community and nation and showed how there has been a continually changing relationship among groups and entities in Mexico throughout history, including latifundio owners, peasants, and the national government. These changing relationships result from the emergence of differential political and economic forces. As new relationships develop, there emerge what Wolf terms cultural "brokers," who mediate between community-oriented groups and national institutions:

The study of these "brokers" will prove increasingly rewarding, as anthropologists shift their attention from the internal organization of communities to the manner of their integration into larger systems. For they stand guard over the crucial junctures or synapses of relationships which connect the local system to the larger whole. Their basic function is to relate community-oriented individuals who want to stabilize or improve their life chances, but who lack economic and political connections, with nation-oriented individuals who operate primarily in terms of the complex cultural forms standardized as national institutions, but whose success in these operations depends on the size and strength of their personal following . . . The position of these "brokers" is an "exposed" one, since, Janus-like, they face in two directions at once. They must serve some of the interests of groups operating on both the community and the national level, and they must cope with the conflicts raised by the collision of these interests. They cannot settle them, since by doing so they would abolish their own usefulness to others. Thus they often act as buffers between groups, maintaining the tensions which provide the dynamic of their actions. [Wolf 1956: 1075–6.]

Guillet reported that in Rumipata the process of brokerage by return migrants has resulted from structural changes brought about by agrarian reform. It would appear that changes in man/land relations brought about by socioeconomic policies such as agrarian reform will ultimately affect the alignment of groups that have articulated between peasant communities and the regional and national political economy. "Such a situation is optimum for the emergence of entrepreneurs who can judiciously manipulate their resources to raise their position in the social structure. If structural change is associated with return migration, then we can expect a high degree of competition by migrants for these choice roles now opened up to them" (Gillet 1976: 301).

Rollwagen (1974: 48) notes that Wolf sees brokers mediating between groups from a community on the one hand and groups representing national-level institutions on the other. He thinks that the specification that there be a definable "group" at the community level causes very little trouble to anthropologists, since the villages they study are usually small and groups are isolable. However, he continues, "when anthropologists turn their attention to the impact of the nation on the community that they are studying, they are more likely to talk about 'forces' rather than specific groups."

Rollwagen argues that Wolf's stricture that these so-called national-level groups must operate primarily through national institutions restricts the kinds of contacts the community might have with the nation and restricts our considerations to those national-level groups that have formal structures (1974: 48). Coupling this argument with Silverman's analysis of Italian local and national groups (1965: 172–89), Rollwagen relates a case of mediation involving *paleteros* (popsicle or ice-cream vendors) in Jalisco, Mexico. His study emphasizes mediation arising in the rural community, not at the national level.

In 1946, a man from the village of Mexticacan opened a small factory for the production of *paletas* (popsicles and ice cream) in Aguascalientas, one of the two large cities relatively near to Mexticacan. His business flourished, so some of his fellow villagers began similar enterprises in other cities in Mexico. Within ten years, Mexticaqueños had established *paleterías* (factories for the production of popsicle and ice cream products) throughout Mexico and had monopolized perhaps 70 to 80 percent of the market in Mexico (Rollwagen 1974: 52). The factory owners generally employed men from their village and thus developed a patron–client relationship between employers and employees of the type described by Wolf (1966: 1–22). Rural–urban migration increased, with the patrons acting as mediators or brokers between clients from Mexticacan and a specific urban population, not an institution or a group representing that institution. The migrant clients from Mexticacan worked at (usually) temporary jobs in ice-cream factories in the region. The patrons gradually lost interest in their role as mediators as their interest in the community diminished, although they still maintained ties with Mexticacan. They began to participate more and more as national-level businessmen assimilated to urban life and less and less as villagers whose social and economic ties necessitated contact with fellow villagers (Rollwagen 1974: 55–8).

Brokerage or mediation can and often does involve complex social and personal relationships. In Tilantongo, there are resident mestizo entrepreneurs and politicians, some of whom are returned migrants, who act as brokers between the community and urban centers. Their influence is primarily limited to minor, usually ineffectual lobbying in the state capital of Oaxaca and relaying information about job opportunities as peons or other low-paid unskilled laborers in nearby towns. The more important brokerage functions, such as finding steady employment and housing in large cities, particularly Mexico City, for village residents, and undertaking ambitious schemes for the improvement of community facilities, are left to the relatively wealthy members of the community who live in Mexico City and Puebla. But the brokers who reside in Tilantongo act as mediators between the brokers in the large urban centers and their own contacts in the local community and local population.

In her study of Chuschi, Peru, Billie Jean Isbell reported that returned migrants have dual identities: They see themselves as members of the national culture as well as members of the village community. They are, in short, "the mediators between the urban ideology of the national culture and the traditional ideology of the village." Their success in this role, Isbell concludes, depends in part upon historical events beyond their control. It also depends upon the degree of resistance they encounter from the nonmigrants (Isbell 1974: 255).

The effects of out-migration on community of origin

The effects of out-migration and return migration on communities of origin have probably received the least attention of any aspect of internal migration. Speaking of the Andean situation, which is generalizable for the rest of mainland Latin America, Preston (1969: 282–4) remarked that it might be reasonable to hypothesize that the very problems that serve to expel people from their home environment are at least partly solved by their exodus. Yet there is little evidence to support this, at least in relation to economic factors. Out-migration seems to keep the pressure on the land constant rather than to decrease it. It is important to distinguish between the effects of those who have *left* the community and those who have *returned*.

Preston points out several problems that arise in communities from which there is extensive out-migration. One of these is the near-universal selectivity of the young that leaves communities decimated by the migration of many of their biologically productive population and with an abnormal proportion of aged persons. Another change that results from migration from village to town or city is a shortage of agricultural labor in rural areas. A third problem associated with out-migration is the quality of the migrants and the question of whether there exists a rural "brain drain" (Preston 1969: 282–4).

This by no means exhausts the list of changes and problems associated with out- and return migration. There is the crucial consideration of land tenure. There are often financial arrangements between city dwellers and their village kin. Social, economic, and political changes in rural villages and towns may reflect the whims and plans of absentee and returned migrants. And these relate to the degree and level of socioeconomic integration of community, region, and nation (see Steward 1963) and the role of cultural brokers discussed above earlier in this chapter.

Loss of the biologically productive population

The loss of young people may not necessarily mean a reduction in population. A continuing increase in fertility rates and, in some instances, in-migration from other villages, may help compensate numerically for this loss. In his overview of migration from Mexican communities, Cornelius (1976a: 13) observed that "the key factor that conditions outmigration's impact on these communities is natural population increase. Many negative economic and social consequences often associated with heavy outmigration have not materialized in most of the communities because it occurred while rates of natural population were increasing considerably. Until recently, natural increase, combined with immigration from surrounding communities, has more than offset population loss from outmigration in most communities."

In his investigation of Aldea San Francisco, Argentina, Richard Wilkie noted that in-migration has taken place consistently since the 1920s but in much smaller numbers than out-migration. Most in-migrants are females married to men from Aldea San Francisco, with the largest volume since 1970 (R. W. Wilkie n.d.: 10; see also Wilkie and Wilkie n.d.: 12).

Another important demographic consequence is the changing sex ratio. Graves and Graves (1974: 127) observed that out-migration of males and the resulting increase in the proportion of women has obvious consequences for sexual behavior and marital patterns. Butterworth (1970: 10) describes the situation for Tilantongo:

Marital infidelity, temporary sexual liaisons, and marriage dissolution are becoming more frequent largely as a result of the breakup of the immediate and extended family through out-migration and the exodus of potential marriage partners. In addition, these behaviors are traditionally more common among mestizos who do not migrate, and they are reinforced by returning migrants ... Many women no longer have family members to turn to in time of need and consequently resort to dispensing their favors to men who will help to support them. It is also becoming increasingly common for young migrant girls to bear illegitimate children in the city, or to be abandoned there by their spouses. They then return to Tilantongo with their offspring where they have little hope of finding a husband and therefore settle for an unstable common-law marriage or other impermanent relationships with men.

The depletion of the pool of potential marriage partners in Tilantongo is dramatically illustrated in the cabecera [roughly equivalent to a county seat] itself. Aside from a few widowers, there are only four unmarried males over sixteen years of age, and all but one of these are still in their teens and dependent upon their parents. Of the twenty-six unmarried females fourteen years and over, only five are "desirable" mates in the sense of being young and childless. The others are widowed, separated, or abandoned women, most of them with children. The situation creates a social atmosphere conducive to marital infidelity, temporary sexual alliances, and separations as young men (and sometimes women) seek out sexual opportunities with married persons.

It is thus readily apparent that the demographic situation that prevails in any given locality is an important underlying factor in social behavior.

Shortage of agricultural labor

The presumed shortage of agricultural labor resulting from out-migration from rural areas is not well documented in the literature. Mechanization of agriculture with a concomitant increase in the number of idle hands has, as we mentioned in our analysis of the push–pull syndrome, often resulted in migration of excess rural laborers to the city. But this is not always the case. Cornelius (1976a: 13) noted that in spite of massive out-migration from the villages he studied, the large natural population increase has ensured that severe labor shortages did not develop. Nor did a shift take place from labor-intensive to capital-intensive mechanized agriculture.

This suggests that there is no single cause-and-effect relationship between mechanization of agriculture and the use of human resources. In some cases, mechanization may force people to leave rural areas; in others, scarcity of manpower may be a powerful inducement to introduce mechanized procedures. The stage of economic development of a region or nation is a strong determinant of these processes.[4]

The rural brain drain

The young and middle sectors of the population that leave their natal base are likely to include many potential innovators and community improvers. As a result, the community may become progressively more conservative, because of both the loss of these people and the ageing of its resident population (Preston 1969: 85). Perlman (1976: 62) states that this selective migration tends to perpetuate a "docile work force" in the rural communities of Brazil. She refers to Octavio Ianni's warning that the migration of these innovators to urban centers represents a loss of "vanguard elements" for the rural areas (Ianni 1970: 52).

Nevertheless, some investigators see positive aspects to the so-called brain-drain process. One of these is the conservation of traditional elements, which permits the maintenance of economic and power relations in a region. Margulis (1967: 100–1) looks upon this as a kind of "defense mechanism" that conserves the traditional structure of communities. However, since migration never occurs in only one direction, the flow of information and economic benefits in such forms as remittances often affect, even if indirectly, the economic and power relations in a locality.

Remittances and other financial aid

Financial aid from migrants to residents of their natal community takes several forms. The most frequent is that of remittances in cash (usually by way of money orders) to members of the immediate family. This may be to wives and children in the case of temporary or seasonal migration, or to parents or other relatives when permanent out-migrants have taken their family of procreation with them.

In Latin America, remittances from abroad have had greater economic consequences than financial aid sent from city to countryside within national or regional boundaries. Cornelius (1976a: 14–15) relates that the most direct and important economic impact on the communities he investigated in Mexico comes from the cash that migrants send back home from the United States to their relatives in Mexico. Remittances from those who migrate to Mexican cities are less important for two reasons: Migrants staying in Mexico generally earn and remit less, and migration within Mexico tends to be more permanent than movement to the United States and to involve whole families. However, when only one or two members of the nuclear family migrate, they retain obligations to their closest relatives. In such cases, family members staying in the community may derive most of their income from migrant remittances.[5]

Most remittances from migrants go to individual families for use in buying goods, rather than for the collective benefit of the community. Migrants from some communities, however, contribute cash to community development projects. The number and amount of contributions for collective goods seems to depend largely on the level of organization among migrants in their destination area (Cornelius 1976a: 14–15) This subject is explored further in Chapter 5.

The problem of land tenure

Since agriculture is, almost by definition, the subsistence base of rural communities (exceptions are villages such as Tzintzuntzan that specialize in crafts or other nonagricultural pursuits such as fishing or tourism), it is surprising that the subject of land tenure and its relation to out- and return migration has received relatively little attention in the literature on Latin American communities. Although for the most part we avoid discussing seasonal and temporary (wage) migration, the same problems often arise with this type of movement as with permanent out-migration. Wiest (1973: 191) has talked about this in relation to wage labor in Acuitzio del Canje, Michoacán, Mexico:

A long-standing tenure arrangement, one conveniently adopted by migrating heads of households who possess small landholdings . . . is to lease to a sharecropper (*mediero*). The arrangement permits the seasonal absence of the landowner while protecting his ownership of land and guaranteeing him a continued agricultural income. It is also used by households with rights to *ejido* land (even though it is illegal), because *ejido* plots are too small to provide an adequate income. The sharecrop arrangement does not jeopardize the household's rights to *ejido* land since the illegality of the widespread practice is overlooked . . . The care of animals is the responsibility of husbands and grown sons, when they are present. The animals are tended by the wife-mother when they are not . . . Almost without exception, arrangements are made to take care of day-to-day tasks through the assistance of the available individuals in the household.

In cases of permanent out-migration, many migrants maintain possession of land titles, often having the land sharecropped in a manner similar to that employed by temporary migrants. In his study of emigration to the United States from nine small communities in the state of Jalisco, Mexico, Cornelius (1976b: 38) points out that, contrary to the fears or beliefs of some Mexican government officials, migration north of the border does not seem to depress agricultural production. If the emigrant owns land, he either leaves other members of the family in charge of cultivating and harvesting the crops, rents it out, or enters into a sharecropping agreement with another resident of the community. "Very seldom does the land actually lay idle during the migrant's absence in the U.S. Even those who move permanently to the U.S. seem to retain their landholdings in their community of origin, and keep them in production using hired hands, in order to supplement the family income." This attachment to the land has both economic and psychological roots. Even when the sharecropping venture proves to be economically unprofitable, the knowledge by migrants that they still own land in their natal village gives a psychological security to the absentee owner.

While the system of absentee ownership by city dwellers and sharecropping by local residents may have benefits for both the migrant and the stay-at-home, tensions may arise when profit-sharing time comes. The

situation that angers some villagers (judging from Butterworth's data) is
when migrants leave their land in fallow. In Tilantongo, at least, the people
deem this a selfish act that deprives the community of needed land;
however, whether by intention or neglect, the practice does mitigate
against exhaustion of the soil.

Other socioeconomic effects

Patterns of return migration can produce widespread changes in the village
economy, provided the opportunities to exploit the increased capital
resources are available. Connell et al. (1976: 131) reminds us that direct
agricultural skills are not the only valued import. Many villagers attach
prestige to outside work because the experience has frequently given the
returned migrant a greater ability to deal in the local and regional
economic and political systems. These economic and social skills are
valuable and respected acquisitions. In San Juan la Laguna, Guatemala,
Sexton (1972: 45) found that villagers who had lived outside the village
were given important roles in the community's relations with external
agents and were also a source for the introduction of new agricultural
techniques.

But what of the productive skills outside agriculture? If the migrant
gains a skill, such as carpentry or motor repair, that can contribute to the
development of the village economy, his migration will seem to have been
even more useful. However, the evidence suggests that most migrants
working in industry are unlikely to gain nonfarm skills useful in the village.
And even most farm innovations, the authors warn, if they represent
substantial changes in agricultural methods and are difficult to fit into the
traditional agricultural cycle, are introduced slowly and are adopted only
after testing and experimentation within the community. Nevertheless,
migrants who return to farming, because of experience outside the village,
are probably more likely to respond to innovations (Connell et al. 1976:
131–2).

In nonagricultural matters, Kemper and Foster (1975: 57) report that
demographic change in Tzintzuntzan – including out-migration – has been
accompanied by major changes in the way of life for the great majority of
villagers. Pottery-making is still the primary occupation of most household
heads, but has declined in relative importance as potters' sons and
daughters abandon the craft for commerce and day labor or leave the
village altogether to seek their fortune elsewhere.

The national economic involvement of the *paleteros* from Mexticacan
studied by Rollwagen had a strong socioeconomic impact on the village. In
the early days of their business, the entrepreneurs remained largely based
in Mexticacan and staffed their production centers with people from the

community. As the business expanded to other locations in Mexico, the paleteros began to recruit more and more fellow villagers as workers. At first, both the owners and workers migrated as individuals. Later, the owners began to move their families to the cities in which their businesses were located. Apparently few workers did so, however, because their jobs usually were not permanent (Rollwagen 1974: 53).

As a consequence, the owners' ties with the village began to diminish in strength and numbers. The mediators had power in the community while they were in the role of brokers, but when the mediation diminished, so did their exercise of power. Money still comes to Mexticacan from owners and workers, but probably now in small quantities. It does not provide working capital for other enterprises as it did in the early days of the paleteros. (Rollwagen 1974: 59).

Social and political effects

The economic consequences of out- and return migration are intimately related to the migration's social and political effects on communities of origin. Migration's effects on social relationships and class consciousness are felt in rural villages as well as in urban settings. The rural scene will be considered here, the urban in following chapters.

As with many other aspects of how and to what extent migration affects small communities, data on this subject are sparse in quantity; nonetheless, some of the qualitative finds in Latin America are intriguing. Looking first at the tensions that inevitably exist in social groupings, it would appear that migration may be one means of resolving conflict, at least temporarily. Browning (1973: 260) argues that internal migration, as it is expressed in the movement out of rural or small urban communities into metropolitan areas, serves to dampen and reduce group and class conflict in both communities of origin and communities of destination. He maintains that both permanent and temporary out-migration relieve potentially explosive tensions:

Out-migration reduces the tensions between subordinate and superordinate groups. Of the two crucial relationships within the economic structure of the community – that between debtor and creditor, and between hired man and employer – migration offers several "outs" to those in subordinate relationships. Debtors can pay off or reduce their debts by working away several months as agricultural laborers or in construction jobs in the city. Day laborers are not "bound" to any one employer in town and the opportunities to go out of town further extends [sic] their options. All in all, the variety of migration patterns introduces considerable fluidity into the social structure, making it difficult for class antagonisms to rigidify. [Browning 1973: 261]

The research of Margulis (1967: 100), Ianni (1970: 52), and Butterworth (unpublished notes) agrees with this evaluation.

This "fluidity" extends into the field of ritual as well. Guillet (1976: 300) has reported on the movement of return migrants into the ritual life of Rumipata, Peru. A new fiesta was organized by a group of residents, the Club San Marcos, originally founded in Lima as a voluntary association of migrants to that city. Some of the founders had returned to Rumipata and reorganized the club:

> The movement of return migrants into the ritual field of community life offered them an opportunity to maximize the resources at their command. Through manipulation of the content of ritual, they were able to present a collective multifaceted identity which distinguished themselves as a "modern," progressive segment of the population. Such an identity has been projected and reinforced in other spheres of community life, but finds its ultimate expression in ritual. Ritual communicates regularities as well as transformation in social structure; in the Rumipata case, migrants, as well as other nation-oriented groups, signalled through ritual performance their entrance as a cohesive self-conscious grouping intent upon participating to the fullest in the community. [Guillet 1976: 300]

Guillet also writes of the part played by returned migrants in the political process, including succession to office and political brokerage. These processes were crucial to the community because of the structural changes brought about by the agrarian reform. Officeholders, many of them returned migrants, were called upon to represent their communities in negotiations with the burgeoning reform bureaucracy (Guillet: 300). Isbell (1974: 244) noted that those who had migrated out of Chuschi, Peru, learned Spanish, and then returned to the village were not incorporated into the prestige system but rather became eligible for bureaucratic positions as appointed or elected officials.

In some communities the political situation appears to have been irrevocably influenced by migrants who reside in urban centers. In Tilantongo, political machinations have been such that it has been difficult for a president to serve his full term. During one period of little more than a decade, eight men held the presidential post (constitutionally a three-year term), two of whom held it twice as "interim" presidents. Structurally, there has been an opposition within and without the community between "progressive" and "conservative" factions. In addition to, and partly congruent with, this fission, there are individual personality factors that affect politics. The result is that a small number of men have retained political power in the hands of their friends, compadres, and relatives, and shuffle the posts about every few years (preferably at election time) among members of the clique without essentially altering the political power structure.

The opposition between progressive and conservative groups cannot be understood from a study of the community as an isolate, for the progressive faction receives its main support from urban centers. Some of the city residents feel that unless drastic political, social, and economic changes are made in Tilantongo the moribund community may expire. These progressive groups in urban centers, particularly in Mexico City, operate both behind the scenes and in the open to manipulate the politics of Tilantongo. They support the progressive faction in the community, but because this faction has consistently lost strength through out-migration, the progressives in the city have turned more and more to their fellow migrant progressives to achieve their ends. So far they have not been successful in electing migrants to political office in Tilantongo.

Because the nonprogressive element in the city does not normally engage in political activity, the urban progressives have little opposition from that side. Their major opposition comes from within Tilantongo itself. This conservative faction fears and distrusts the progressives but depends upon them for the few improvements that come to the community and for which the conservatives indirectly claim credit. For humanitarian reasons these improvements (money and materials to build a basketball court, repair the rectory, paint the schoolhouse, etc.) are not withheld by the progressives in the city. Although the progressives know they are probably abetting the political stranglehold of the conservative group in power, they have a genuine sympathy for the plight of their paisanos. In addition, the constructions represent in material form the identification of the migrants with their beloved homeland. The factor of personal gain is by no means entirely absent among this group, but, on the whole, the interests of the community come first.

The progressives want to put an end to the vendettas, bickering, and eternal disputes over land boundaries in order to unite the people and work together for a better Tilantongo. They look askance at the pressuring of ignorant Indians and mestizos through unjustified jailings and fines and demand that an end be put to the institutionalized *mordida* (bribe, literally "bite") and the practice of pocketing income from taxes and state and national funds channeled into the community for road and school construction. They rightfully maintain that a good road would have connected Tilantongo with the Pan-American Highway twenty-five years ago if the funds had not been misappropriated.

The conservatives are not against improvements and progress as such, but are hesitant and at times adamant to relinquish their own power and authority to permit changes to occur. On the one hand, they deny the charges of abuses of power, theft, and extortion made by the progressives; on the other, they submit that the progressives have done and would do the same thing given the opportunity. They wash their hands of responsibility for the collapse of the road construction project, theft of money to rebuild the church, and other fiascos.

Although their popularity within the community is far from widespread (and many people dismiss their actions as typical of what any politico would do), the conservatives have a strong trump card that they astutely use to their advantage. This is the general distrust by the people of the progressive element in the city. Tilantongueños fear that if the progressives get political control of the municipio, they will instigate changes of such a far-reaching nature that Tilantongo would never be the same again. The city-dwellers are often looked upon as big-town bullies who, if put in positions of power in the village, would avenge past political and social crimes, liquidate anyone standing in the way of their march toward progress, and transform the population into city slickers. Thus the conservatives are able to entrench themselves at critical times through their rallying call of "Tilantongo for Tilantongueños."

One consequence of out-migration, then, is a continuing conservatism in the sending community. Potential agents of change, particularly those who are deemed radicals, often leave their villages because of frustration, ostracism, or threats to their lives or property. Stuart and Kearney (n.d.: 28–9) report for San Jerónimo Oaxaca, Mexico, that the impact of migration is primarily conservative; in its absence, massive changes would occur and traditional village structures would not have survived.

The eminent anthropologist A. L. Kroeber once made this comment on human conservatism and rationalization:

The fact is that we have become so habituated to the existing method that a departure from it might temporarily be a bit disconcerting. Consequently we rationalize our cumbersome habit, taking for granted or explaining that this custom is intrinsically and logically best, although a moment's objective reflection suffices to show that the system we are so addicted to costs each of us, and will cost the next generation time, energy, and money without bringing substantial compensation ... The most civilized [as well as] the most savage nations tend to believe that they adhere to their institutions after an impartial consideration of all alternatives and in full exercise of wisdom, whereas analysis frequently reveals them as equally resistive to alteration whether it is for better or for worse. [Kroeber 1948: 527]

5. Migrant adaptation: kinship, networks, and small groups

Any study of social and cultural adaptations among rural migrants in the city should be based on some conception of the nature of urban social organization. Since good empirical data (with the exception of some family studies) and good theory on the effects of urbanization on social life are in short supply, however, it should come as no surprise that social organization in the city is the weakest aspect of the literature on rural–urban migration in Latin America. Extending the tradition of community studies into the urban setting, most investigations have focused on particular places of one kind or another: *vecindades,* squatter settlements, barrios, colonias, and so forth. We do not wish to deny the contributions made by these neighborhood or settlement pattern studies, for ecology obviously is an important component of urbanization. But the rapid proliferation of such studies in recent years has led to an overemphasis on place phenomena and an underemphasis on elements of social organization. In this chapter we bring together current research findings on migrant social organization, ignoring for the time being the important variables of housing and settlement types that are discussed in Chapter 8.

The only truly comprehensive theory of modern urban social organization currently available derives from such great nineteenth-century thinkers as Henry Maine, Georg Simmel, Emile Durkheim, Max Weber, Ferdinand Tönnies, and others. Based at the University of Chicago in the first decades of the twentieth century, the sociologists Robert Ezra Park, Ernest Burgess, Roderick McKenzie, and Louis Wirth, together with the anthropologist Robert Redfield, synthesized a number of strands of classic sociology into a concept of urban social structure. To this day, the best exposition of their position is Wirth's paper "Urbanism as a way of life" (1938). Wirth and his colleagues viewed the city and its impact on human behavior negatively when contrasted with so-called rural forms of organization (idealized by Robert Redfield in his companion piece "The folk society" [1947]).

Wirth (1938: 12–17) stressed the pulverizing effect of the city on social relationships, which became, in his view, increasingly impersonal, superficial, transitory, and segmented. Social disorganization afflicts many urbanites in the form of anomie or normlessness. A high degree of residential mobility among city dwellers leads to a general acceptance of social instability and personal insecurity. The urban mode of life fosters "the substitution of secondary for primary contacts, the weakening of bonds of kinship and the declining social significance of the family, the disappearance of the neighborhood, and the undermining of the traditional basis of social solidarity" (Wirth 1938: 21). Under such conditions, Wirth felt, social solidarity in the city is achieved primarily through membership in voluntary organizations, which will be discussed in Chapter 7. Only by joining such clubs and interest groups can urbanites establish identities for themselves and avoid the anomie and individual impotence fostered by the disintegration of family, kinship, and neighborhood ties.

In attempting to place Wirth's ideas in perspective in light of current thinking in the field, it is clear that the notion of a single urban way of life is mistaken. Urban centers in different times and places are clearly dissimilar; a variety of urban forms must be distinguished. Even more vexing, however, is the problem of urban heterogeneity. If we posit social heterogeneity as a cardinal characteristic of cities, as Wirth does, how then can urbanites be expected to follow a common way of life? Finally, the weakness of Wirth's position is shown by a large amount of empirical data gathered in recent decades. There is ample evidence from all areas of the world that the urban environment in its many forms is not nearly so pernicious as was once thought. Family and kinship ties remain strong and significant in hundreds of large cities, neighborhoods do not disintegrate (unless demolished by urban renewal programs), and close personal relationships are just as important in the city as they are in the country.

David Jacobson (1975) has shown that the notion that the geographical and residential mobility that are so common among urban dwellers today *cause* social instability is questionable at best. Social stability, he points out, is not based primarily on frequency and duration of contact, but on people's future expectations that certain relationships will continue. It is quite common, in this urban world of ours, for stable relationships to be latent much of the time and activated only sporadically on special occasions. Jacobson's point serves to emphasize that the study of place phenomena in themselves may tell us little about the principles of urban social organization.

Studies of migrant adaptation in Latin American cities have been instrumental in showing the lack of fit between empirical cases and the hypotheses of the Chicago School. Oscar Lewis (1952) found, in a pioneering study, that migrants from the peasant village of Tepoztlán adapted to life in Mexico City with relative ease and "without breakdown" of their traditional forms of social relations. More recent studies have confirmed Lewis' findings. Yet, while the classical theory of urbanism and its negative implications for migrant adaptation have been empirically refuted in many respects, no alternative scheme has taken their place. We still lack an adequate theoretical framework that can account for migrant adaptation to the urban environment. Recent research has made it clear that a multitude of factors are involved, and in this chapter we will call attention to some of the most important and best understood. We turn first to a brief exposition of a few important concepts and research tools, next to the case materials themselves.

Groups, networks, and relationships

One of the reasons that the classic concept of urban life has proved to be unsatisfactory is that it fails to recognize the structured quality of social interaction that occurs outside of the group context. As Jacobson (1975: 361) has observed, group membership is a critical aspect of Wirth's theory. Where individuals remain detached and do not belong to formal, corporate groups of one kind or another, Wirth predicted the breakdown of social control and social solidarity. But we know now that a significant portion of social life, especially in cities, occurs between pairs of people (dyads) who may interact only sporadically. And then there are those fleeting forms we may call "cliques" or "factions," in which social interaction usually centers on one person or a coalition of persons, the central ego. These are not true groups, for their members may not know one another or have any common consciousness of kind; cliques may dissolve quickly when the central ego disappears from the social scene (Boissevain 1968: 542).

Another type of structured social relationship that occurs outside the group context is the network relationship, also based on a central ego. A network is simply the set of personal links an individual (ego) builds up around himself – a social field or web of relationships that is not governed by any specific role expectations. Some of the people in ego's network may know one another and others may not; some of them may come together at times for a specific purpose while others remain isolated except for their contacts with ego. Obviously, no two individuals will possess identical networks, although there may be considerable overlap. The network concept is a promising approach to problems in urban research, particularly the study of migrant adaptation, for it allows us to take the individual as the starting point for analysis in a situation in which groups may be absent or not immediately apparent. The idea behind network analysis is deceptively simple: "that the configuration of cross-cutting interpersonal bonds is in some unspecified way causally connected with the actions of these persons and with the social institutions of their society" (Barnes 1972: 2).

It is important, then, that we keep an open mind and not limit our analysis of urban life to a search for groups, as Wirth did, but that we recognize a whole continuum of forms of social interactions, from interacting dyads through personal networks, cliques, and factions to the corporate group (Boissevain 1968). In taking such an approach, the focus is necessarily on the individual and the adaptive strategies he employs in coping with the urban environment in which he finds himself. The systemic nature of social life, in this view, is not based solely on group membership or formal structure but derives from "active individuals generating patterns by their own decisions in all contexts of interaction" (Whitten and Wolfe 1973: 719).

Adaptive strategies of migrants in the city may also be analyzed along two more general dimensions (see Graves and Graves 1974: 128–32). Strategies may be individualistic – the migrant relies on his own resources or initiative, or group-oriented – he relies on others (kinsmen, fellow villagers) for help. Strategies may also be classified as formal versus informal. In the first case, the migrant makes use of formal channels of organization and urban bureaucracies in finding a niche for himself in the city; in the second, he is more apt to rely on more informal contacts in his own personal network.

Kinship and the family

Without exception, studies show that the family and kinship networks play a crucial role in migrant adaptation to Latin American cities. Relatives are apt to be the principal source of personal security and the primary locus of social control for most migrants, whether they are married or single. More often than not, newcomers to the city arrive at the doorsteps of kin, where they may live *arrimados* (as guests) rent-free while they look for jobs and housing of their own. In fact, it seems that few people would seriously consider migrating to a particular city unless they had relatives there. But the significance of urban kinship goes far beyond the first few weeks or months of adjustment. Kinship strategies are regularly employed to find jobs and housing, secure loans, provide child care, procure godparents to baptize the newborn, facilitate dealings with urban bureaucracies, purchase consumer goods at lower prices, place children in school, and provide information. It is often said that in Latin America the only people that can be trusted are relatives and compadres (co-parents or fictive kin), a statement perhaps even more true for migrants than for other sectors of the urban population. In Monterrey, for example, Balán, Browning, and Jelin (1973: 163) found that the more agrarian the migrant's background, the greater the importance of kinship networks in the city.

The vast majority of Latin Americans participate in a bilateral kinship system that rests on the nuclear or extended family, and the migrant population is no exception. Significantly, the personal kindred among lower-class migrants seems to lack the cohesion and importance of the family. (The case of San Lorenzo, Ecuador, discussed in Chapter 6 is an outstanding exception.) Family structure varies from city to city and within different sectors of the same city, but a few generalizations can be made. Recent studies have shown that far from becoming atrophied in the city, the extended family remains strong among migrants, and in some cases even increases in significance. This is particularly true for Mexico – in both the capital and the provincial city of Oaxaca – where independent nuclear families may even be in the minority among urban migrants. It is quite common for a married couple and its children to be embedded in a larger unit that may include the parents of one of the spouses, a married sibling, or both (cf. Lomnitz 1974). In a survey of migrants from the mestizo village of Tzintzuntzan in Mexico City, Robert Kemper (1974: 27–8) found that extended families gained in importance with the move to the city, and actually slightly outnumbered the independent nuclear units.

Extended family solidarity depends to some extent on facility of communication, however, and in an environment in which automobiles and telephones are the prerogative of the privileged few, it appears that extended families among migrants are most often clustered in the same or adjoining neighborhoods. Few of them live together in the same household, nor do they wish to; a far more common and desirable arrangement is a sort of extended family enclave in which two or more economically independent households, frequently composed of a married couple with children, or of an elderly couple, live near each other and comprise a single family unit (Chance 1971: 133; Kemper 1974: 28). Thus, although the financially independent unit of husband, wife, and children remains the preferred household form – the unit of residence – the familial network within which daily kinship relations take place is often broader in scope, although rarely does it encompass more than three generations. The formation of such enclaves, however, is dependent on the availability of convenient housing for the component household units, and we would expect them to be most common in young neighborhoods that are still expanding. The value of extended family ties to incoming migrants seems obvious. There may be a tendency for family size to diminish with length of residence in the city, as Gino Germani (1961: 214) found in Buenos Aires, but very few studies have controlled adequately for the time factor.

There is no evidence that urban residence inevitably affects the stability of the marriage bond. Almost universally, free unions are common among lower-class migrants, sometimes exceeding 50 percent of the population studied. But most anthropologists have found such marriages to be no more stable or unstable than legal ones. In some cases (Buenos Aires, Lima) the preference for free unions is said to reflect rural patterns, while in others (Rio de Janeiro, Popayán) it is apparently a concomitant of the migration process. In any case, it is important to realize that common-law marriage has several adaptive advantages for members of the urban lower class, migrants and urban-born alike. It is especially well-suited to economic instability, for in case of hardship or prolonged unemployment, free unions may be dissolved at will. It may also make it possible to avoid potential conflict over property rights. When there is little at stake economically, women sometimes favor common-law marriage, because it imposes fewer restrictions on them and allows them to have a more equitable relationship with their husbands (D. Foster 1975: 214). Added to this is the fact that in some countries, especially Colombia, divorces are very costly and difficult to obtain (M. Whiteford 1976b: 75).

Continuity and change in roles within the migrant family have also been the subject of a number of inquiries, but there is surprisingly little agreement among researchers on the effect of urbanization on family relations in Latin America. The pioneer in this field was once again Oscar Lewis, who noted the following changes in the Gómez family after seventeen years' residence in Mexico City:

Displacement of the father by the mother as the dominant figure in the family; increased freedom for the children; a steadily rising standard of living on the basis of installment buying; a higher aspiration level, added leisure, and greater opportunities for diversion; broader social contacts; and a gradual modernization of many beliefs. [Lewis 1959: 14]

Other studies have since confirmed most of Lewis's findings. His first point regarding the dominance of the mother bears closer examination, however.

Much has been written by North American social scientists about the prevalence of the matrifocal family or female-based household among the urban poor, particularly in the Caribbean area and the United States. Briefly, the pattern consists of an emphasis on the female line in kin relations, a transient relation between husband and wife, and a marginal position for the husband (if he is present at all) with respect to economic support and socialization of the children. Like common-law marriage, this pattern of family and household arrangements can be seen as adaptive when jobs are lacking and husbands cannot adequately support their families. Wives can often more readily find work performing domestic services, but by doing so they may pose a threat to the male role. The most extreme examples of matrifocality reported for Latin American cities come from Ciudad Guayana, Venezuela, and San Juan, Puerto Rico. In both cases, one-fifth of the households studied (most of them inhabited by migrants) were headed by women (Peattie 1968: 48; Safa 1974: 38). These tended to be among the poorest and most unstable families in the respective cities. In Ciudad Guayana, the focus on the mother–children tie has resulted in household groups that form small, three-generation matrilineages composed of a woman, her daughters, and their children (Peattie 1968: 48). In his Mexico City cases, in contrast, Lewis discusses a much milder variety of the pattern and refers to a tendency toward "matricentered" families. Here the husband is present and able to hold down a job, but it is the mother who "provides the most solid and stable nucleus for family life" (Lewis 1959: 390).

These findings are contradicted by others, however. William Mangin (1967: 81) reports that the rural Peruvian tendency to reinforce the male line in kinship relations continues unchanged in the squatter settlements of Lima, where matrifocality is relatively rare. And in many neighborhoods in Mexico City, Butterworth (1972) and Lomnitz (1974) have found that even the poorest migrant families tend to be male dominated, closely approximating the traditional Latin American patriarchal pattern.

Finally, in still other cases (Mexico City, once again, and São Paulo) rural–urban migration seems to have fostered an egalitarian trend in family living in which neither husband nor wife dominates. This pattern has been described best by Robert Kemper (1974: 33) for migrants from Tzintzuntzan in the Mexican capital:

Husband–wife relations in migrant families tend to be egalitarian and mutually supportive: most men assist and cooperate in domestic chores and progressive, younger women are career- as well as family-oriented. Regardless of their specific arrangements for income production and domestic duties, nearly all families demonstrate a low level of male authoritarianism and a high degree of "democratic" conflict resolution between spouses.

It seems unlikely that the factors behind these three contrasting portraits of family relationships will be unraveled until research is undertaken that pays closer attention to the multiple variables involved. We need more information on the places of origin of the migrants, their possible preadaptation to urban living, whether the families in question were formed before or after the move, the age of the families (place in the domestic cycle), employment histories and class status, housing arrangements, and so forth. For example, it may be that matrifocality has been reported only rarely for migrants to mainland Latin American cities because most research to date has been carried out in suburban squatter settlements (in contrast to Lewis's inner-city research). As William Mangin (1970: 26) has remarked, the fact that in such settlements the couple often shares an investment in a lot and a house may keep some husbands at home who might otherwise desert in an urban slum rental. Even if the husband does desert, the wife's prospects for remarriage are good, for she is the "owner" of a house and a lot.

We must conclude that the relationship between urbanization and family structure in Latin America remains only imperfectly understood. All that can be said with certainty at present is that: (1) the family serves as the primary point of reference in the migrant's social network; (2) the extended family is strong among first-generation migrants; and (3) in some cases the family is actually strengthened in the city. There is little evidence to suggest that urbanization inevitably selects for the nuclear family, as some sociologists have argued. The increased variety of economic alternatives available in the city does favor the nuclear household as the unit of production and consumption, for parents and children are not apt to have a common stake in a source of capital as they frequently did back on the farm. But as we have seen, preference for independent nuclear households need not entail any negative sanctions against the extended family.

In keeping with the inherent variety and heterogeneity of modern urban life, it seems most reasonable to hypothesize that Latin American cities (and migrants to them) will inevitably display a number of family and household types determined by a wide range of factors. It is up to researchers – current and future – to better isolate these variables and determine the conditions that give rise to the various family forms.

Social networks and the rural–urban interface

Thus far, migrant adaptation to city life has been portrayed as responding only to urban situations and stimuli, as if what has been left behind in the country is of no further consequence. This is not always the case, however, and urban life for many migrants involves continuing social and economic relationships with their home village or region. Urbanization is not an all-or-nothing event. Some migrants become more urbanized than others, in the sense that their identities, social contacts, and aspirations are focused on the city and involve a variety of associates with widely different backgrounds. In contrast, there are those who strive to surround themselves with paisanos (fellow villagers or people from the same general region) in the city and keep up strong ties with their homeland, even though they have no intention of returning to live there. Rarely does urban adaptation occur without significant changes in the lifestyles of the people involved, but these changes may be only partial and may include only specific aspects of the persons' lives. Many migrants have found it possible, for example, to adapt to new work situations in the city while still maintaining rural styles in their social relations, recreation, and family life. Nor can we overlook the other side of the migration process: that cities themselves change and adapt to the people who come to live in them. In many areas the sociocultural boundaries between city and country are eroding and the cities are becoming "ruralized" in some respects (Butterworth 1971: 97).

In studying the adaptations of migrants in the urban milieu, therefore, we must sometimes focus our attention away from the city itself. To insist on a rigid dichotomization between rural and urban lifestyles may simply cloud the issue and introduce into the analysis artificial categories that are meaningless to the people being studied. For example, it is common for urban squatter settlements to hold community labor parties every Sunday to make needed repairs or improvements to paths, roads, and drainage ditches. Sometimes these gatherings are referred to by the same names used to describe similar social mechanisms that have existed for centuries in the rural peasant villages from which the migrants have come (cf. D. Foster 1971). But to maintain that these urban work parties are simply transplants of a basically rural institution – that they are rural "holdovers" in the city – is to miss the point. In both city and country, jobs need to be done and a way has to be found to mobilize the necessary labor. Migrants in squatter settlements, if they had a choice, would rather spend their free time in other activities, but they are forced to work on Sundays because help or funds have not been forthcoming from the city government. Under such conditions, weekend work parties are not symptomatic of a low degree of involvement in city life or lack of an urbanized mentality. To the extent that the work is accomplished efficiently, they constitute successful adaptive strategies in the urban environment. If they originated as rural institutions, they are now urban as well.

One way to avoid becoming entangled in such spurious distinctions is to conceive of the city and its rural hinterland as complementary aspects of a single social system or network. By placing both city and country within the same analytical framework, we can examine the personal networks of migrants and obtain a balanced picture of the extent of their participation in both urban and rural spheres. We can find out where their loyalties lie and begin to measure concretely their degree of attachment to their places of origin and how this attachment (if it exists) affects their daily lives in the city. In short, the network concept permits us to formulate propositions about the interrelationships between city and provinces in a more sophisticated fashion. It is the network, viewed as a field of activity, that constitutes the social environment of the individual, and its content and scope are more important as determinants of behavior than its spatial location (Roberts 1974: 208).

Although few such studies have been undertaken so far, it appears that migrant adaptations in Latin America range from group-oriented, relatively formal strategies at one extreme to more individualistic and informal ones at the other. Migrants closest to the formal end of the continuum customarily display a strong in-group orientation and spend much of their time in association with fellow villagers. Basically conservative in outlook, these people strive to preserve what they can of their native culture in the context of family life and kinship and friendship relations. They maintain close ties with friends and relatives in their home communities and visit them frequently. In the city, they are apt to belong to an organized migrant association and may identify more strongly with their place of origin than with their current residence or nationality. The personal networks of such migrants can be described as highly connected (Bott 1975: 142) in the sense that there are many relationships among the component members, all of whom know one another well and participate in a variety of activities together. Spatially, such networks are commonly quite far flung, for they simultaneously include contacts in the city and back home. In extreme cases, migrants may spend almost all of their time in the company of their paisanos and attempt to keep the rest of the city at arm's length. Such people become encapsulated within the urban environment, by choice socially and culturally isolated from many aspects of city life (see Mayer 1962 for an illustration from South Africa).

At the opposite end of the adaptive continuum are the individualists – those migrants who employ more informal strategies in coping with the urban environment. Such people tend to associate little with fellow villagers, and sometimes may lose track of them completely. They identify more with the city than with their place of origin and rarely return there for any reason. They spend most of their time with people whose backgrounds differ from their own, people who are not likely to know one another. In other words, the network of this type of migrant is dispersed, for there are few relationships among the individuals who comprise it. Each set of activities – work, home life, recreation – involves the migrant with a different set of people and frequently with different expectations regarding social comportment. The personal networks of these individualists also tend to be more urban-based than those of the conservatives, for they include fewer contacts in the migrants' home provinces.

The first of these contrasting strategies of adaptation is best exemplified by migration to Lima, Peru, much of it originating in the Quechua-speaking Indian provinces of the highlands. To a markedly greater degree than their counterparts in other Latin American cities, migrants in Lima have preserved much of their native identities and a sense of group orientation. Paul Doughty (1972: 40) maintains that Andean culture is actually reaffirmed in the city and given new value in the face of urban ridicule. Pride in one's home village and region is maintained and often strengthened, frequently through membership in one of the approximately one thousand migrant associations that exist in Lima. Bryan Roberts has shown that city and country have interpenetrated each other to a remarkable degree in Peru and that village organization remains important to the ways in which migrants cope with their environment:

A substantial section of the population of Lima organizes its social and sporting activities in terms of associations based on place of origin. Fiestas that are organized in forms customary in provincial villages and towns are common in Lima among fellow migrants and among urban occupational groups, such as, for example, market traders, chauffeurs or policemen. Migrants return home frequently and especially to celebrate local fiestas; they also exchange produce with friends and relatives in the village and establish trading links there. [Roberts 1974: 207]

A comparable and perhaps more extreme example of the way in which urbanization can result in highly connected and spatially diffuse networks is seen in the case of migrants from the Mixtec Indian village of Tilantongo in Mexico City (Butterworth 1970; 1972). Most of these people are still Tilantongueños first and mexicanos second, despite many years of residence in one of Latin America's largest and most cosmopolitan cities. While they regard their urban-born children as mexicanos (mestizos), the migrants still consider themselves to be indios. Ties among fellow migrants are close; they help one another in time of need, and the better-established ones find jobs for the others. There is an extreme preference for and insistence on primary face-to-face relationships with fellow paisanos, and friendships are rarely formed with anyone else. Marriage with a fellow villager is preferred, and many men go back to Tilantongo to find a wife. Migrants with wives from Tilantongo outnumber those with spouses from elsewhere by more than two to one. When a child is born, more often than not its godparents of baptism will be Tilantongueños as well.

Economically and socially, the migrants have adapted successfully to city life, yet they cannot be termed fully urbanized or citified. This is best illustrated by a group of men that meets regularly at the home of Alfonso, the informal leader of the Tilantongueño community in Mexico City. Most of the eight core members of this collectivity (there are about twenty-four peripheral members) obtained jobs at a large manufacturing firm in the city thanks to Alfonso, and all of them at one time stayed with him as guests (*arrimados*) before establishing their own homes. All are related by ties of kinship or *compadrazgo* and regard themselves almost as one large extended family. The primary purpose of the group is social, and gatherings are held at Alfonso's home every weekend. Over beer or tequila, news about Tilantongo and its migrant population is disseminated and problems of the community discussed. The group also takes upon itself the task of introducing new arrivals from Tilantongo into the complexities of urban life, thus acting as an instrument of socialization. Surprisingly, the men spend little time discussing their own problems in the city. They are oriented emotionally more to their homeland than to the city:

The most popular topic of conversation among members of Alfonso's group is their *tierra*, Tilantongo. The men recall their childhoods in the village, the way things have – and have not – changed, and most importantly, the current state of affairs in the community. They deplore the decline that has taken place and fear that Tilantongo will soon become a ghost town. They recount tales of the former glory of their homeland, when Tilantongo was the seat of a small empire. If an outsider is present, he may be told the history of Eight Deer, the famous Mixtec conqueror from Tilantongo who is said to have exercized suzerainty over more than one hundred towns; or the story of Ita Ndewy, a beautiful Indian princess whose tragic end almost seems to adumbrate the current demise of Tilantongo.

After the men have been drinking for a while, someone invariably brings forth a guitar to accompany sentimental songs about their beloved *tierra*. A favorite is the "Cancion Mixteca." ("How far away am I from the land where I was born / Immense nostalgia fills my thoughts . . . "). Hardly a dry eye remains as the melody concludes: "I would like to cry / I would like to die / of sentiment." With tears streaming down his cheeks, one of the men is likely to stand and shout, "I'm from Tilantongo!" [Butterworth 1972: 39]

The networks of these migrants are extremely close knit and contain few people who are not from Tilantongo or other nearby towns in their home state of Oaxaca. Aside from attending an infrequent movie or soccer match, the men in Alfonso's group rarely go anywhere except to the homes of other fellow migrants. They lead encapsulated lives and constitute a sort of defended group in a sprawling metropolis in which they live but which they will never regard as their home.

In comparison to the Indians from Tilantongo, the mestizos from Tzintzuntzan evidence considerably less in-group solidarity than their counterparts from Oaxaca. Only 24 percent of the migrant households in the city maintain strong ties with others, and knowledge of fellow migrants from Tzintzuntzan varies tremendously. The basic organizational strategy of the migrants is the individualistic dyadic contract, with an emphasis on kinship and friendship ties. The initial adjustment of new arrivals in the city customarily involves maintenance of strong ties with fellow villagers, but after a few months these are replaced by a search for other patrons who have more power and can perhaps be of more help. Individual families are largely on their own, and social interaction among paisanos in the city is limited. Personal networks are consequently relatively dispersed and broadly based, the overall adaptive strategy being "pragmatic analysis of social options rather than extension of initial dependence on migrants with greater urban exposure" (Kemper 1975: 234).

More important than place of origin for most Tzintzuntzeños is class status, for the migrant population is far from socioeconomically homogeneous. Most migrants tend to interact with others of similar class standing and feel uncomfortable in the presence of paisanos who are above or below them on the social scale. As one informant put it, there is a growing rift between "los inferiores" and "los superiores" (Kemper 1975: 240).

To round out the picture, we conclude our survey with a brief look at ladino (non-Indians of Spanish cultural heritage) adaptive strategies in Guatemala City, by far the most individualistic and informal case of urban adaptation yet described for Latin America (Roberts 1970; 1973; 1974). The networks of these migrants are dispersed to a degree not reported for any other city. Roberts found that residential turnover and intraurban mobility are considerable, reflecting the lack of stable relationships based on occupation, ethnicity, or place of origin. Kinship is of some importance, but its scope is limited; aunts and uncles are treated as close kin, but relations with cousins are often distant. Collective organization is weak, there being no intensively interacting groups except for a few religious sects.

In this unstable urban environment, the migrant's social relationships become highly specialized:

Heads of households operate within one set of relations at work, within another in their religious activity, within another when cooperating for community organization, and within yet another when active in a national political party. Few relations are common to these different situations. There is thus little social pressure for people to be consistent in their behavior from one situation to another. [Roberts 1970: 371]

Place of origin is surprisingly insignificant to most ladino migrants once they establish themselves in Guatemala City. They are not particularly interested in seeking out other paisanos, and only a minority of marriages in the city are between migrants from the same town. Social and sporting activities are organized by neighborhoods or workplace, never by place of origin. Visits back home are rare and participation in village fiestas rarer still. In comparison to the one thousand migrant associations in Lima, Guatemala City can boast only four or five, and these are regional associations that represent important regional capitals. Unlike Lima and the case of Tilantongo, migration in Guatemala is not well integrated with the social and economic fields of activity of the rural communities. People who decided to leave their native villages tend to sever their ties there and are soon forgotten by the next generation. In the city, migrant's networks are correspondingly urban-based and greatly dispersed socially, although they are spatially restricted. For these poeple, the urbanization process has not bridged the gap between city and country as it has for many migrants in Lima and Mexico City. The Guatemalan capital and its rural hinterland continue to represent very different situations that are not meaningfully linked by interdependent enterprises, despite the considerable cityward migration of the last few decades.

Determinants of urban adaptation

Although we now know that most migrants adapt more or less successfully and without trauma to city life, we have as yet no satisfactory theoretical model that can explain this adaptation and its variations. Despite this fundamental handicap, however, recent research has uncovered a number of factors or variables that together affect the outcome of the migration process. They are: (1) the ethnic and cultural background of the migrant; (2) the ecological, political, economic, and demographic characteristics of the migrant's place of origin; (3) selectivity of migration – the personal characteristics of the migrant, such as personality, skills, wealth; (4) the size, density, and social heterogeneity of the city; (5) the availability and type of urban housing and neighborhood; (6) the urban class status of the migrant; (7) the availability and type of urban employment; (8) the nature of urban bureaucracies and political structure; (9) the time factor – length of residence in the city. We will not comment at length on all these factors (several are dealt with elsewhere in this book) but will discuss only a few in relation to the case studies presented in the preceding section.

Some of the differences in adaptation noted in Lima, Mexico City, and Guatemala City, for example, are related to the contrasting ethnic and cultural backgrounds of the migrants. It is not coincidence that the most individualistic and informal strategies are favored by mestizo or ladino migrants. In comparison with the Indian populations of Mexico and Guatemala, the rural mestizos and ladinos are likely to identify more strongly with the nation, participate more fully in national culture (or at least be more knowledgeable about it), and have broader social contacts and more dispersed networks. In short, they are better preadapted to urban living than the Indians, because they have had to overcome fewer linguistic and cultural obstacles in order to understand the city. Indians in Lima and Tilantongueños in Mexico City, on the other hand, bring with them to the city a different sort of cultural heritage that includes an indigenous language, a strong identification with their home community, and different conceptions of how social relations ought to be conducted.

There are further differences, however. Of considerable importance are the economic and political conditions in the hinterland and the various social relationships that they engender. Bryan Roberts (1974) has focused on these variables in comparing migrant adaptation in Lima and Guatemala City, attempting to explain why city dwellers in Guatemala do not consider their rural origins relevant to their urban identities. His analysis is complex, but it rests on the contrasting patterns of regional development found in Guatemala and the Mantaro Valley of Peru (which he takes to be representative of the regions that supply most of Lima's immigrants).

In brief, the pattern of organization in the Guatemalan provinces is conservative, while that of the Mantaro area of Peru is progressive. Rural Guatemalan communities are noted for their rigid stratification of ladinos over Indians. With the line between these two segments tightly drawn, custom is oriented toward protecting the economic status quo, and "social-relationships are less likely to extend economic opportunities than to reinforce economic differences" (Roberts 1974: 211). In addition, economic and political developments in Guatemala have provided few outlets for labor or opportunities for regional expression. The provincial and local levels are tightly organized by the federal government, thus discouraging regional autonomy. As a consequence, Roberts found that ladino culture in rural Guatemala reflects an "undynamic, socially stratified situation" (1974: 213). This society has little hold over the allegiances of its members, and those who decide to emigrate to the capital take no particular pride in their place of origin.

The Mantaro region of Peru, in contrast, is the product of a very different set of circumstances. Its inhabitants vary in the amounts of wealth and resources they control, but there is no rigid social separation comparable to the bifurcation between ladinos and Indians in Guatemala. Furthermore, Peruvians in this area perceive more local economic opportunity than do their Guatemalan counterparts. The Peruvian region is more ecologically varied and there has always been a variety of ways of making a living and greater labor opportunities. In addition, the Mantaro Valley has a long history of regional autonomy, and local residents have exercised more effective control over their immediate environment than appears to be the case in Guatemala. Under these conditions, those who emigrate to Lima do so with some pride in their origin and with the conviction that some aspects of their native culture will prove useful in the city. And so they have. For this region, at least, migration has become a regular part of village organization, with a constant exchange of people, products, and ideas back and forth between city and country.

Two remaining variables that affect the migration process deserve further comment: the size of the city itself and the migrants' length of residence there. The full effects of these factors on migrant social organization are not well understood, but one final example may serve to illustrate their relevance. During the course of his research on Tilantongo, Butterworth found that migrants in the city of Puebla (a state capital with a population of about five hundred thousand) have adopted significantly different patterns of behavior than those in Mexico City described above. The differences are most evident in network structure and group solidarity: Whereas these are closed and tight in Mexico City, the opposite appears to be the case in Puebla. Migrants in Puebla tend to perceive the social ambiance as less hostile; their fellow Pueblans are less ready to "eat them up," as they say. There is a minimum of mutual aid among Tilantongueños in Puebla, and personal networks are considerably more dispersed than in the capital. Many migrants from Tilantongo in Puebla do not know one another. In Mexico City, Butterworth contacted more than sixty families from Tilantongo very quickly, but it took much more work to locate just twenty in Puebla. There are other differences. Fewer than one-third of the children born to Tilantongueños in Puebla were baptized by godparents from the village, reversing the pattern found in Mexico City. Fewer men in

Puebla choose Tilantongueñas as their mates, and none of them participate in any migrant associations or get-togethers analogous to Alfonso's group in the capital. The migrants who do get together regularly in Puebla are almost always relatives.

In trying to account for these differences in adaptation, the contrasts between the two cities become immediately important. Perhaps the impersonal vastness of Mexico City acts as a threat (albeit not consciously perceived as such) to these migrants, thereby encouraging a high degree of in-group solidarity. Puebla, on the other hand, is much smaller, less industrialized, and less impersonal. Migrants in Puebla also enjoy greater job security, and perhaps for that reason perceive their urban environment as less threatening. Length of residence of the migrants in Puebla is also longer than of those in Mexico City, and it appears that more time to gain job and housing security lessens the migrants' dependence on one another.

Still other factors may be relevant to the differences observed. Puebla has attracted considerably fewer migrants than the capital, and consequently fewer social and economic resources are controlled by Tilantongueños. Finally, migrant selectivity seems to have operated differently in each case. Migrants in Puebla are old-timers for the most part, among the first to leave Tilantongo when the heavy migration process began in the 1940s. On the whole these pioneering individuals are more adventurous, more self-reliant, and therefore better selected for success in the city than many migrants who left the village in recent years. In short, such individuals are less apt to feel that they need one another's company in the city and are more inclined to go their separate ways.

Although we have not exhausted all the variables pertinent to social and cultural urban adaptation in this chapter, we have reviewed what we consider to be the most important ones. Of the nine factors identified, length of residence in the city is probably the least understood; it certainly deserves more attention from social scientists than it has heretofore received. Few studies have tested adequately for the time factor (Germani's 1961 work in Buenos Aires is an exception), and what data we have tend to be contradictory. Even more glaring is the total lack of information on generational differences. How do children of migrants organize their social environment? Are they no different than sons and daughters of city-born residents, or are the constraints on their behavior different because of their parents' background? These and related questions have not been the subject of inquiry, and we hope that future researchers will take up this challenge.

In conclusion, when placed in world-wide perspective, migrant adaptation in Latin America is on the whole more individualistic and informal than that in many other parts of the Third World. In areas with large tribal populations (particularly sub-Saharan Africa), group-oriented, formal strategies in the city are considerably more in evidence than they are in any of the cases reviewed here. Group activities and ethnic consciousness are crucial characteristics in much of urban Africa, but it is their weakness (with some exceptions, such as Lima) that is noticeable in Latin America. Many centuries of indigenous urbanization, followed by over four hundred years of Iberian dominance, have created a society in which few inhabitants are complete strangers to the city, and in which both rural and urban populations have long participated in a common network of relationships.

6. The urban class structure

Approaches to the study of class in Latin America

In a paper that synthesized a wide variety of materials on Latin American subcultures, Charles Wagley and Marvin Harris (1965: 55) remarked that "the problem of class differences in the Latin American urban centers presents one of the most pressing and difficult challenges to students of Latin American culture." This assessment is still true today. Research on social stratification has been small in quantity and has shown little cumulative development. There is still a lack of agreement among investigators as to how social classes should be defined: whether on the basis of income, education, occupation, social prestige, or cultural traits. Consequently, many of the studies we do possess are highly idiosyncratic and subjective, each writer taking a somewhat different approach (Stavenhagen 1974: 29). Another problem is the lack of comparability between urban ethnographic studies of social class that focus on particular cities and the macro-oriented statistical studies that often attempt to encompass whole nations. [1]

Following the distinctions drawn by the people under study, ethnographic studies of stratification have customarily defined class differences in terms of the prestige associated with certain styles of life. They have paid scant attention to such variables as wealth and power, except insofar as the people see them as important, and therefore employ the concept of class differently than we have in Chapter 1, where it is defined in the strict economic sense. The statistically based studies, on the other hand, are more apt to define class boundaries in an arbitrary fashion, based on some quantifiable index such as years of schooling, income, or occupation, or even the number of rooms in dwellings. Some but not all of the authors of these analyses have not carried out any systematic fieldwork and are content to rely on statistical manipulation of census data. As anthropologists, we must express our skepticism about such an approach, which places greater emphasis on statistical analysis than on the reliability and quality of the data. In this chapter, while we shall occasionally refer to some of these quantitative studies, no attempt is made to review them systematically. Emphasis is placed on the more qualitative contributions made by anthropologists.

Clearly, we have a long way to go in the analysis of social stratification in Latin American cities. Much remains to be done in sharpening our concepts and definitions, making them operational for purposes of empirical research, and achieving the kind of well-rounded "quantitative–qualitative mix" (Pelto 1972: 11) that is so important for studies of complex urban societies. For the sake of clarity and consistency, in this chapter we shall continue to use the term "class" in the Weberian sense of an economic interest group, even though this usage differs from that found in some of our sources (cf. Reina 1973 and A. Whiteford 1964; 1977, who conceive of classes essentially as status groups). Power and power groups have been studied primarily by sociologists and political scientists at the national rather than the local level and will not be dealt with here (see Horowitz 1970; Johnson 1958; Lipset and Solari 1967; Wolf and Hansen 1972). Since other chapters in this book deal extensively with the lower class – a majority of which consists of migrants in many cities – this discussion will emphasize the middle and upper classes in order to round out the portrait of Latin American cities as much as possible.

At the outset, we wish to state our disagreement with a still widely held stereotype of class stratification in Latin America. This is the view that most stratified Latin American communities, whether rural or urban, exhibit an essentially two-class structure in which a small, exclusive elite controls considerable wealth, monopolizes the prestigious occupations, and dominates a vast proletariat composed of manual workers. The middle sector, if admitted to exist at all, is regarded as small, unstable, and of only recent origin. Often implicit in this view are the assumptions that (1) the dual class structure derives from a similar colonial system that was largely feudal in nature; and (2) because a large middle class patterned after the sort found today in North America and Western Europe is lacking, no middle class exists in Latin America. We believe both of these assumptions to be faulty and wish to stress the necessity of viewing Latin American stratification systems on their own terms. Classes and status groups in urban Latin America do not take the same form they do in the United States and Europe, nor is there reason to expect them to. We must therefore scrupulously avoid any attempt to place Latin American data into North American molds, and we should not be surprised if variation and divergence are found. At the same time, our concepts (the concept of class, for example) should be flexible enough to be useful both north and south of the Rio Grande and in other complex societies as well, for any theoretical construct that applies only to Latin America or any other single region would be of doubtful utility.

A number of recent studies of colonial Latin America have cast considerable doubt on the feudal model of urban society, a point that was stressed in Chapter 1. There is evidence that even in rural Brazil, where feudal patterns are thought to have been strongest, the stratification system was far more fluid and complex than any rigid two-class model would allow. Emphasizing the criteria of slave ownership and occupation as recorded in censuses of ten localities of the *capitania* of São Paulo in 1822–4, Emilio Willems (1970) has documented the existence of a sizeable rural middle class. In contrast to the popular stereotype, the population of all ten localities was highly differentiated. To be sure, there was a small group of wealthy plantation owners at the top and a large block of slaves at the bottom but in between there was a strikingly heterogeneous population of free peasants, many of them slaveowners. Willems (1970: 47) points out that there was a significant degree of social mobility and that in no sense can colonial southern Brazil be classified as a rigid caste society.

Much the same can be said for the Mexican city of Oaxaca in colonial times. In Chapter 1 we saw that Oaxaca was characterized by a significant amount of racial and socioeconomic mobility and that its class structure was more capitalistic than feudal by the late seventeenth century. In 1792 the city's occupational structure contained some 141 different classifications with a sizeable "preindustrial middle group" that accounted for 20 percent of the employed non-Indian males (Chance 1978: 159–74). The middle sector included many professionals such as minor royal officials, physicians, lawyers, barber-surgeons, druggists, and schoolteachers, as well as almost three hundred high-status artisans, including gilders, painters, and silversmiths. All these people ranked above the lower-status artisans such as the carpenters, shoemakers, and tailors, and many of them were able to use their occupations as springboards for upward social mobility. Conversely, this middle sector also absorbed a significant number of downwardly mobile sons of *hacendados* who had lost or divided their small estates.

While we do not have enough information to define the precise boundaries of the middle class in colonial Oaxaca, there seems little doubt about its existence. Angel Palerm (1952: 29) reached similar conclusions regarding the capital and other northern Mexican cities in the late eighteenth and early nineteenth centuries. These historical precedents laid the foundation for the modern urban class structure, which today exists within the framework of an essentially capitalist socioeconomic system (Cuba excepted), although state intervention and control is increasing in many nations.

Economic classes and cultural sectors

Although we think it most appropriate to speak of a middle class in Latin American cities, the total cultural configuration is nonetheless quite different from that found in North America and Europe. This is due in part to a lack of a congruent system of cultural values and ideology in much of the region. Although analysis in terms of a dichotomy between rich and poor greatly oversimplifies the economic basis of class, even in some large cities many people tend to perceive the class system, and formulate their aspirations within it, in terms of a dual division of upper and lower segments. The principal means of division, one long recognized by anthropologists, is the distinction between those who work with their hands and those who do not. Ralph Beals (1965: 360) has aptly expressed the significance of this important feature of the Latin American lifestyle by contrasting it to the North American:

The middle-class family with two cars and no servants, the banker who washes windows in preparation for his wife's tea party, the professor in overalls wielding a shovel in his garden – all are incomprehensible in Latin America. Unless an individual occupies an impregnable social position, there are certain manual activities which may *never* be engaged in even for recreation, certain implements which must *never* be touched.

This value pattern has deep Hispanic roots, and the related dichotomous view of socioeconomic differences also seems to have European origins. In colonial Mexico, despite the elaborate racial hierarchy and emergent middle class in many cities, urbanites customarily distinguished only two socioeconomic or class segments: the *gente decente*, or respectable people, and *la plebe*, the populace or common people (Chance 1978: 127). Under colonial conditions, this two-class world view and its associated value system were continually reinforced by the necessity of distinguishing between the rulers and the ruled, the Spanish and the non-Spanish, the white and the nonwhite. That this cultural dichotomy continues today in many areas, despite the existence of a centuries-old middle class, underscores the continuing influence of Latin America's colonial heritage on its modern social values.

Richard Adams (1965: 266–70; 1967: 47–69) has sought to account for the modern situation with a model of two value sectors: the power–prestige sector and the work–wealth sector. Each of these, according to Adams, represents a profoundly different view of the stratification system and the means by which one's place in it is secured or improved. In the lower sector, the only way to get ahead is through wealth, and this means hard work, usually of the manual variety. Few manual workers are able to cross the boundary into the upper white-collar sector, and while a degree of intrasector mobility is possible through the accumulation of wealth, few can expect to move out of the lower sector by work alone. The upper or prestige sector includes both the upper and most of the middle classes and is defined by a different set of values. Wealth is desirable and a certain amount of it is necessary to remain within this sector, but money is less an end in itself than it is a means to the acquisition of prestige symbols such as a car, a stylish home, fashionable clothes, large landholdings, a professional title or college degree, and exclusive club memberships.

Wealth is only one of several ways by which these symbols may be acquired, but in Adams's analysis all such means come under the umbrella of "power" (not to be confused with the Weberian usage): "Just as work provides the surest way to wealth in the work sector, so power is the clearest way to prestige in the prestige sector. Power lies in the ability to manipulate events and people so that things turn up to your advantage" (Adams 1965: 268). Thus it is possible for some people to operate successfully in the prestige sector even with modest financial means. Individuals of this sort may call on a number of friends and relatives for help, particularly for career advancement. In order to remain in the prestige sector it is also necessary to engage in correct public behavior, to use the right sort of language, and to be at ease with an extensive repertoire of "refined" manners that is often difficult to learn if one has not been born into this social milieu or at least participated in it for some time. In Paraná, Argentina, these social graces are summed up in the concept of *cultura*, which Ruben Reina (1973: 189) feels may be best defined as a well-developed ability "to communicate verbally an image of one's level of literacy."

Important in setting off the sector with cultura from the one below it is the negative value attached to manual labor and work in general. Work becomes something to avoid whenever possible, and if the valued prestige symbols can be acquired through other means, so much the better. This is why the American "Protestant ethic" makes little sense to middle- and upper-class Latin Americans, although it may be admired by those of the lower class who operate within the work sector. A vivid example of the negative value placed on physical labor by those in the prestige sector (or those aspiring to enter it) comes from Popayán, one of Colombia's smaller and more traditional cities, located in the Andes. In this city even struggling artisans of the lower middle class are careful not to engage in stigmatized manual activities away from their shops, and no one with prestige aspirations would think of carrying a package through the streets. Social activity may be disrupted if a servant or other suitable person cannot be found to do the moving, carrying, or lifting, as Andrew Whiteford (1977: 152) found during his stay in Popayán in 1950:

A university student, whose father was a plumber, was not able to bring his guitar to our house for a serenade, because he could not find a boy to carry it. He was afraid to be observed carrying his guitar, because people might think that he was so poor that he was playing for money, or that he was taking his instrument to the pawn shop.

Because the work and prestige sectors entail different ways of looking at the stratification system, upward mobility from the lower to the higher sector is difficult, although it does occur. Adams (1965: 269) believes that the process of mobility normally requires two generations, although he points out that it happens more quickly in the cities than in the country-side. Most commonly, mobility today tends to increase the numbers of people in the middle ranges of society rather than at the top. But Adams cautions against regarding this expansion of the middle range as presaging a new cultural entity. Rather than giving birth to a new cultural recognition of the middle class, mobility instead serves to expand and further differentiate the two existing cultural sectors. The result, says Adams, is "an expansion of the old social structure, with many kinds of changes that seem to parallel the development in Europe and North America, but which structurally is holding the basic form it has always had" (1965: 269).

Adams's contribution is an important one, for he has given us a sophisticated analysis of the values surrounding stratification in Latin American cities while at the same time recognizing that the economic realities of class are separate from the cultural ones. The dual-sector model does not deny the existence of a highly differentiated class system; rather, it emphasizes the incongruities between the economics of social differen-tiation and what people see as desirable and worth striving for. Nowhere is this more evident than in the cities, where the relationship between value sectors and economic classes may become highly disjointed so that people holding the values of one sector may find themselves in an inappropriate class (Adams 1967: 51). Particularly in the smaller cities, it is not unusual to find that some of the wealthiest individuals are hardworking entrepre-neurs who owe everything they have to their business acumen and hard work. They may follow a lavish life style yet still never gain full acceptance in the prestige sector, because they lack the necessary disdain for work, the proper family background and social connections, and cultura. On the other hand, there are individuals who are descendants of illustrious colonial families and who possess impeccable credentials in exactly those areas in which the self-made tycoons are lacking. That much of their families' wealth is now dissipated does not exclude such aristocrats by birth from the prestige sector, although, depending on their income, it may relegate them to its lower levels. In other words, the owners and controllers of the means of production are likely to be found in both the prestige and work sectors. At the same time, there are many in the prestige sector who own or control very little, such as the large number of salaried bureaucrats who qualify for this sector by virtue of their nonmanual occupations (Adams 1967: 51).

The dual-sector model does not apply uniformly to all urban areas in Latin America, however. Countries that are predominantly European in their cultural orientation – including Argentina, Uruguay, Chile, and Costa Rica – constitute significant exceptions. In the first three of these, heavy European immigration during the nineteenth century stimulated the development of a sizeable urban middle class that now approaches the classic Western form. Many of these immigrants entered the occupational structure at the middle level or soon worked their way up to it. Consequently, a strong middle-class ideology has developed in a number of cities, as Ruben Reina (1973) has shown in detail for Paraná, Argentina. In addition to immigration, another factor that accounts for the cultural recognition of the middle class in this region is the lack of a large, colonized indigenous population, which appears to have been so important to the maintenance of a dichotomized value structure in Mesoamerica and the Andes.

In still other regions, the dual-sector model is further complicated by racial considerations. In many cities in the coastal areas of Ecuador, Colombia, Panama, Venezuela, and Brazil, perceptions of class are inextricably linked to racial status. The complex nature of this relationship will be discussed later in this chapter.

Finally, Adams's prediction that a new middle-value sector is unlikely to develop may well prove inaccurate in the near future. Evidence is accumulating that in a number of localities undergoing rapid urbanization and industrialization the value sectors are indeed changing significantly. The deeply entrenched dichotomy between manual and nonmanual labor is on the wane in a number of cities. This is perhaps most evident in Mexico. In the heavily industrial northern metropolis of Monterrey, Jorge Balán and his collaborators found very little deprecation of manual labor and an egalitarian tone to interpersonal class contacts that stands in sharp contrast to the traditional Latin American pattern (Balán et al. 1973: 306).

Monterrey is unusual in that it has a large industrial labor force and a relatively small bureaucratic white-collar sector, but another study carried out in the still largely nonindustrial city of Oaxaca reports similar findings. Michael Higgins (1971: 31) found the manual–nonmanual distinction to be irrelevant in Oaxaca, at least in the opinion of the lower class. When they were asked to rank their neighbors, what mattered most to lower-class Oaxaqueños was the amount and control of material wealth people had. How the wealth was obtained, the sort of job one had, or one's amount of education was not found to be an important determinant of prestige. Frank Miller (1973: 118) has also noticed a shift in class attitudes among industrial workers in Ciudad Sahagún in the state of Hidalgo, and his observation would probably hold for many other industrializing cities in Latin America: "With the process of modernization, levels of income, education, and the sophistication of industrial labor have all increased, and the traditional middle-class [and upper-class] sense of superiority has become increasingly difficult to maintain."

The upper class

The composition of economic classes in Latin American cities, as elsewhere, is defined by the division of labor and differential access to and control of wealth. At the risk of overgeneralizing, we shall here briefly sketch the broad parameters of the upper and middle classes in urban Latin America and mention a few salient aspects of the lifestyle associated with each.

The upper class or elite is one of the least-known and least-studied segments of modern Latin American society. Anthropologists have customarily paid closest attention to the urban poor and migrants from the countryside. Moreover, few middle-income social scientists possess the requisite financial resources and social connections to engage in participant observation among the upper class for any extended period of time, and only a small number of ethnographic studies of the elite have accumulated to date (Gonzalez 1974; Goode 1970b; Leeds 1965; Reina 1973; Scheele 1956; Strickon 1962; A. Whiteford 1964; A. Whiteford 1977). Studying the rich presents a number of unique problems for the fieldworker in addition to the obvious financial ones. As Richard Adams puts it (1967: 58), the ethnographer of the upper class will be subject to sundry restraints on what he may write, and his work is likely to be "thoroughly criticized and perhaps shredded by his subjects." In a candid report of her field experiences among the elite in a small city in the Dominican Republic, Nancie Gonzalez (1974: 28) describes the difficulties she encountered:

Potential upper-class informants were busy with their own affairs, they accorded me only a moderately high social standing, and they were not interested in my work. Although I was at the time an associate professor at a state university in the United States, I was continually asked if I were not writing my "thesis." One part of the problem was the inability of the people of this class to understand why a scholar, having earned the doctorate, would want to continue with research. Another part of the problem undoubtedly had to do with my gender. The fact that I was divorced also detracted from my social standing, although in the eyes of some of the males it enhanced my initial attractiveness. Finally, my standard of living was clearly much lower than theirs, and worse, it was far below the average of North American officials and businessmen then living in the Dominican Republic. It was obvious to the upper-class Dominicans that I neither worked for a prestigeful organization which would pay my expenses, nor did I have personal resources to maintain a higher standard of living on my own. In either case, I was obviously a person of little consequence.

It is possible to divide the upper class in most Latin American cities into two segments: the aristocratic and the commercial/industrial. The aristocratic elite derives its wealth primarily from large estates devoted to agriculture or stockraising, or from the management of other inherited properties, frequently urban real estate. Many of the men have university degrees and may lead professional lives as politicians, doctors, and lawyers, spending only a small fraction of their time tending to their inherited estates. The traditional ideals of this group are those of the aristocratic landed gentry, with its characteristic disdain for work. Great emphasis is placed on courtly manners and verbal and written expression. Until the 1930s, France was generally looked to as a source of cultural ideals, although it is now being replaced by the United States (Wagley and Harris 1965: 56). Much importance is attached to kinship ties and intermarriage between elite families as ways of preserving upper-class access to the means of production. Family genealogies are carefully traced and preserved.

In Popayán, Colombia, where commerce and industry are still little developed, virtually every upper-class family owns at least one hacienda and most can trace their descent to important personages of colonial times. Each aristocratic family carefully preserves its *pergamino* (pedigree) in a vault or chest, and some can trace their noble titles as far back as the fifteenth century. Coats of arms are prominently displayed and often appear on silver services, in colored leather on the backs of chairs, embossed on stationery, carved in stone and wood, and wrought in iron on patio gates. Almost all upper-class men in Popayán refer to themselves as *hacendados* or *ganaderos* (cattlemen), but they devote most of their energies to their medical practices, their law offices, their posts in the local university, or their political activities. During his fieldwork, Andrew Whiteford found that a distinguished ancestry was still a prerequisite for true upper-class status and that the only way an outsider could effectively penetrate this stratum was through marriage to one of its sons or daughters. To be part of the elite in Popayán was by definition to be *clase alta por abolengo* – upper-class by lineage – and a large landowner. Commercial activity was still somewhat frowned upon, and the city's two or three richest men – all of them merchants – were not members of the aristocratic status group, because they lacked the necessary *pergaminos* (A. Whiteford 1977: 112–42).

By 1950, however, Popayán's aristocracy was changing and becoming more open to talent and money from without. Most Latin American cities have another upper-class segment that is increasingly phasing out much of the seigneurial elite. This group consists of the families of generals, wealthy bureaucrats, industrialists, merchants, and bankers. As the tempo of urbanization and industrialization increases, there has been a decline in the importance of land as the most valued source of wealth; today more than ever before, the real fortunes are to be made in commerce and industry. Many analysts have referred to this sector as the new or industrial upper class and view it as essentially a nineteenth- and twentieth-century phenomenon (Iutaka 1971: 262; Willems 1975: 257). To the extent that this segment depends on new wealth and new jobs opened up by industry, these researchers have a point. But in Mexico, at least, merchants always comprised the wealthiest sector of the upper class in colonial times, and there is every reason to believe that they continued to occupy this position through the nineteenth century. Far from being a recent phenomenon, this part of the upper class has a long history, one that is riddled with booms and busts, with meteoric ascents and plummeting declines.

Because of the vicissitudes of trade and international finance, this division of the upper-class has until recently had less continuity through time than the landed sector. New families have tended to come and go every few generations, and for this reason entrepreneurs are often frowned upon as nouveaux riches by the seigneurial families who depend to a much greater extent on inherited wealth. Sometimes, of course, these two sorts of elites are united in a single family, but there is much variation from country to country. It seems clear, however, that these two upper-class groups – one depending largely on its inheritance and the other on its business acumen – have coexisted for some time. In any given city, one or the other was likely to be dominant at any given point in time, and the commercial/industrial elite did not begin its eclipse of the seigneurial upper class until the advent of industrialization. Today, the days of the landholding elites seem numbered, but there are signs that its structural position is continuing in some cities. Wealthy industrialists now bequeath factories to their descendants rather than haciendas.

Whatever the composition of the upper class, in a few cities the powerful and propertied can still be found in residences that cluster around the central plaza much as they did in colonial times. This pattern is still discernable to some extent in such provincial capitals as Oaxaca and Popayán, but the best-documented case is Paraná, Argentina, where the traditional social ecology of the city remains virtually intact. El Centro, an area encompassing the central plaza and five surrounding blocks, is the province of *los dueños de la ciudad* (the owners of the city), as one Paranense put it, and is regarded by the people as standing in opposition to the poorer outskirts, *la zona de los barrios*, where most of the lower class resides (Reina 1973: 42). Paraná's sizeable middle class lives in a belt of neighborhoods that occupies an intermediate position between the center and periphery. Reina found that some discomfort occurs in the few cases in which a family's place of residence does not match its social or class status. "The variables of profession, income, housing, level of aspirations, participation in public life, membership in clubs and other voluntary organizations, and level of education stand in direct relationship to the city areas" (Reina 1973: 65). Paraná, like Popayán, is a relatively small and still nonindustrial city, however. In most of the larger urban centers the upper class has abandoned the central area as a place of residence, although many people continue to work there in their offices and commercial establishments. The exodus from the central city to suburban residential areas was already well underway by 1900 in some cities, and the process appears to be virtually completed in urban centers of five hundred thousand or more. Although wealthy and prestigious neighborhoods have been carved out in suburbia, mixed residential areas are now becoming more common than exclusive upper-class barrios (Willems 1975: 238–40).

The middle class

The middle class is by far the most heterogeneous and complex component of the socioeconomic hierarchy. Unlike the other two classes, the middle class is overwhelmingly a product of urbanization and owes it existence to commercial and industrial development. Today the middle class is strongest in the cities of Argentina, Uruguay, Chile, Costa Rica, Mexico, Venezuela, and Brazil, and with the exception of Brazil these are also the countries with the highest indexes of urbanization and literacy (Wagley 1963: 202).

There has been much uncertainty and confusion about the place of the urban middle classes in Latin American society. They are more highly differentiated than their counterparts in Europe and North America, and their boundaries fluctuate considerably from region to region and city to city. In general, the middle class is composed of three types of occupational groupings. First are the rank-and-file of salaried and professional people, including office workers in government and private business, university professors, bank managers, many doctors and lawyers, and middle-level managers in business firms. All of these people enjoy the prestige that comes from holding a nonmanual job, and most of them are wholly dependent on their salaries for their livelihood. Second, there are those with a direct stake in private property and free enterprise. These are the entrepreneurs, who are either in business for themselves or preside over small service and manufacturing firms. Third, the middle class also includes a number of skilled artisans in various trades. These people do hold manual positions, and although their work may be nearly identical to that of many lower-class workers, the middle-class artisans stand out as the owners of small shops or *talleres*: they are the bosses, and the employers of others. The most successful artisans are frequently able to leave all the actual work to their employees and devote their time to supervision, bookkeeping, and maintaining good relations with their clientele. Of the three sectors, that of salaried professionals and white collar workers is still the largest at present, although the sector of self-employed artisans is growing. The self-made, independent entrepreneurs so common in Europe and North America are much fewer in Latin America, due to shortage of capital and the lesser degree of industrialization. But to the extent that industrialization increases, so will the middle class, for new kinds of jobs, both technical and managerial, will be created and must be filled. In some cities this process is already quite advanced, and in others it has hardly begun.

Given the paucity of empirical studies and lack of agreement among scholars as to how the middle class should be defined, it is probably futile to attempt any realistic estimate of the size of this segment in Latin America. Almost three decades ago, the Pan-American Union endeavored to do this by commissioning a collection of articles on the middle classes in all the Latin American nations, most of which were penned by native scholars (Crevenna 1950–1). The project proved to be overly ambitious; the papers produced very little agreement, because they were for the most part statements of opinion rather than reports of research findings. Few actual studies were carried out and the result was "a wealth of penetrating insights, brilliant commentaries, skilled syntheses, but very few facts" (A. Whiteford 1964: 95). Estimates of the size of national middle classes ranged from 8 percent of the population in Venezuela to 50 percent in Uruguay, the average for all of Latin America falling in the neighborhood of 20 percent (Gillin 1960: 25). Lamentably, in recent decades social scientists have continued to ignore the middle class (as they have the elite) and only a handful of ethnographic studies have been carried out to date (Leeds, 1965; Lomnitz 1971; Reina 1973; A. Whiteford 1964; A. Whiteford 1977).

Despite the lack of research, most observers agree that one of the major characteristics of the Latin American middle class is its government dependency. This is true especially for the large numbers of directors, technicians, administrators, and other people who work for large organizations, many of which are either created by or sponsored by the state. Much of the middle class, in other words, works for the government and enjoys the benefits of job tenure, pension plans, special medical care, and social security, perquisites that are usually not guaranteed for equivalent white-collar positions in the private sector.

This pattern is especially prevalent in the national capitals, which have the largest middle class bureaucratic sectors. In Rio de Janeiro, for example, Sugiyama Iutaka (1966: 129) found that over one-third of his sample of upper- and middle-class workers were employed in the city's public bureaucracy. In Lima, government white-collar workers are said to outnumber those in the private sector (Chaplin 1969: 431), and in Santiago the state is by far the principal employer of the middle class (Lomnitz 1971: 94). Especially in cities with limited employment possibilities in industry, government jobs are highly sought after even when salaries are low. The important thing they have to offer is security, a most attractive quality in today's cities with their serious problems of underemployment and spiraling rates of inflation. An extreme case is reported for Rio where "the importance of a public job is so great that people prefer to descend socially than to be upwardly mobile in the private sector" (Iutaka 1966: 130).

Under these conditions, it is not surprising that members of the Latin American middle class tend to be politically conservative. They are apt to side with those in power and support the status quo, for many of them realize that their livelihood depends on the government. Career advancement is most likely to come to those who conform to elite demands. The Mexican sociologist Rodolfo Stavenhagen (1974: 30) maintains that the middle class constitutes the chief base of support for military dictatorship in Latin America. Together with this dependency on power elites, much of the middle class shares a value system and life-style closely patterned after those of the upper class. Using Adams's terms, all but the lower artisanal stratum of the middle class belongs to the power–prestige value sector rather than the work–wealth sector. In terms of dress, language, etiquette, housing, and general style of life, the middle class in most cities consciously strives to follow the standards set by the elite.

There is a constant struggle to keep up appearances through conspicuous consumption and the acquisition of items of high display value such as fashionable apartments, stylish clothing, expensive automobiles, and television sets (Wagley and Harris 1965: 57). Many are successful in maintaining their positions as long as they can hold on to their jobs. They can avoid the degradation of manual labor and be attended daily by at least one household servant, thanks to the presence in the cities of vast numbers of migrant poor, many of whom are underemployed. But these high aspirations inevitably place middle-class families in a financial bind, for with the exception of a few well-off entrepreneurs, their salaries are all they have. Consequently, they are always running out of cash, and many families are forced to cut corners and make real sacrifices in order to continue sending their children to the best private schools and to maintain their high consumption level. More than one observer has remarked that the middle-class families of most modest means tend to entertain most lavishly (A. Whiteford 1977: 152–3).

The overall picture that emerges is quite distinct from the classic pattern of the North American or European middle class. Especially in the United States, the middle class is thought to constitute a majority of the population and to set general standards for the rest of the nation. In Latin America, however, where the lower class constitutes the majority (or at least a plurality), it is the upper class that sets the standards and the middle class that is forever trying to catch up. As a result, the middle class has not developed an emphasis on saving or a distinctive ideology of its own (Wagley and Harris 1965: 57).

In addition to the penchant for jobs in the public and private bureaucracy, there is another distinctive aspect of Latin American middle-class careers that deserves mention. This is the often cited tendency for many persons to hold more than one job simultaneously. There are a number of reasons for this, most of which are related to the expanding nature of the economic and occupational structure of so many Latin American cities. There is a rapid proliferation of new economic sectors, occupations, and statuses, and a continual shortage of personnel to fill them. Because the forms of curricularized training and specialized skills have not yet had sufficient time to develop, many of these newly created jobs, such as market analyst or computer programmer, are filled by self-trained people, and many persons hold more than one position (Leeds 1965: 381–2). There is yet another reason for multiple job-holding, however: many middle-class occupations do not pay well and struggling breadwinners must often work more than one job simply to make ends meet. For example, high-school teachers in Rio sometimes teach in five or six different schools every day (Wagley and Harris 1965: 57).

Multiple job-holding seems to be more common at the higher occupational levels, however (Iutaka 1966: 127), and many individuals are motivated by status aspirations as well as economic necessity. According to David Chaplin (1969: 431), in middle-class Peru the "ideal" combination of occupations would be "a university professorship for prestige, a government position for power and prestige, and various private jobs related to the government post for income." The social organization of this occupational pattern has been perceptively studied by Anthony Leeds (1965) in six Brazilian cities. He found that career advancement in this setting operates less through training and qualifications (though of course these are not wholly unimportant) than it does through the manipulation of kinship and friendship networks.

In keeping with Brazil's rural-agrarian heritage, which stresses face-to-face relations among kin and pseudo-kin in particular localities, middle- and upper-class career patterns in the cities are organized on a strikingly personalistic basis, despite the often highly industrialized and commercial backdrop. Relatives frequently provide the steps to new connections and new jobs for many urban professionals and bureaucrats. Many aspiring young men depend heavily on an uncle, father-in-law, or cousin for initial entry and subsequent advancement through the occupational structure (Leeds 1965: 387–8). Business is accomplished and influence wielded not through formalized, impersonal bureaucratic channels, but through membership in *panelinhas*, or cliques, that exist at the middle and upper levels of the occupational hierarchy. These are informal alliances composed of men in different careers, all of them power equals, who stand in a position to help one another in business matters, cut red tape, and otherwise grant favors when needed. *Panelinhas* are of different types and can cover many different activities. A typical politico-economic clique may consist of a customs official, an insurance man, a lawyer or two, a businessman, an accountant, a municipal, state, or federal deputy, and a banker. The number of *panelinhas* in a given city is proportional to its size and level of economic and political development. Small cities may have only one or two, while large industrial centers have many dozens (Leeds 1965: 393–4).

Larissa Lomnitz has described a similar pattern for the middle-class bureaucrats in Chilean cities (1971). Because such people have neither much capital nor control over the means of production in their society, one of their major resources lies in their personal networks of social and family connections. An elaborate system for the reciprocity of favors exists for such services as job placement, loans, the waiving of priorities and red tape, admissions to schools, legal and political favors, and social introductions. This is more than just nepotism, for relatives are rarely involved in such transactions. Rather, it is a complex network composed of chains of dyadic contracts between pairs of individuals who regard each other as friends and agree to act as go-betweens for each other. Initial favors are bestowed without any overt indication of return, but the obligation thus created "is stored in a sort of savings account of future services to be rendered to various persons and drawn upon as the need arises" (Lomnitz 1971: 94).

What role are the Latin American middle classes currently playing in the processes of urbanization and economic development, and what does the future hold for them? These questions have attracted considerable comment, much of it polemical, from North American social scientists during the past three decades. Until fairly recently, many of these observers were of the opinion that "Latin American development is the work and creation of a nationalist, progressive, enterprising, and dynamic middle class, and the social and economic policy objectives of the Latin American governments should be to stimulate 'social mobility' and the development of that class" (Stavenhagen 1974: 29). For the most part, this point of view has proved to be wishful thinking by those who insist on seeing Latin America from a North American viewpoint. It is also factually inaccurate, and Rodolfo Stavenhagen (1974) includes this viewpoint in his list of seven "fallacies" about Latin America. The fact that a Latin American middle class exists does not mean that it will follow the same route as its North American counterpart, as some have mistakenly assumed. In most Latin American cities today the middle class still lacks cohesion, power, and a consciousness of kind, and we have seen that its composition and boundaries can fluctuate widely from place to place.

The role of the middle class in national development has been much discussed for Mexico, for example. A country with a relatively open class system by Latin American standards, Mexico has undergone a phenomenal amount of urbanization, industrialization, and population growth since World War II. Research findings on the role of the Mexican middle class tend to conflict. Some researchers have argued that a new "ideology of modernization" is coming out of the middle sector, based on a belief in the need for rapid economic development, a commitment to education, and a sense of nationalism (Miller 1973: 119; see also Stern and Kahl 1968: 26). This may well be the case, but there is also compelling evidence against the overly optimistic conclusion that the middle class is destined to expand greatly in size through upward mobility from the lower class. Jorge Balán and his collaborators (1973) have shown that there is no evidence for such a trend in Monterrey, the second most industrialized city in Mexico. Even in this relatively egalitarian urban center with its moderate degree of upward social mobility, the middle class is still small and emergent and dependent upon the business elite for its existence. It is weak, rather apolitical, and tends to accept the work and community ethic of the upper class (Balán et al. 1973: 304).

Mexico as a whole is an instructive example, for its industrial plant has been called one of the most dynamic and successful in Latin America (Stern and Kahl 1968: 8). Yet despite its growth, Mexico has one of the most extreme concentrations of income of the large countries of the world. In 1963 the poorest 40 percent of the population received only 11 percent of the total national income, and the richest 10 percent of the populace received almost half the wealth. In recent years there have been some small gains in purchasing power among the middle-income groups, but industrialization has not resulted in a numerical predominance of the middle class in urban areas, nor has it reduced the wide gap between the rich and the poor. Moreover, this appears to be the result of a widespread pattern of industrialization in Latin America that rests on a large supply of unskilled, lower-class labor (which grows through migration from rural areas), a slow rate of labor absorption in the technologically modern sector, and a reluctance of national governments to formulate effective income redistribution policies (Balán et al. 1973: 240).

Louis Casagrande looked at urbanization in Zacapu, Michoacan, from three interrelated perspectives. First, he described the evolution of the three major social strata or classes: the *clase obrera*, the *clase humilde*, and the *clase media* (the last including, in particular, the local comerciantes). Casagrande discovered that there is a polarization of workers in Zacapu. The unionized workers at a large factory in the city have used their closed shop *sindicato* (union) to advance their economic security, solidify their class consciousness, and exclude outsiders. Meanwhile, the members of the encapsulated, marginal sector (known locally as the *clase humilde*), have used kin-based work groups, classic patron–client relationships, and strategies of legal and illegal migration to cope with their relative – if not absolute – deprivation (L. Casagrande 1979: 164–73).

It appears that the urban middle class in Latin America as a whole is very gradually increasing in size and is beginning to obtain a larger share of the wealth. These trends are proceeding at a much slower rate than some have predicted, however, and a well-grounded middle-class ideology has yet to develop, although there are signs that something of the sort is beginning to emerge in a few cities. At present, the Latin American middle class seems to lack the internal dynamism necessary to become a catalyst of change. While it may be developing an ideology of modernization, it is not the only sector of society to do so and it still takes its cues and much of its sustenance from the upper class. It is within the commercial and industrial sectors of the upper class – not the middle class – that the most important innovators and promoters of economic development are currently found.

Social mobility

Up to this point the class structure has been described as if it were rigid and unchanging, but this is rarely the case. Both downward and upward mobility occur continually. Cases of downward movement include members of the elite who have abandoned social interests or lost much of their wealth. They may be able to remain within the prestige value sector with the help of relatives and friends, but if a certain level of wealth is not maintained, their descendants will be less fortunate. For members of the middle class, loss of income or reputation always have more immediate consequences, and downward movement is almost inevitable. Because we have no systematic studies of downward mobility in Latin America, it is impossible to judge its frequency in any meaningful way. We shall thus confine our attention to upward mobility as it affects the lower and middle classes.

Barriers to upward mobility are still stronger in all of Latin America than they are in Europe and North America, but they tend to be most permeable in the cities. Social mobility has occurred steadily on a moderate scale for some time and it is clearly increasing (Willems 1975: 249–51). Judging primarily from the Pan-American Union studies (Crevenna 1950–1), Ralph Beals (1965: 351) believes that the most open class system is to be found in Mexico, followed by Argentina, Chile, and Uruguay.

The industrial cities in southern South America and new cities founded there and elsewhere provide striking examples of social mobility. In large industrial urban centers such as São Paulo and Buenos Aires, the impact of European immigration during the nineteenth century cannot be underestimated. For Argentina, Gino Germani (1970: 303–4) states that the middle layers of the occupational structure increased from less than 11 percent in 1869 to more than 30 percent in 1914. Most of this growth was due to immigration, and today both the Argentine middle class and most of the manual workers (at least in Buenos Aires) are overwhelmingly of foreign origin. More important, however, is the fact that the vast majority of immigrants came from lower-class European backgrounds. For many decades, then, social mobility became an accepted pattern in the central Argentine cities and most of the middle class up until 1950 can be said to have lower-class origins (Germani 1970: 305). Few of the immigrants seem to have penetrated the upper class, however. In Paraná, Reina (1973: 238) found that both the wealthiest and poorest inhabitants of the city are more Argentine and have been in the area longer than the middle-class citizens, most of whom are of Italian, German, Swiss, or Spanish ancestry. Iutaka (1971: 265) has noted a similar pattern in Brazil, where immigrants and their descendants are more likely to be upwardly mobile than the Brazilians. Whereas many new industrial occupations are shunned by traditional Brazilians as not up to their prestige aspirations, immigrants are more inclined to fill them, because they are less bound by the traditional value system. Consequently, immigrants and their descendants have been absorbed into the industrial plant at a greater rate and are more upwardly mobile in the class structure.

Social mobility has also become almost a way of life in what Willems (1975: 251–2) calls Latin America's urban frontier – the literally hundreds of new cities founded during the nineteenth century in formerly undeveloped or sparsely populated regions. The largest number of these are in the western region of São Paulo State in Brazil and the north and west of the neighboring Argentine state of Paraná. Willems himself has worked in the city of Pereira, Colombia, which was founded by a group of small farmers in 1863 but is today a bustling community of over 230,000 with a highly differentiated class structure. The growth of Pereira's class system has been almost entirely an internal development involving extensive social mobility, because most migrants arriving in the city come from lower-class, agricultural backgrounds (Willems 1975: 251–2).

In all the major urban centers, it is the upper class that is most difficult to penetrate. In an article written twenty-five years ago, Ralph Beals (1965: 355–6) provides a good comparative discussion of the difficulties involved. He notes that the urban elites of Peru and Brazil tend to be the most closed and define themselves in quasi-racial terms. Entry into the upper class is easier in Mexico, Chile, and Argentina. Only in Mexico, however, has there been a thorough reorganization of the upper class in terms of power and wealth, due to the upheavals of the Revolution of 1910. It is still true in many cases that money is not enough to gain admission to the highest status groups; as we have seen in Popayán, marriage is usually involved in mobility from the middle to upper levels.

It is one thing to say that social mobility has occurred but quite another to document how it actually takes place. There is much unanimity among researchers, and among their informants as well, that education is the single most important means to mobility today (Chaplin 1969: 433; Iutaka 1971: 264; Reina 1973: 334; Tumin and Feldman 1971: 7). The possession of a high-school or college diploma or formal training in specialized skills is bound to become even more necessary for the most desirable positions in the future. A spiral effect may be predicted. Although many young lower-class males today have more education than their fathers, this will enable them only to maintain their fathers' occupational statuses, for the educational requirements for many skilled and semiskilled jobs are continually rising (Balán et al. 1973: 244).

Important as it is, education is only one part of the mobility process. Particularly in the prestige value sector, once one's education is completed, successful careers may be determined less by one's specific qualifications and abilities than by the quality of one's friends and relatives (Iutaka 1971; Leeds 1965; Lomnitz 1971). Patronage is extremely important at all levels of Latin American society, and aspirants to higher rank who have not taken steps to cultivate or strengthen personal relationships with the right people will always find their paths blocked, even though their credentials may be impeccable. In general, it appears that reliance on relatives in the mobility process is greatest at the upper levels of the class hierarchy. Strong cognatic ties and large kindreds are present among the upper classes, while the kinship networks of the poor are likely to be much more constricted. In a very real sense, the wealthy can affort to keep track of larger groups of relatives, and mobility at the higher levels is determined to a large extent by the number and quality of collateral kin one can draw on (Adams 1965: 270–1).

Social mobility may involve different sets of actors, ranging from the isolated individual to whole families and even larger kinship units. From the few data available, it appears that, barring mass upheavals and revolutionary change, mobility in most cities is a highly individualistic phenomenon and that Latin Americans tend to view it as such. In San Juan, Puerto Rico, the urban poor see the class system as open and believe that anyone can better his position if he tries hard enough. They view the process of mobility as largely determined by an individual's own life history (Safa 1974: 35, 103). Mobility in Paraná, Argentina is also an individual undertaking and can at times place a strain on family solidarity:

If a person attempts to improve his social standing, this causes social imbalance within the family. The father may be a skilled worker, oriented toward his neighborhood and active in a neighborhood club; one son is attending secondary school, and another the Escuela Industrial. In situations like that, a natural social distance emerges; there may be some embarrassment when the persons are socially sensitive. Families with one son working while another is enjoying the life of a student have more acute problems. One solution is that the son who has been working and helping the family finally chooses to move to another town or province. [Reina 1973: 334]

The most fascinating and unique case study of social mobility in Latin America has been carried out in a northwest Ecuadorian port town by Norman E. Whitten, Jr. (1965; 1969). San Lorenzo is a predominantly black community that at the time of Whitten's initial research in 1963 had a population of only 2,418. It nevertheless exhibited a diversified occupational base and a well-developed, three-tiered class hierarchy. Stressing the overriding importance of kinship ties, Whitten has proposed a developmental cycle model of strategies of social mobility employed by members of the lower class to enter the middle class (few blacks make it to the upper). Upward movement in San Lorenzo is a group undertaking and is achieved by "consolidating social capital to exploit economic and political opportunity" (Whitten 1969: 231). A four-generation cycle can be discerned, and the unit that makes mobility possible is the kindred. The lower-class personal kindred is ego-oriented and includes the core individual and his siblings plus other consanguineal, affinal, and fictive kin. Although it tends to be based in a particular locality, many members are dispersed in different towns and thus make possible the spatial mobility that is so common along the Ecuadorian coast, especially among the males. Collateral extension of the personal kindred rarely extends beyond one's second cousins (Whitten 1965: 139–47).

The mobility cycle begins when a lower-class family establishes itself in a particular town. During this first generation, the leveling effect of reciprocal obligations tends to keep the family poor, but the family does manage to put down roots in the locality. In the second generation, ties to the large dispersed personal kindred are severed by a core group of siblings; contacts within a small, localized segment of the kin group are intensified as all members contribute to one another's economic advance. At this point members of the kindred cross the threshold into the middle class and become important economic middlemen in the community.

The third generation represents a stage of consolidation. Sibling bonds are strengthened and the kindred increasingly resembles a business enterprise as it is transformed into a true corporate group, the "stem kindred": "a corporately functioning, self-perpetuating kindred, united by consolidated socioeconomic interests and obligations" (Whitten 1965: 139). At this time the kindred expands in size, draws together in one section of the town, and consolidates its economic position through social and political connections. United by its economic interests, it functions corporately without coercion or authority. Each small urban community in the area tends to have one dominant, middle-class stem kindred.

But the period of ascendency of these collectivities is short-lived in the boom-and-bust environment of the Ecuadorian littoral. By the time the fourth generation has come of age, the economic and political control of the group has begun to weaken. The kindred has expanded more rapidly than the economy, and when economic contraction sets in, its members cease to be useful as middlemen between the upper and lower classes. Factions develop, fissions ensue, and the kindred reverts to lower-class status as other family groups struggle to launch new developmental cycles of their own (Whitten 1965: 156–8). Whitten found that during his stay in San Lorenzo in 1963, the dominant stem kindred encompassed half the middle-class black population as well as a few light *costeños* and mestizos. No budding local entrepreneur would think of launching a serious economic or political undertaking without the support of the dominant kindred.

In some respects the pattern just described is reminiscent of the machinations of the Brazilian *panelinha*. But the fact that in San Lorenzo only relatives are involved and that a true corporate organization is achieved makes this case unique. San Lorenzo is significant for at least two reasons. First, it shows that anthropologists can make important ethnographic contributions to the study of social mobility, a field too often approached solely through the statistical manipulation of occupational classifications. And equally important, the case of San Lorenzo suggests that conclusions about social mobility as well as other aspects of urban social organization that hold for the large primate cities may not apply to the smaller towns, where the economy is less stable and urbanization is still in the incipient stage.

Race and class relations

Social stratification in many Latin American cities cannot be adequately understood without considering racial factors. This is particularly true in the coastal provinces of Ecuador, Colombia, Venezuela, Guyana, Surinam, Brazil, and Central America, all of which contain significant populations of black ancestry. In this section we shall discuss the relationship between race and class insofar as blacks and whites are concerned and the effect of urbanization on this sphere of social relations.

The colonial background of the Latin American racial system was touched on in Chapter 1, where we emphasized the phenomenon of racial mobility and the fact that racial identity per se is affected by class status and other factors. Charles Wagley (1965: 531–2) has pointed out that "race" is defined differently in different parts of the Americas. While in the United States ancestry is the key factor in distinguishing between black and white, in Latin America physical appearance and other sociocultural criteria play a more important role. The result is that in many regions of Central and South America today there is a broad continuum of physical types that do not in themselves form social groups or possess clearly defined ethnic identities. This gradient is very much like the one described for colonial Oaxaca in Chapter 1. A person's class standing (wealth) influences his "race" just as do his features, hair and skin color, education, family background, and occupation. Even siblings may be classified as racially different if one is slightly darker than the other, or makes more money, or holds a more prestigious job. Where race is important, the relationships between the class and prestige hierarchies are far more complex than they are in cities that lack significant black or mulatto populations. In the latter communities, which have furnished most of the examples given until now in this chapter, there is likely to be more congruity between one's wealth and one's social status, although we have seen that rarely if ever is there complete overlap.

In some South American coastal cities it is not unusual to find that all economic classes are racially heterogeneous to some degree and that complex calculations lie behind the determination of racial status. In the Ecuadorian town of San Lorenzo, a *blanco* (white) is defined as "any middle- or upper-class mestizo, Caucasian, or mulatto who is held in some degree of respect" (Whitten 1965: 91). White status here does not depend on one's genes alone but on a multitude of ways by which a person may earn the respect of his neighbors. However, although mulattoes can become blancos in San Lorenzo, blacks cannot. And researchers have found that members of the same community are apt to disagree on the racial designations of others. In their study of Cartagena, a large Colombian port city of some three hundred thousand inhabitants, Mauricio Solaún and Sidney Kronus (1973: 165) showed fifty-two photographs of individuals to sixty-two respondents of all class levels. The photographs covered the full spectrum of racial types and patterns of dress in the area and the investigators themselves established an objective classification of ten physical types. When the pictures were shown to the respondents, however, no fewer than sixty-two different racial categorizations were elicited!

In a similar experiment in Brazil, Marvin Harris (1970: 76) showed a deck of seventy-two face drawings to 100 people and obtained a total of 492 different categorizations, with the range extending from two to seventy per respondent. Space does not permit a full discussion of the complexities of Latin American race relations, but it is sufficient to emphasize the crucial significance of the racially mixed sector in these coastal areas. Miscegenated people are regarded as different from blacks, unlike the system in the United States, where they would be classified as light in color but blacks nonetheless.

The urban structure of race and class in coastal South America can be illustrated with the case of Cartagena. Solaún and Kronus (1973: 105–19) define an elite, a middle class, a "working class," and a lower class, and show that persons of color – the miscegénated – are found in all of them. Skin color darkens as one descends the socioeconomic ladder, however: there are virtually no blacks in the upper class (though there are mulattoes) and no whites in the lower class. Most Cartagenians with nearly pure Caucasian ancestry can trace their descent back to Spain, but they are a small group. The great bulk of the people have some distinguishing Negroid characteristics, and unlike the pattern in some Brazilian cities, even the Cartagenian elite recognizes that it is not purely white. The most racially heterogeneous stratum is the middle class, which tends to be dominated by miscegenated persons, although it has a substantial number of whites and a smaller proportion of blacks.

Latin American race relations have been described as neither totally closed (an extreme that the system in the United States approximates) nor totally open, but "infused" and "eclectic." (Solaún and Kronus 1973: 22) On the one hand, endogamy and hierarchical rules separate the whites and blacks who occupy the polar extremes of the system, and blacks are clearly discriminated against. On the other, many individuals of mixed racial heritage are accepted in the upper levels of the class hierarchy, marry white spouses, and compete on equal terms with one another for scarce resources (Solaún and Kronus 1973: 22). Thus there is a degree of racial integration of a significantly greater magnitude than in the United States. This system works against the formation of racial groups by permitting a degree of individual mobility for some people of color, although upward mobility is always more difficult for blacks than for lighter individuals. The rise of such persons within the class system does not mean, however, that Latin America is a racial paradise or that its cities are racial "democracies." The relative numbers of light and dark people in the various classes of any coastal Latin American city (Cartagena is typical of many) are sufficient proof to the contrary.

While it may be applied in a very subtle fashion, discrimination makes itself felt. Indeed, there are indications that racial tensions and discrimination are increasing in the competitive atmosphere of large cities such as São Paulo and Rio de Janeiro, which are filling up with migrants looking for work (Degler 1971: 281–7; Fernandes 1969: 440–7; Wagley 1963: 155). Rapid urbanization today appears to be promoting a heightened awareness of racial differences, and insofar as people of color become increasingly conscious of their position in society, antagonism with whites is likely to increase. In tracing the changes that occurred in San Lorenzo, Ecuador between 1965 and 1968, Whitten (1974: 183–201) has noted a disturbing trend toward black disenfranchisement. In this brief period, San Lorenzo underwent rapid urbanization: Its population doubled, exploitation of the natural environment expanded greatly, and more money entered the local economy. The concomitant social changes were reflected in the changing residential pattern of the town: Whereas prominent blacks had once occupied the central portion, by 1968 they had been pushed out to the less prestigious periphery and the center had been taken over by recently arrived blanco-mestizos. Middle-class blacks were also being pushed out of their entrepreneurial activities – disenfranchised, to use Whitten's term – at a rapid rate.

As long as the blanco-mestizos are in the clear minority we could say that race relations are most fluid, and that individual relationships do not reflect the white ideational constructs which derogate the black frontiersmen. But a change in the numerical ratio of mestizo-blancos to black frontiersmen plus the differential access of the former to capital resources renders a crucial transformation in the pattern of race relations, and the case of San Lorenzo shows how very rapid this transformation can be. [Whitten 1974: 193]

Paradoxically, while urbanization and economic development may have the effect of promoting racial and economic mobility for the miscegenated – mulattoes, mestizos, and so forth – they may be erecting barriers for the blacks and the Indians. As Whitten has observed (1974: 198), the process of development in South American nations is normally conceived of in part as a process of ethnic mixture, one that categorically excludes blacks and Indians who do not enter the "melting pot." Consequently, blackness is cognitively relegated to the bottom of the class hierarchy, even though a few individual blacks are able to enter the middle class. With Whitten, we too "cannot help but wonder whether countries such as Ecuador and Colombia are entering a phase of 'preadaptation' to contemporary industrial economy, where segregation along color lines is one relatively convenient, though deplorable, means of sorting aggregates into access classes" (1974: 199–200). We would go one step further and extend this speculation to urban Brazil as well.

Migration and the urban class structure

Our discussion of the urban class structure would be incomplete without a statement about its relationship to the migratory process. Although research in this area has been limited, two general types of questions may be posed. First, how do rural migrants in the city compare with city natives in terms of their class position and social mobility? Second, to what degree do migrants assimilate to the urban class system and lose the regional or local identities that may have been important in the rural setting? The second question obviously has many ramifications, some of which are addressed in Chapter 7.

A common assumption made by many students of urbanization in Latin America is that because most migrants are of rural origin, most are therefore to be found at the bottom of the urban lower class; frequently it is also assumed that differences in socioeconomic status between city natives and migrants are likely to be pronounced (Balán 1969: 4). Recent research has shown, however, that this is not always the case and that the relative position of migrants vis-à-vis urban natives is not all that inferior. A comprehensive approach to this question must take into account a number of variables, some of which have been dealt with in preceding chapters. Among them are the nature of migrant selectivity, the kinds of communities migrants come from, the rate of creation of new jobs in the cities, and the level of skill or qualifications needed for urban occupations (Balán 1969: 5). But the key factor for understanding the socioeconomic position of migrants in the city lies in the occupational opportunies open to them as compared to those open to the urban-born.

In their analysis of survey data from Buenos Aires, Santiago, and six Brazilian cities, Bock and Iutaka (1969: 348–51) conclude that migrants are not disadvantaged occupationally in the urban setting. Measured on a six-tiered scale, the mean occupational level of the migrants is only slightly lower than that of urban natives. Furthermore, judging from a comparison of fathers' and sons' occupations, migrants appear to be as socially mobile as the city-born. If migrants in these cities are at first disadvantaged in comparison to urbanites, they appear to overcome their handicaps within the first generation. Donald Foster's study of six poor barrios in the port city of Barranquilla, Colombia (1975: 259-60) confirms these observations. Although in this city urban natives have a slight edge in semiskilled occupations, the unemployment rate for migrants and natives is about the same, as are their incomes.

The best available study of migrant–native socioeconomic differences in any Latin American city is that of Jorge Balán, Harley L. Browning and Elizabeth Jelín for heavily industrial Monterrey (1973). Here the city-born were found to have an advantage over the rural migrants, especially those coming from agricultural backgrounds, but the differences are not great. Unskilled laborers in Monterrey tend to remain at the same level for their entire lives, regardless of their place of birth. Job changes among this sector of the lower class usually entail a shift from occupations that require physical strength to ones that are less physically demanding but are essentially dead-end positions that carry no chance for advancement (Balán et al. 1973: 198–200).

Occupational mobility is intimately related to the migrant's age. The more capable and motivated men usually arrive in Monterrey in their late teens or early twenties, and those who come before the age of twenty-six actually have a higher mobility rate than city natives (although the natives enter the occupational ladder at a slightly higher level). The older migrants, because they have spent much of their lives in rural communities with few job opportunities, are less mobile, but not less mobile than the urban natives. In general, migrants to Monterrey enter the occupational structure at a lower level than the city-born; if they migrate as young men they are likely to overcome this handicap, but if they wait until their thirties or forties they will be less successful (Balán et al. 1973: 201–7). The single greatest hurdle that rural migrants in Monterrey and many other cities face today is lack of education. The amount of educational credentials needed for many jobs is on the rise, a trend that places country dwellers at a disadvantage because of the general lack of rural educational facilities. Today, young migrants from the country are finding it increasingly difficult to rise above the level of the unskilled manual laborer. Formerly, work experience provided a means of upward mobility, but this is less true today.

Whether Monterrey can be said to be "typical" of Latin American cities is impossible to say. In their South American study, Bock and Iutaka (1969: 349) obtained consistently low correlations between age at migration and urban social mobility. However, it seems that the assumption of sharp socioeconomic differences between migrants and the urban-born is a dubious one, especially for large industrial cities. Reviewing survey data from São Paulo, Santiago, Mexico City, Monterrey, San Salvador, Guatemala City, and Buenos Aires, Balán (1969: 12–23) found evidence of significant contrasts between migrants and urban natives only in the last case. He attributes this primarily to a slackening of the pace of industrialization since 1950. (Note that his findings for Buenos Aires contradict those of Bock and Iutaka cited above.) These considerations suggest that anthropologists should pay more attention to migrant preadaptation to urban life (Gulick 1973: 998–9), especially in Latin America, where cities and their hinterlands have been interacting for centuries within essentially the same sociocultural framework. Whether such preadaptation will continue to be a significant factor in the years to come will depend largely on the degree of commitment of national governments to improving their rural school systems.

Having considered the socioeconomic adaptation of migrants to the urban class structure, we turn finally to the cultural and ethnic dimensions of the process. There is certainly little doubt that class factors are very important in determining the behavior and outlook of urban Latin Americans. Emilio Willems (1968: 75) has suggested a conceptual framework for relating the study of migration to the urban class structure. Willems proposes that classes be regarded as distinctive subcultures that influence peoples' conduct and motivations. His basic hypothesis is that "the acculturation of these [migrant] groups, regardless of their cultural origin, may be considered synonymous with their absorption into the existing class system which in turn does not remain unchanged in the process" (Willems 1968: 75). While Willems points out that there are factors that may inhibit migrant acculturation to the class system (such as poverty or lack of employment opportunities), he seems to feel that, in general, most migrants shed their previous ethnic or cultural identities and in place of them develop a high degree of awareness of their class position. We might call this the melting-pot theory of urbanization. It holds that the incorporation of newcomers proceeds along class lines and that ethnicity is bound to be less important than class consciousness in the long run.

This point of view does indeed have some merit in explaining the urbanization of European and Asian immigrants in a number of South American cities. While Old World ethnic identities are normally strong among first-generation European migrants, their descendants are less conscious of their ancestry. Figures for Brazil and Chile indicate that ethnic endogamy is no longer prevalent and that most people identify more with their class than with any ethnic group (Willems 1968: 80). Paraná, Argentina, with its long history of immigration of Italians, Russian-Germans, French, Swiss, Basques, Irish, and English, provides a good example. Ethnic associations were strong and numerous in this city at the end of the nineteenth century, but they have been on the decline for some time and since 1930 have had little influence on the urban social structure. Only among the grandparents' generation today does ethnic identity remain strong; their children and grandchildren for the most part consider themselves to be simply Argentinians and members of the Paraná middle class (Reina 1973: 74, 143–6).

While the melting pot theory seems to hold up well for many cities in Brazil, Argentina, Chile, Guatemala, and perhaps some in Mexico, when we turn to other countries we are immediately confronted with problems. Contrary to the theory, we find that ethnicity as well as class is an important component of migrant adaptation to many urban centers. Indian identity and cuture as yet show few signs of disappearing among migrants in Lima, Peru (Doughty 1972; Roberts 1974), and the same appears to hold true for La Paz, Bolivia as well (Buechler 1970). In sprawling, industrial Cali, Colombia, Guy Ashton (1974) studied a new government-sponsored housing project settled by three distinct groups: mestizo migrants from the Central Cordillera, black migrants from the coast and the Cauca valley, and urban mestizos native to the metropolitan area. Far from melting into a single, class-conscious group, however, after several years this lower-class population remains divided into ethnic enclaves within the housing project. Each maintains a clearly defined subculture of its own based on place of origin, and the corresponding ethnic identities show no signs of erosion. The mestizo migrants initially expressed a desire to become assimilated into the urban labor force, but the city-born mestizos in the housing project refuse to accept their country cousins as equals, because they signify lower social status and unwanted competition for jobs (even though the two groups do not differ racially). The result so far has been a reinforcement of the mestizo migrants' regional subculture and identity, and much the same can be said for the blacks (Ashton 1974: 883, 892).

Although in many Latin American localities there may be a near identity of class and ethnic status, especially in the cities, the cases just discussed show that "a stratification that is based on both ethnicity and class is fundamentally different from one that is based on class only" (van den Berghe and Primov 1977: 259). While ethnic distinctions are not as sharp in Latin American cities as they are in their counterparts elsewhere in the developing world, especially in tribal sub-Saharan Africa, they are nonetheless important and cannot be ignored. There is little evidence thus far that urbanization in and of itself has any inevitable "homogenizing effect" on racial and ethnic differences. In fact, there are signs that just the opposite is occurring. Whatever the future brings for the urban class system in Latin America, it is clear that the racial and ethnic dimensions of inequality will remain part of the urban scene for quite some time to come.

7. Voluntary associations

In some countries, notably Argentina and the United States, mass immigration from Europe in the nineteenth century led to a proliferation of voluntary associations of all kinds. Groups concerned with mutual aid, medical care, ethnic consciousness, politics, and sports and other entertainment have historically played an important role in the lives of many urban migrants in these countries. Louis Wirth (1938) was no doubt influenced by what he observed in his native Chicago when he placed so much emphasis on voluntary associations in his theory of urbanism. Outside of the southern South American countries, however, voluntary organizations in Latin America are not important vehicles of migrant adaptation to urban life. (Lima is an important exception to this generalization.) A good many groups of all kinds proliferate in the urban setting, but they are usually short-lived, and their memberships are relatively inactive except for a few enthusiastic individuals.[1]

Many associations arise to accomplish specific projects – the "instrumental associations" of Gordon and Babchuk (1959: 22–9) – only to disintegrate when the goal is achieved or near completion. Political interest groups respond to crises but have difficulty sustaining themselves and frequently degenerate into recreational associations (Goode 1970: 164). The most important type of association among the lower classes – among migrants and the city-born alike – is devoted to sports and takes charge of organizing the ubiquitous Sunday soccer match or baseball game. On the whole, however, a good many voluntary groups in Latin American cities might be more accurately described as cliques or collectivities that depend on a key person or persons for their existence. Participation in organizations also varies considerably with class status, as Floyd Dotson (1953) found in Guadalajara, Mexico. Of the 415 adults he interviewed, 58 percent of the men and 68 percent of the women belonged to no association at all, and members of the city's lower class (which contains most of the migrants from rural areas) participated much less than those higher up on the socioeconomic ladder.

Outside of the family context, most social relationships in urban Latin America are not built on corporate models. Much more significant in the social fabric is the relatively informal, ego-centered network of relationships, which is more amorphous and has no sharp boundaries. Friendship and kinship are apt to be much more important to migrant adaptation than membership in clubs, political parties, or unions. Keeping these limitations in mind, we now proceed to look at the distribution and functions that *can* be ascribed to voluntary organizations.

Functions of voluntary associations

In his review of studies of voluntary associations as adaptive mechanisms in situations of social, cultural, ecological, and technological change, especially in change involving rapid urban growth and large-scale migrations of rural populations to towns and cities, Kerri (1976: 23) notes that social scientists have found that kinship and territory are no longer effective means for the organization of new social groups or the reorganization of existing ones. He argues that voluntary associations are more pliable than kinship and territorial units of social organization.[2] Based on voluntary participation and communality of the interests of members, voluntary associations generally lack the rigidity that may characterize kinship or territorial organizations. Because people are born or adopted into kin groups, there is little or no choice or volition in kinship group membership. Although kinship group membership can be renounced, such renunciation may invoke sanctions and involve complex procedures.

Kinship group members need not have common interests, except where ownership of land, duties and obligations, or social exchange and reciprocity, are concerned. Because of these features, new types of kinship-based groups are not easily formed, and existing types are not easily manipulated and adapted to deal with new domains of experience. "This is where voluntary associations, usually formed by people interested in problems of mutual concern and on their own volition, have become more useful, in adaptive terms, than kinship groups ... Similarly, territorial units, because of their political organization, have much more definite, but again much more rigid, features than voluntary associations" (Kerri 1976: 24). This dichotomy, which opposes kinship-territorially based groups and voluntary associations, fits our previous emphasis on networks, dyads, and small groups as intermediate forms of formal and informal interaction (see Chapter 5).

Voluntary associations, which Kerri classifies as "common-interest" associations satisfy two conditions: (1) they are based on common interests; and (2) their membership is entirely voluntary (Kerri 1976: 24). Kerri argues that it is important to distinguish between those aspects of human experience from which an interest is derived and the interest itself. In other words, groups with common interests can and should be differentiated from associations whose existence is based upon other criteria. Take, for example, ethnic associations. The fact of shared ethnicity may or may not be the raison d'être for these groups. As Kerri (1976: 24) phrases it, "although we may find that in an urban area the members of an association belong to the same ethnic group, this does not automatically mean that the bond of ethnicity is what brought them together. It is their interest in survival in the midst of the complexities and strangeness of the urban area, and not their ethnicity per se, that accounts for the formation of the association."

This statement, however, overlooks the time factor, because the purpose or function of an association may change over time. Further, many ethnic associations have as a primary purpose the welfare of their members' hometowns, not their survival in the city, although these groups may have a latent function of acting as buffers between inexperienced newcomers and a potentially hostile urban milieu.

Since the 1950s, social scientists working in Latin America have recorded the existence and functions of regional voluntary associations, particularly in Peru. Some of the earliest and best studies were done by William Mangin (e.g. 1959). While admitting the limited amount of anthropological literature about social clubs at the time of his initial investigations (1951–3), Mangin was impressed by the proliferation of these regional associations or clubs in Peru. He thought their proliferation extreme, both in regard to the number of clubs and the intensity of the members' participation. Although there are many kinds of these associations – occupational clubs, sports clubs, drinking clubs, professional clubs – Mangin dealt mainly with the type of social club organized around a locality, usually the place of birth or early residence of its members. There are clubs representing different villages in almost every town and city in Peru.

Club members often defend local interests in the various government ministries and are usually in the forefront of attempts to obtain new schools, roads, sewers, water, and other public services and advantages for the town or district. Lobbying among the bureaucratic institutions in Lima is an important function of these groups. Considerations of kinship, *compadrazgo* (ritual coparenthood), and regionalism are of the utmost importance in getting things accomplished at all levels in every ministry. Kinship, *compadrazgo,* and friendship within the club carry over to Lima from the hometown and provide security for the migrant (Mangin 1959: 27–8).

One of the most important aspects of the clubs is the role they play in acculturating the *serrano* (inhabitant of the high sierra) to life in Lima. Few of these people come to Lima completely naive; the club's influence is often felt before leaving the town. Clubs in towns are modeled on Lima clubs and there is frequent interchange of members and many dual members as people move back and forth from Lima to their towns and villages (Mangin 1959: 28).

Club membership carries many material and social benefits. Members have access to lawyers, doctors, politicians, and businessmen that they might otherwise never meet and there is frequently a feeling of obligation on the part of the professional members, who gain clients in the clubs. The political uses of the organizations, as well as the social advantages, are obvious (Mangin 1959: 29–30).

Mangin interprets the role of regional associations or clubs formed by migrants from common regions of origin as playing an important role in the process of adaptation to the urban environment. This view has received support from Doughty's work in Lima (1968; 1970; 1972). Ronald Skeldon (1976: 233–4) has looked at the Lima situation and agrees that there is considerable evidence to support this interpretation. Mangin and Doughty consider that the clubs have two major roles: First and most important, they act as buffers that cushion the shock of the impact of urban life on recently arrived migrants by providing them with a familiar environment in an otherwise novel situation, a point put forth earlier in Kerri's appraisal. Second, the clubs promote modernization of communities of origin through their stated goals of hometown improvement. These associations are therefore seen as contributing to the social and political integration of the nation.

True as this may be, the situation is not as clear-cut and unchanging as it might appear. Jonkind's (1971: 1) investigation of regional associations or clubs in Lima threw doubt upon the importance of these functions. His analysis of the data demonstrated that the proportion of the total migrant population of Lima who are regional club members is considerably less than is generally supposed; the regional clubs organize fewer activities than is commonly supposed; very few of these organized activities are related to the aims that might produce the supposed functional results; and participation of members in the institutional activities is substantially less than is normally supposed.

Doughty (1979: 30–46) has referred to the lifeways of club members in Lima as "provincial life behind the back of the city." Jonkind (1974: 481) takes exception to this, arguing that the regional (ethnic) association is, with respect to its organization, recruitment of members, and activities, an urban institution. He maintains that it is misleading to claim that regional associations significantly contribute to the development of their regions of origin. These associations, he contends, are not manifestations of a "rural residue," but are "essentially elitist, composed of well-adjusted and successful migrants. That they are united in regional associations is not a result of feelings of solidarity with the *copaisanos* of the homeland or in Lima, but is probably more a result of prestige motivations" (Jonkind 1974: 481).

In a pair of recent articles, Skeldon (1976; 1977) attempts to integrate these two interpretations. He questions the assumption that the role or function of regional associations remains constant over time and that their role is similar no matter how far distant the association may be from the hometown. He hypothesizes that "the role of regional associations does change systematically through time and that this change is intimately related to the degree of development of population migration from a particular community, which in turn is related to the accessibility of the hometown to the particular urban center in question" (Skeldon 1976: 234). Skeldon concludes that:

1. Regional associations are set up during semipermanent and early stages of migration to Lima (or an intermediate city). The migrant community (usually located in the central part of the city) will be fairly tight knit and will have great interest in the hometown. The club will probably take steps to stimulate hometown development. Return visits of migrants are important and more formal steps to institutionalize aid to new migrants may be made. Thus the role of the association becomes that of a buffer.

2. As early migrants are established in the city they become friends with those in other parts of the country and move from crowded inner-city slums to *barriadas* (squatter settlements) on the outskirts. Club membership thus declines. A new generation of migrants comes, probably of lower socioeconomic status, and factions develop in the weakened association. The role of buffer declines and the clubs become small social and recreational associations.

3. Information filtering back to the village increasingly prepares the youth of the village for cityward migration. "The villagers no longer look to the village but are increasingly oriented toward the city." The role as buffer has become irrelevant and there is little interest in hometown development.

4. The more dynamic club leaders try to promote consolidation or cooperation between district (*anexo*) clubs to form provincial clubs. "At this point the role of the club appears to be almost purely recreational with activities organized to try to ensure the survival of the club itself."

5. In time, even these clubs may fade as separate, broader-based barriada associations arise.

Skeldon sees clubs as "reflecting the process of urbanization: They are an integral part of the change from a primarily rural society to one that is dominated by cities" (1976: 246–7). We will further discuss the barriada movement in Chapter 8.

In other parts of Latin America, where voluntary associations are less numerous, or at least less intensively studied than in Peru, we find some evidence that lends support to the Mangin–Doughty approach, to Jonkind's appraisal, as well as to the Skeldon hypothesis. Drake (1972: 46–51) observed that in Manizales, Colombia, a city of over a quarter of a million people, there were at least 600 voluntary associations of all kinds (including trade unions) in the late 1960s. But there were no "regional associations." The majority of the organizations formed earlier in the century and still functioning in 1967 – that is, those that had persistence through time – were made up of persons who had the time and resources to participate in giving charity to the less fortunate. In other words, these organizations represented the interests of the elite. (See Conniff 1975).

In Tulcán barrio of Popayán, M. Whiteford (1976b: 65) noted that there are virtually no barrio-wide associations, not even mutual aid societies; voluntary associations are limited to a barrio soccer team and a group of men who compete for Tulcán in the city *tejo* championships (tejo is a Colombian game similar to quoits). There is, however, a socioreligious lay organization sponsored by upper-class women from Popayán, the Acción Católica, that has a number of female participants from the barrio. Women from Popayán meet with women from Tulcán once a week to talk about their problems, to socialize, and "to squeeze in a little religious training, emphasizing mainly the desirability of marriage for Tulcanés women living in free unions" (Whiteford: 111). Belonging to this organization provides lower-class women with potentially powerful patrons who otherwise would be unavailable to them. The upper-class women help their lower-class associates if their requests are not too great and are made in connection with the organization (Whiteford 1976b: 111).

The families that Roberts studied in Guatemala City were not strangers to the more formally organized activities of urban life: they attended sports and the cinema films and frequented public health clinics and government and municipal offices. "Indeed," Roberts remarked, "the limits on participation appear to be placed more by the nonavailability of organizations catering to these families than by their nonutilization of facilities" (Roberts 1973: 195–6). Many government and voluntary associations that include low-income people in other parts of the world are, according to Roberts, not available in Guatemala. It is difficult, however, to conceive of the "nonavailability" of a voluntary association. Social security exists, but it serves only the small part of the labor force employed in large-scale enterprises, and labor unions are available to an even smaller fraction of the laboring population. In one of the neighborhoods investigated, there are various community betterment organizations and the usual football clubs and even a mothers' club, but voluntary associations of any substance are apparently absent or rare (Roberts 1973: 196–8).

Kemper (1977: 162) reports that no formal or informal association of migrants from Tzintzuntzan existed in Mexico City until the summer of 1975, although a basketball team flourished briefly among some young migrants earlier.

Absence of such a voluntary association provides an important clue to understanding the migrants' participation in the urban social world: first, it means that social integration among the migrants has rested solely on kinship, friendship, or *compadrazgo* ties, often established prior to migration; second, limiting social relations among migrants has encouraged an outward search for potential urban contacts; finally, urban adaptation has depended on a pragmatic analysis of one's social options rather than on an extension of initial dependence on those migrants with greater exposure to the city. If the new migrant association is successful, perhaps it will provide a forum for those social relationships.

Carlos Orellana (1973: 273–83) has reported on the existence of a voluntary association formed by Mixtec migrants from Soyaltepec, Oaxaca, in Mexico City. The *Union Vecinal* was formed by the migrants in Mexico City "in order to facilitate adaptation to the city in terms of employment, housing, and community solidarity." The organization has achieved legitimacy from the home community by carrying out major construction projects in the village and providing employment for migrants in the city.

A case study of another voluntary association in Mexico City, probably the largest regional association in Mexico, illustrates the complex nature of these organizations.

A case study from Mexico

The Coalición de Pueblos Mixtecos Oaxaqueños (CPMO) (Coalition of Mixtec Oaxacan Communities) was founded in Mexico City in 1951 by members of small voluntary associations from villages in the Mixtec region of the state of Oaxaca, Mexico.[3] Its first and only president has been Dr. Manuel Hernández Hernández, a medical doctor with a practice in Mexico City and former state deputy to the capital from the state of Oaxaca.[4] Because of the leadership and influence in political circles of Dr. Hernández, the Coalición grew rapidly. By 1961 it claimed representatives from thirty-nine villages in the Mixteca.[5] By the 1970s its number of representatives had doubled.

The main activities of the CPMO include obtaining services for member villages, particularly potable water, electricity, dams, roads and other communications, schools and school supplies, and health care. Officers in the CPMO are elected by fellow members. In the 1970s the Central Executive Committee consisted of eleven offices: president; secretary general; secretary of organization and publicity; secretary of social, cultural, and sporting activities; secretary of legal affairs; secretary of social and rural medicine; secretary of the treasury; secretary of acts and agreements;

foreign secretary; secretary of women's affairs; and a technical consultant. The existence of an office of women's affairs is noteworthy. It was, of course, held by a woman, as was the office of acts and agreements.

The organization and main purposes of the CPMO were outlined in the first constitution of the association, drafted in September, 1952. Its Declaration of Principles reads as follows:

The Oaxacan Mixtecs unite and organize in a spirit of progress, taking upon themselves problems of an economic, educational, social, and political character of the Oaxacan Mixtec Villages; with the object of soliciting the attention of the Federal and State Governments, taking as our model the Federal Laws and the Postulates of the Mexican Revolution. The acts that are brought together today will be ruled by the love of serving faithfully the populations of [place of origin] as well as the Coalición [La Entidad] and our fatherland, eschewing anything that would damage the Coalición and our Oaxacan Mixtec villages, taking as our motto, "For the Progress and Superiority of the Mixtecas."

There are four types of membership in the CPMO: (1) Allied members – Mixtec organizations who, without losing their own autonomy, affiliate themselves voluntarily with the CPMO and agree to obey the statutes of the latter. (2) Representative members, who are elected by their home community to serve the interests of that community in the CPMO. They are usually migrants living permanently in Mexico City or Puebla. (3) Individual members who are Mixtec men and women without official representation of some body. (4) Honorary members, who are interested in the activities of the organization and offer their support to the CPMO.

The original constitution has undergone a number of modifications, but it has remained essentially the same document that was drafted in 1952. Meetings are held on the last Sunday of each month in a modern auditorium in Mexico City or in the offices of the National Indian Institute (Instituto Nacional Indigenista – INI). In addition to the Central Executive Committee, representative and individual members are expected to attend the meetings. A roll call is taken at each meeting and absences noted. Attendance is, on the whole, remarkably good.

Each representative and individual member is obliged to pay dues; the amount is determined by ability to pay. There are also monetary quotas assigned or volunteered for extraordinary expenses. During the roll call the present status of dues payments of each member village or individual is announced, an apparently effective means of keeping members from falling too far in arrears in their dues.

Each member of the Executive Committee is asked to report on his or her activities since the previous meeting. The most important and detailed accounts are those of the secretary general, secretary of the treasury, and president. The secretary general or a deputy reviews the month's correspondence. The review emphasizes the latest efforts of the Coalición to acquire goods and services for member communities and notes new requests for assistance. To the outsider, these reviews seem tedious in their detail but to village representatives they represent the influence they have exerted on President Hernández and the efficacy of his actions to government agencies.

The treasurer reports on finances, listing, again in great detail, the income and expenditure of funds – ranging from five pesos for a bus ticket to perhaps a donation of several thousand pesos from a sympathetic benefactor. Announcements by other secretaries may include a scheduled dance sponored by the CPMO, a tribute to one of its benefactors, or an announcement concerning the long search for a permanent home for the CPMO.

The CPMO publishes a monthly newspaper entitled *Monte Albán* (named after a famous archeological site). The price of *Monte Albán* is twenty pesos per year or two pesos per copy at the meetings or at Dr. Hernández' office. The paper is aimed at members of the Coalición and their hometowns. Its contents include both national news and reports on conditions in and news from Mixtec communities. Much of the news from the Mixteca is obtained by Dr. Hernández during his frequent visits to that region.

The highlight of any meeting of the Coalición is Dr. Hernández' report. A magnetic individual possessed of great rhetorical power and charm, Dr. Hernández reviews his activities during the month and his efforts on behalf of Mixtec villages (he was born in the Mixtec community of Teposcolula). He tries to make at least one trip a month to the Mixteca, travelling the mountainous routes and humid lowlands by truck, jeep, and even mule. He listens patiently to the requests of local authorities for assistance and notes their most pressing needs.

The meetings of the CPMO end with representatives of Mixtec communities making solemn pronouncements and supplications about their beloved tierra. The communities they represent are at all levels of development and have various types of social and political organizations. However, they are mostly poor, fragmented politically, with no history of strong viable communal systems. At no time at these meetings are needs of migrant families or individuals in the city discussed. The Coalición is entirely dedicated to the amelioration of conditions in the Mixteca.

The unofficial headquarters of the CPMO is Dr. Hernández' medical offices. When he is in Mexico City, his door is open to members of the Coalición and other Mixtecs from about 6:00 P.M. onwards – sometimes as late as midnight. (This of course follows his normal office hours). For a nominal fee he cares for his Mixtec paisanos and dispenses medicine and medical advice. He also listens to the personal and familial problems of his fellow Mixtecs. These are acts by Dr. Hernández as a private individual and not as the president of the CPMO who also happens to be a medical doctor.

On Thursday or Friday evenings, or whenever else it is necessary, officials and influential nonofficeholders of the Coalición meet in semiprivate session in Dr. Hernández' office to discuss needs and future actions of the group. Topics range from the latest correspondence to contents of the next issue of *Monte Albán* to the appropriate time and place to arrange a formal dinner in honor of some government dignitary. The CPMO is, in the last analysis, a lobbying organization, so the buttering up of officials in a position to help achieve the goals of the Coalición is often as important as the use of formal channels. In both respects, Dr. Hernández is a man of no small influence. The *personalismo* of Latin American politics is nowhere better reflected than in Dr. Hernández' attempts to solve the problems of his tierra.

In summary, the Coalición de Pueblos Mixtecos Oaxaqueños has brought together into a viable operating unit a cross-section of Indian and mestizo communities with little in common except their ethnicity and regional origin. That the organization functions so well suggests that the relation of traditional communal systems to effective village associations in the city postulated by Orellana is without basis. The political actualization results from effective leadership in the city rather than from hometown social or political organization. The death or retirement of Dr. Hernández will be a difficult shock for the CPMO to withstand, but there are other able, if less charismatic, officials in the association.[6]

To Skeldon's analysis of the developmental cycle of voluntary associations, we may briefly add S. Whiteford and R. N. Adams's view of migrants' organizations:

We argue (1) from a general axiom that human beings seek to improve their control over the environment; (2) that consequently, when there are no constraints to the contrary, individuals will seek participation in a more complex organization. A secondary product of exploring the adaptive process of migrants is the realization that in the case of migrant organizations in particular, ethnicity appears to govern membership during phases of less complex organization, whereas increased complexity of organization will be accompanied by a decrease in the importance of ethnicity as a criterion of participation. [S. Whiteford and Adams 1975: 179]

The thesis of these authors concerning the decrease in importance of ethnicity as a basis for organization seems plausible; however, there is no evidence of this occurring in the CPMO. On the contrary, there appears to be considerable growth in pride in being a Mixtec and consequent organization around this status. As Julian Pitt-Rivers stated concerning the subject of race in Latin America:

The tide seems to be turning today and we see everywhere a reassertion of regional sentiment, the legitimacy of the pre-eminence of the centre put in doubt. Though the movement towards economic centralisation continues in a certain sense, by the very nature of such a movement the division of labour between centre and periphery is destroyed. Just as the economic expansion of the eighteenth century led to the rebellion of the colonies and the foundation of the modern nations of

Latin America, so the economic expansion of the twentieth seems to be leading to conflict between national centre and periphery, and where Indians remain, we see the new Indian middle classes emerging and yet retaining their Indian identity. The centre loses its power to command emulation and middle class Indians sometimes hang on to their regional ethnic affiliation even after they have moved to the capital – like the Isthmus Zapotecs in Mexico City. [Pitt-Rivers 1973: 30]

8. Housing, poverty, and politics

There will be about six billion (American billion) people on earth by the year 2000 and as many as one-half of these will be living in conglomerations of five thousand people or more (Dwyer 1975:15).

The staggering task for the second fifty years of the present century has been and is to provide a tolerable urban environment for an increment of people four times as large as that which was added to world urban populations in the 1000 years before 1950. This is in addition to making up past deficiencies in urban facilities of massive proportions ... Serious physical deficiencies are all too obvious in almost every city, but in no aspect of provision is the task so daunting as in housing. The towns, both large and small, are increasing in population at rates generally not less than 2.5 per cent a year and often up to 10 per cent a year ... Yet the numbers in spontaneous settlements, the makeshift housing areas erected by urban squatters, are growing at even greater rates ... In Latin America recent estimates have included a figure of 800,000 squatters, or one-fifth of the total urban population, in Rio de Janeiro in 1965. This compares with figures of 203,000 in 1950 (8 per cent of total population) and 600,000 in 1964 (16 per cent) and implies that the growth rate of population in the *favelas* has reached four times that of the city as a whole. Santiago, the capital of Chile, had one-quarter of its total population in *callampas* in the early 1960s, while the figures for Lima, the capital of Peru, show 800,000 in the *barriadas* in 1970 (one-third of the total urban population) compared with 500,000 in 1965 and 100,000 in 1958. Over 40 percent of the population of Mexico City is currently living in *colonias proletarias*[1] ... Besides the sheer size of the problem today, and its relatively sudden onset, two further features are worth noting. First, rates of growth of spontaneous settlements are still accelerating in relation to rates of growth of urban populations as a whole. In other words, the problem, huge though it is, is not yet as serious as it will undoubtedly soon become. Second, although most of the estimates given above are for very large cities, spontaneous settlement has become a major urban form in Third World towns and cities of all size ranges. [Dwyer 1975: 15–19]

Laquian (1971), cited by Roberts (1978: 137), reports that squatter settlements provide housing for between 10 and 20 percent of the population of many large cities in Latin America. In Asia, 25 percent of the population of Djakarta and Kuala Lumpur, and 26 percent of Singapore's population, are said to be living in squatter settlements.

The so-called North American pattern outlined by Park, Burgess, and other members of the Chicago School, in which central city properties are converted to commercial uses and lower-class housing and higher-status and higher-income groups retreat to the most prestigious city locations and particularly to the less densely settled urban fringe, seems to be emerging in some Latin American cities as well, as Portes and Walton (1976:

147

117–18) have shown for Cali, Colombia, and Monterrey, Mexico. A common aberration in this pattern south of the Rio Grande is, somewhat ironically, a concomitant movement of lower-status, lower-income people to the fringe areas. This has been documented for the above two cities, Mexico City (Lomnitz 1977; P. Ward 1976). Oaxaca, Mexico (Butterworth 1973; Higgins 1971), Bogotá, Santiago, and Quito (Amato 1970), Lima (Amato 1970; Mangin 1967; Mangin 1970; Mangin and Turner 1968; Turner 1967; Turner 1968), Rio de Janeiro (Leeds 1969), and others.

Unfortunately, little work has been done by anthropologists on the subject of housing and residence patterns within cities. The focus of social and political scientists has been almost exclusively on the marginal areas settled by squatters (see Chance 1980).[2] This is unfortunate because, as Anthony and Elizabeth Leeds (1970: 230–1) observed:

Squatter settlements cannot empirically or theoretically be understood unless they are looked at in detail as parts of a larger system and as products of the operation of the system. Specifically, we – as well as those who have done field work in the barriadas – have learned, largely from empirical experience rather than from theory, that neither favelas nor barriadas can be properly understood without understanding a whole range of other socio-residential types concurrently, since movements into, between, and from favelas or barriadas constitute part of the process of favela-barriada development, rural-urban migrations, and the urbanizing of non-urban persons, and so on. According to ... our review of virtually the entire literature on housing in Rio (and elsewhere in Brazil), no studies exist for Lima or Rio on these other residential types except Patch's (1961). Generally, they are unknown except through Oscar Lewis' work on *vecindades* in Mexico. The best materials we have for Rio and Lima are impressionistic because they are based only on brief forays into these and other housing types. Consequently, all pictures of the social structure and social process involved are, to date, incomplete, whether for Argentina, Brazil, Chile, Columbia (*sic*), Guatemala, Mexico, Nicaragua, or Peru – the Latin American countries in which the most extensive studies of such phenomena have been undertaken.[3]

Oscar Lewis "stumbled across" the *vecindades* – slumlike inner-city housing tenements – by locating migrants to Mexico City from the village of Tepoztlán, which he had been investigating for some fifteen years. Many of the Tepoztecans (people from the village of Tepoztlán) were poor and lived in *vecindades* in downtown Mexico City. The unusual patterning of life in the *vecindades* caught Lewis's attention: Not only were the *vecindades* like small, almost self-contained societies within the metropolis, but different vecindad societies seemed to share many cultural features. These aspects of life in an urban slum led Lewis to promulgate his concept of the "culture of poverty" (1952: 31–41).

The culture of poverty

The basic concept of the culture of poverty was that under certain conditions in some societies a portion of the society would be so impoverished and lacking in participation in the values and goals of the larger society that it would develop a subculture of its own.[4] As Lewis phrased it initially:

Poverty becomes a dynamic factor which affects participation in the larger national culture and creates a subculture of its own. One can speak of a culture of poverty, for it has its own modalities and distinctive social and psychological consequences for its members. It seems to me that the culture of poverty cuts across regional, rural-urban, and even national boundaries. [O. Lewis 1958: 387]

The culture (or subculture) of poverty is thus a design for living shared by many (but not all) poor people and passed on along family lines. As such, it is an adaptation to the conditions of various, although similar, socioeconomic environments. Lewis later specified that these settings are class-stratified, highly individuated, capitalistic societies (O. Lewis 1968: 5).

Lewis discussed the culture of poverty in terms of economic, social and psychological, and "other" traits. The economic traits supposedly characteristic of the culture of poverty include a continual struggle for survival, work for low wages at a miscellany of unskilled occupations, child labor, the absence of savings, a chronic shortage of cash, absence of food reserves in the home, pawning of personal goods, and borrowing from local moneylenders at usurious rates of interest.

Among the most common social and psychological traits are: living in crowded quarters with lack of privacy, gregariousness, a high incidence of alcoholism, frequent resort to violence in the settlement of quarrels, use of physical violence in the training of children, wife beating, consensual marriage, a high incidence of abandonment of mothers and children, a trend toward mother-centered families, and a strong predisposition toward authoritarianism. Other traits include a belief in male superiority, which reaches its highest form in the cult of machismo, and strong feelings of marginality, helplessness, dependency, and alienation (O. Lewis 1961: xxvi–xxvii).

As with any classification, Lewis's categories may be questioned as arbitrary. "The entire ordering of traits," commented Leeds, "lacks conceptualization and logical ordering. In short, it makes no theoretical sense" (Leeds 1971: 242). A more important consideration, however, is that many of the traits supposedly typical of the culture of poverty are merely descriptions of poverty. Others, such as alcoholism and unstable marriages, are probably no more characteristic of the poor than of other classes.

Insofar as gregariousness and lack of privacy are concerned, Leeds has pointed out that lack of privacy is entirely a function of crowdedness and that gregariousness among the poor is a function both of crowdedness and of continually mobilizing family, ritual kin, friends, and neighborhood networks. He adds:

Gregariousness functions to create communications networks . . . It also necessarily reduces privacy, but privacy, as a characteristic value of American middle and upper classes engaged in competition for socio-economic rewards in career structures involving upward mobility, may be more or less irrelevant. Privacy is not, as such, a *value* of the poor, although . . . the poor [may] explicitly formulate the contexts in which they like privacy. However, privacy is a positive *dis*advantage to the urban poor, as a large number of them recognized when helter-skelter urban renewal, or removal to other residential locations without regard to prior community living patterns, broke them away from their old neighborhood ties consisting of linked kin- and non-kin domiciles and friendship networks . . . which operated as mutual information and security systems. [Leeds 1971: 253–4]

Valentine notes that much evidence indicates that families living in poverty are more often unconventional in form than families in higher income strata. He maintains that "these statistically unusual family patterns can generally be traced to externally imposed conditions impinging on the poor from the society at large. Consensual unions may be regarded as a flexible adaptation to certain conditions of poverty. These conditions include fluctuating economic circumstances which may make it advisable for mates to separate and contract alternative unions, either temporary or lasting. And female-centered households may be more functional under conditions of poverty than 'normal' patterns" (Valentine 1971: 207–8).

Lewis emphasized the multiplicity of relationships between the culture of poverty (or people living in it) and the larger external system that generates it. However, as Eames and Goode (1977: 308) pointed out, Lewis frequently confused the two: that is, he included as part of the culture of the poor aspects of life that are characteristic of the external system, not responses to it. For example, he wrote of unemployment as a trait of the culture of poverty, although it is the generator of poverty itself.[5]

Sound as the logic of its critics may have been, the notion of a culture or subculture of poverty was popular and to some seemed to explain why the poor stayed poor. Daniel P. Moynihan picked up the idea and carried it to an extreme in the so-called Moynihan Report.[6] The report dealt with a "Negro subculture" and the "tangle of being entrapped" from one generation to another in matriarchal families. The most eloquent spokesperson for a view of eternal entrapment in a vicious web of poverty was Barbara Ward:

In the slums of the great cities live the families for whom poverty has become a melancholy, self-perpetuating wheel of incapacity. Poor workers who save little become still poorer in old age. Unskilled workers lack the means of self-betterment either for themselves or their children. Children in crowded, filthy, often fatherless homes have not the discipline to learn and once they are "dropouts" they fall below the level of possible self-improvement. If they are Negroes, resentment is added to despair and violence to both. This subculture of the poor lies like a bitter sediment at the base of urban living. Stirred up, it could poison the whole civic environment. [Ward 1964: 191]

Turning closer to our own immediate interests, Ward continues:

All over the world, often long in advance of effective industrialization, the unskilled poor are streaming away from subsistence agriculture to exchange the squalor of rural poverty for the even deeper miseries of the shanty-towns, *favellas* [*sic*], and *bidonvilles* that, year by year, grow inexorably on the fringes of the developing cities. And they, too, are the core of local despair and disaffection . . . everywhere undermining the all too frail structure of public order and thus retarding the economic development that can alone help their plight. Unchecked, disregarded, left to grow and fester, there is here enough explosive material to produce in the world at large the pattern of a bitter class conflict finding to an increasing degree a racial bias, erupting in guerilla warfare, and threatening, ultimately, the security even of the comfortable West. [1964: 191–2]

Is there truth in the words of this prophet of doom? Oscar Lewis, architect of the notion of a subculture of poverty, thought not. Referring to Frantz Fanon's contention (1963: 103) that the lumpen proletariat, "this mass of humanity, this people of the shanty towns," constitutes one of the most spontaneous and radical revolutionary forces of any colonized people, Lewis observed:

My own studies of the urban poor in the slums of San Juan do not support the generalizations of Fanon. I have found very little revolutionary spirit or radical ideology among low income Puerto Ricans. On the contrary, most of the families I studied were quite conservative politically . . . [Lewis 1968: 15]

It is thus appropriate for us to review the political attitudes and activities of this "mass of humanity" in the shantytowns. To do this, we must place the politics of the poor in the perspective of squatter formations.

Squatter settlements

Squatting as a so-called problem is of fairly recent origin. Neither rural nor urban clandestine or forcible land settlement was common in Europe during its industrialization periods. Land titles were established fairly early there and have, for the most part, remained clearly defined. The United States has experienced some amount of squatting, but it occurred primarily in frontier contexts where land rights and titles were still unclear. As these were established, squatters were assimilated into the dominant structure. Today squatting is virtually unknown in the United States (Abrams 1966: 23–6).

As it exists today, squatting is predominantly a Third-World phenomenon that became prominent after World War II (Mangin 1972: 423) and has been increasing at a steady rate ever since. Almost all Latin American countries have experienced a sudden and massive confrontation with the squatting situation. It has primarily resulted from rapid urbanization and industrialization (R. Lewis 1973: 1; Mangin 1972: 423; Matos Mar 1968: 14; Turner 1968: 355) coupled with the inability of nations to cope with the resulting housing needs (Casasco 1969: 87).[7]

There were a few studies of squatter settlements in the late 1930s and 1940s (for example, Pierson 1939), but no serious interest appears to have been generated until the mid and late 1950s, with the bulk of the important pioneering literature making its appearance in the 1960s (for example, Abrams 1964; 1965; 1966; Leeds 1966; 1969; Mangin 1963; 1967; Mangin and Turner 1968; Turner 1968).

Shantytowns[8] are by no means of a single type and generalizations concerning them must be qualified by careful analysis of individual settlements, with emphasis upon the factors that entered into their location and formation – in short, squatment biographies are needed. Flinn and Converse (1970: 457) classified squatter settlements in Colombia into three types, and Butterworth and his associates (1973: 229) showed that there are at least four distinct types of shantytowns in Oaxaca, Mexico. The types reflected the different histories of the settlements.

Although squatting implies illegality, negotiations almost always inevitably take place with government officials or private owners to secure land tenure rights to the squatters. These squatters may have established their residence through forceful invasion or peaceful, often clandestine, settlement. Organized invasion seems to be much more common in Peru than elsewhere in Latin America.[9]

Observers and investigators of shantytowns have tended to fall into two camps insofar as their views on the physical and moral properties of these settlements are concerned. The first of these uses the "festering sore on the urban body" metaphor, deploring the inhumanity and very existence of these conglomerations. Bonilla (1970), for example, writes of how Rio's favelas "crawl in cancerous disorder up the steep *morros*" (hills) of that city. While other metaphors are employed ("dirty beehives," "rats' nests of communism"), medical analogies seem to be the preferred image of these observers. Thus we are advised of "cancers," "eyesores," "endemas," and told that the cure involves therapy and even surgery.

As an antidote to these descriptive excesses, an opposing camp was formed, led by William Mangin, an anthropologist, and John F. C. Turner, an architect. They see squatter settlements, or at least many aspects of them, in a positive light. Mangin has been unequivocal: He views squatter settlements "as a process of social reconstruction through popular intitiative . . . The problem [of squatter settlements] is the solution to the problem" (Mangin 1967: 67, 85). The attempts of Mangin and those of similar persuasion to correct serious misinterpretations of the nature and function of squatter settlements are laudable. There are, as we shall see, probably more positive than negative things to be said about shantytowns. However, by magnifying the positive characteristics of squatter settlements, we may encourage government to evade its responsibility to attack the structural barriers to urban improvement (Butterworth et al. 1973).

However, Mangin and other writers, such as Flinn and Converse (1970), have performed an important service in refuting some of the myths about these "festering sores."

Among the general misconceptions are:

1. Squatter settlements are formed by rural people coming from peasant villages to the cities. However, although the majority of inhabitants of shantytowns may be of ultimate rural origin, many are from towns and small cities and others proceed in traditional stepwise fashion from village to town to city. In some shantytowns, more residents are urban- than rural-born (Flinn and Converse 1970: 460; Matos Mar 1968: 5). A difficulty in making a simple evaluation is that migration to a barriada often includes a stopover in the central city before the move to the outskirts. This, in fact, seems to be the usual pattern (Boyce 1970: 6; Butterworth et al. 1973: 220; Cardona Gutiérrez 1968: 69; Chance 1971: 128–9; D. Foster 1971: 155; R. Lewis 1973: 27; Mangin 1972: 423).

2. A corollary to the above belief that squatter settlements are inhabited by recent migrants from rural areas is the idea that shantytowns are rural enclaves in the city (Bonilla 1970: 73–4; Matos Mar 1961: 174; Medina 1964: 73). In fact, although these self-built settlements often have a rustic physical appearance, their inhabitants usually have urban values. As the Leedses (1970: 252–3) stated for Brazil:

> ... among most favela residents, especially the men, a generalized preference for the city is expressed. The country is backward, sad, paralyzed, without any special attractions as country or living place. Except for some women, most people say, when asked, that they do not want to go back. Why? Because it is better here. Life is better, one feels better, economically it is better, it is not *atrasado* or *parado* ("backward" or "at a standstill"), etc. In other words, the city atmosphere and environment are, in an inchoate, almost sensory way, felt to be desirable and, for those familiar with the rural areas, the more desirable.

3. Squatters are "marginal" to the larger society. They do not participate in the socioeconomic life of the city.

4. They are, therefore an economic drain on the nation.

These first four beliefs apply not only to squatters but to the urban poor in general, although they are often applied specifically to migrants from rural areas. It had long been assumed that migrants were disappointed and frustrated by economic conditions in the city. However, Nelson (1969: 15) pointed out that this assumption was not only modified but contradicted by the evidence. A decade later, her contention that survey findings are virtually unanimous on the point that most migrants consider themselves better off, and probably are in fact better off, than they were before they moved, has remained true.

As Perlman has shown, the concept of marginality is another myth that has grown up in urban studies.[10] Marginality is both a myth and a description of social reality: "As a myth it supports personal beliefs and social interests, and is anchored in people's minds by roots that will remain unshaken by any theoretical criticism. As a description of social reality, it concerns a set of specific problems that must be treated in an alternative theoretical way in order to be correctly understood" (Perlman 1976: 242). Squatment residents may not be the most economically productive sector of the nation, but they do participate in the economic life of the city to the extent that their skills and the economic and political structure permit. Putting aside for the moment the skilled laborers and professionals who are by no means absent from these settlements, there are innumerable "penny capitalists" who operate small stores, hawk wares in the streets, and perform various services. Abrams (1966), Hoenack (1966), and Mangin (1967) have suggested that building by squatters is a major contribution to the construction industry of developing nations. Their dwellings are erected at a much lower cost than government housing and they do not cripple the already fragile economic state of squatter residents, because squatters generally erect a minimal shelter at first and improve it only as they can afford to do so.

In specific instances we have documentation that squatters have made critical contributions to the nation's socio-economic system. A case in point is the building of Brasília. The creation of Brasília in the heart of the nation was to accomplish more than to provide a new capital city. It was hoped that it would open up the hinterlands and spur the economic development of the nation. As it turned out, Brasília was built almost entirely by squatter labor, because high priority was placed on construction schedules and low priority was placed on the needs of the laborers. The result was the springing up of vast numbers of squatter settlements in the new capital. These settlements met several needs. They provided shelter to the laborers and their families and provided the labor necessary for the construction at minimum cost to the government (Epstein 1973: 151–5).

Other common misconceptions:

5. Squatter settlements are areas of high crime and low morality. Evidence has shown that this is simply not true. Shantytowns do not have a higher crime rate than any other population and rates vary according to settlement just as they would with any neighborhood. Considering that most squatter settlements do not have the protection of a city or municipal police force and must rely primarily on their own internal policing strategies, squatter settlements police themselves remarkably well. The charge of low morality is most often made about prostitution within the settlement. More often than not, prostitutes who reside in the squatter settlements ply their trade elsewhere in the city.

6. Squatter settlements are chaotic and unorganized.

7. Squatters are present-time oriented.

These are among the greatest misconceptions about squatter settlements. Because of the massive amount of data to the contrary, they are the most easily repudiated charges.

One of the most clear-cut examples of organization among squatters is the organized "invasions" that have occurred in Peru (Mangin 1972; *El Rescate* 1972). These are situations in which groups of people, consisting mainly of young families, plan and execute the invasion of a particular piece of property. These invasions often require months of preparation. Frequently the squatters recruit the aid of lawyers or law students, clergy, and members of the press. Most often the land to be settled is public unused land. Less often the land may be privately owned or the title of the land may be in question. (In Mexico and Peru many land titles go back to immediate post-conquest land grants.). Lawyers are invaluable in determining the status of the property, and the sanction of the clergy is frequently sought to strengthen the squatters' moral claim to the land. Squatters attempt to capture the attention and support of the press in the hope that if their invasion or clandestine move is favorably covered, police retaliation will be minimized.

There are other ways in which squatters have demonstrated their ability to organize. The voluntary associations discussed in the previous chapter are generally well established in shantytowns, and voluntary work groups (*tequios*), at least in Mexico, are salient features of squatter organization (see D. Foster 1971). Informal organizations among squatters include credit systems, burial aid groups, child-care arrangements, and well-developed gossip and information networks.

Cheleen Mahar's study of a colonia on the outskirts of the city of Oaxaca demonstrates the way the colonos manipulate kin, *compadradazgo,* and friendship ties to achieve ends otherwise judged to be unattainable (Mahar n.d.). Mahar notes that social contacts are particularly important for devising economic and health strategies. The problems of unemployment and underemployment is dealt with, in part, by small business operations that depend to a large extent on social contracts. Then too, in Oaxaca the role of the formal welfare agencies is filled largely by a system of reciprocal agreements – agreements between kin, friends, and compadres and the individual, as well as between individuals and some of the institutions, primarily small businesses within the colonia. Thus by creating a social network of economic ties that are legitimated by colonia residents and that persist from generation to generation, the lack of formal economic dependence on the wider social institutions is compensated for.

Similarly, medical and child-care problems find a partial resolution through the same social contracts. Compadre ties with doctors or members of other professional classes are important. Mutual dependency between mothers in the colonia plays a major role. The specialization of certain individuals in the ability to deal with sickness is a further adaptation, and one that increases the value of the individual concerned in exchange relationships. All these ties, as far as they are effective in coping with illness and with child care, are informal attempts to fill the gap that the formal institutions leave among this population.

The consequence of these informal networks is to insure households against economic and medical danger. Through these processes, women clearly provide themselves with a source of power. The networks are of lasting importance, because they constitute a set of alternative institutional arrangements for the colonia poor. Because access to banks, hospitals, lending institutions, and so forth, are largely limited to members of the middle class, these new arrangements are necessary for survival.

The idea of present-time orientation seems to be a spinoff from Oscar Lewis's formulation of the culture of poverty. Information available on squatter settlements, however (which Lewis did not study), suggests just the opposite. Most squatters interviewed indicate that they have come to live in shantytowns in order to send their children to school, to save on rent either by improving their present house or building another one, or to start a small business. None of these is a short-range goal, and all indicate a hope or an ability to plan for the future.

8. Squatter settlement residents are a socioeconomically homogeneous group. The truth is that most self-built communities contain highly heterogeneous populations (see Butterworth et al. 1963). Residents may range from the illiterate and chronically unemployed or underemployed to professionals such as lawyers and doctors (Higgins 1971: 19–38). There are also a wide range of blue-collar and white-collar workers. Level of education varies accordingly. Pendrell's study of Salvador, capital of the state of Bahia, Brazil (1967: 7–8) states that the four squatter settlements she investigated contained a continuum from almost wholly proletarian residents to almost wholly upper middle and upper classes. This is supported by Butterworth and his colleagues (1973) and by Safa (1974). Safa relates that squatters who have been relocated in housing projects often wish to return to their squatments. (In this regard, see O. Lewis's portrait of a young woman forced out of her slum dwelling in San Juan who pined to return to her former life (1966b). In other words, many residents of squatter settlements do so out of choice, not necessity.

There is a continual flow of people into the shantytown studied by Safa from rural areas, and from the shantytown to other urban neighborhoods. Length of residence in the slum (Los Peloteros) varies greatly, from twenty-five years to less than five years. Despite this continual turnover of people, however, the core of old timers, made up of some of the original settlers of the squatter settlment, contributes greatly to neighborhood stability. "These old timers form a stable nucleus to whom new migrants can attach themselves and they also provide an important source of leadership and continuity for the community" (Safa 1974: 13).

Similarly, in the settlements studied by Butterworth and his colleagues, residence was much more stable than one would have anticipated. The most important reasons for this stability were employment and construction of permanent residences. However, political stability was also frequently effected by incorporation into or affiliation with official government structures (Butterworth et al. 1973: 223–32). This is discussed further in the section on politics later in this chapter.

Donald Foster's research on low-income housing in Barranquilla, Colombia, relates that informants see their current residence as a permanent thing. "When economic stability is achieved, it is not accompanied by residential mobility" (D. Foster 1975: 243). Foster concludes that "the phenomenal growth of owner-built settlements and their evolution into orderly neighborhoods demonstrates the success of this response to the stress of the urban environment" (1975: 254). This would seem to be a validation of the so-called Turner hypothesis.

The Turner hypothesis

John F. C. Turner proposed that there is a functional relationship between social needs and environmental forms. He argues that urban migrants have priorities by which they evaluate their dwelling requirements and that determine in part their physical movements in the city. Although he made some adjustments in his priorities over the years, these priorities have remained essentially the same: (1) location; (2) security of tenure; and (3) amenities (Turner 1967; 1968). "As the migrant becomes integrated into the urban milieu and gains growing economic security, the relative importance of these priorities changes" (J. C. Brown 1972: 11). Brown continues:

For the newly arrived bridgeheader wishing to gain a foothold in the city, *location* close to sources of employment is the critical variable in his search for housing. Turner states that home at this stage of the migrant's life is in a rented central city slum room or in a provisional shack which he builds himself in the central city area. Only when the migrant gains an economic cushion and begins to consider consolidating his position in the city does *security of tenure* and the search for an appropriate site to construct a permanent home become a functional priority. Turner hypothesizes that, at this stage of the migrant's stay in the city (which may take 10 or 15 years to reach), he generally moves to an urban fringe location where he can squat or buy a piece of inexpensive land to create a stable dwelling environment. It is only when he gains economic security, title to his land, and the minimal beginnings of a permanent dwelling structure that *amenity* in the living environment becomes a priority for the migrant consolidator. At this point he may begin to make substantial improvements on his dwelling by substituting more permanent construction materials for temporary ones, by installing plumbing, or by purchasing appliances and other "luxury" items. [Brown 1972: 164–5]

Brown's findings in Mexico City show that Turner's priorities appear to be valid for the Mexican case and that the intraurban settlement pattern that Turner suggests appears to have been characteristic of Mexico City until about 1950. Today, however, Turner's priorities may not be valid for Mexico. Brown concludes that the Mexican data indicate that the model may be accurately descriptive only for limited historical periods in a country's urban development (1972: 165).

Cheleen Mahar (n.d.) takes a similar point of view and is even less sanguine about the positive aspects of shantytowns. She contends that enthusiasm for the possibilities inherent in squatter settlments may be well founded in the early stages of settlement growth but perhaps is less so during later stages of their existence. In highly institutionalized developing countries, the solution of socioeconomic problems is left in the hands of governmental agencies of various kinds, with or without the help of private corporations. The question of who decides, and who does what for whom in this process of delivering social services is an area on which Turner (1977) and Turner and Fichter (1972) have commented. In *Housing by people,* Turner criticizes these centrally administered social programs, with their emphasis on production. His point is that those who organize such agencies along the lines of a factory assembly conception of social services limit the possibilities for real change in a situation that desperately needs immediate change. Housing, claims Turner, "has commonly come to mean the current stock of dwelling units and the capability of large building and management organizations to provide more" (1977: 4).

The use of institutions to define and seek to meet basic needs in the areas of employment, education, health, and housing removes the mass of the client population from the areas of decision making that determine the answers to questions about who decides and who does what for whom. The institutional attack on human needs thereby leads to a future in which the potential for human intervention and social transformation is severely reduced. Fichter, Turner, and Grenell (1972: 241) are unequivocal in their position:

When dwellers control the major decisions and are free to make their own contributions in the design, construction, or management of their housing, both this process and the environment produced stimulate individual and social well-being. When people have no control over nor responsibility for key decisions in the housing process, on the other hand, dwelling environments may instead become a barrier to personal fulfillment and a burden on the economy.

Elizabeth Petras's study of urban slum dwellings in Santiago, Chile

(1973) examines how housing needs are met within a framework of direct political strategies. Petras argues that a class of squatters has developed from collective political and economic attempts to gain adequate housing. Like other slum dwellers and urban migrants who have organized squatter settlements, the squatters experienced considerable institutional opposition, often violent confrontation, long periods of ill health, and inadequate housing and nutrition. But unlike the squatters' own previous experiences in the settlements, conditions improved. After long, costly battles and exchanges with authorities, housing improvements began slowly; medical aid, although partial and inadequate, was provided; and talk of educational opportunities – a somewhat unrealistic expectation in earlier times – began (Petras 1973: 39–59).

Petras's study provides an alternative perspective to the now almost fashionable extolling of the benefits of shantytown living. Mahar (n.d.) states that Mangin and Turner seem to imply that squatter settlements are little more than somewhat impoverished middle-class neighborhoods, with all the preoccupations of middle-class residents elsewhere in the world. Mahar (n.d.) believes that this view of squatter settlement life "merely disguises the agonizing poverty of most true social conditions and provides a further barrier to their amelioration."

In sum, it seems that squatter settlements may be marginal in a geographical sense, but the nature of their integration into urban, regional, and national life remains problematical. Writing of her experiences in Rio's favelas, Perlman stated:

Our data indicate that the presuppositions and predictions of marginality theory are almost universally untrue. Brazilian society may well be divided into two sectors but ... characterizing these as "marginal" and "integrated" is deeply deceptive. It allows analysts to avoid the recognition that both sectors are integrated into society, but on very different terms. Favelados are not marginal to Brazilian society, but integrated into it in a manner detrimental to their interests. *They are not socially marginal but rejected, not economically marginal but exploited, and not politically marginal but repressed.* [Perlman in Peattie 1974: 108]

"In short," Perlman concludes, "*they have the aspirations of the bourgeoisie, the perseverance of pioneers, and the values of patriots*" (Perlman 1976: 243; emphasis in both quotations hers).

Peattie thinks the very notion of "marginality" is invalid because it runs counter to the idea of a complex social system with patterned inequalities. Peattie argues that the idea of "marginality" takes the perspective of dominant sectors for granted, making other sectors marginal to them. Thus, the policy consequences are considerable (see Levine 1979: 176). "If we conceive of the city – as some Latin Americanists have done – as a kind of fortress of high culture, European and elitist, in an Indian or peasant hinterland which it dominates, we will tend to move toward certain kinds of public policy. We will tend to perceive large in-migrations to the city from the rural hinterland as an 'invasion.' We are led to think of the problems of urbanization basically as pacification efforts" (Peattie 1974: 108).

A final myth:

9. Squatter settlements are breeding grounds of radical political activity. It is difficult to trace the origin of this myth. Presumably it harks back to Marxist philosophy, but its advocates make little attempt to provide empirical evidence of its truth. Our final section deals with this question in some detail.

Political involvement of the urban poor

Speculations concerning the political involvement of the urban poor in Latin America range from assessments of the poor as disorganized and apathetic or apolitical to assumptions that they constitute a huge frustrated and angry mass, a potential revolutionary force. Belief in such assumptions on the part of the elite and the policy makers inside and outside of Latin America appears to be based on a body of political and sociopsychological theories nonspecific to Latin America. The ready acceptance of these theories may represent a projection on to the poor of the values, motivations, and behavioral strategies of the elite.

Wayne Cornelius (1971: 102) refers to the widely accepted ideas about the sociopolitical implications of urban migration as "eclectic" and as "borrowed theory":

There is no integrated, formal theory of migrant assimilation and political behavior which informs textbook discussions and other non–data-based treatments of the subject by Latin Americanists. What has been widely diffused through the literature is, rather, an amalgam of generalizations and propositions derived from the work of European social theorists, North American urban specialists and political sociologists, and political scientists in the American politics and political development fields. The borrowed propositions appear to cluster around three basic themes: (1) Material deprivation and frustration of mobility expectations; (2) personal and social disorganization; and (3) political radicalization and disruptive behavior. Migrants entering urban centers are assumed to experience instigating conditions (1) and (2), become alienated toward the existing socio-political order, and undergo political radicalization leading to various forms of disruptive activity. Reduced to barest essentials, this is what has served as the most commonly accepted "working theory" regarding political correlates of migrant assimilation in contemporary Latin America. Intervening variables are sometimes introduced, but these are generally regarded as mediating conditions which may influence the degree of radicalization or intensity of disruptive activity, which are still regarded as the most probable outcomes of migrant assimilation into Latin American urban environments under existing circumstances. [Cornelius 1971: 97; see also Cornelius 1969: 833–6]

During the past three decades, ethnographic research in squatter settlements in Latin America has provided data that contradict the widely accepted postulates cited by Cornelius.[11] Empirical evidence has led anthropologists to challenge these postulates.[12] Existing notions regarding the homogeneity of the urban poor in their political attitudes and behavior also must be regarded as myths. (See Cornelius 1975; and Goldrich, Pratt, and Schuller 1970). Differences in measure and mode of political participation occur among settlements in different nations, among settlements in the same city, and among individuals within the same settlement. Political responses of individuals or of a population constitute an aspect of the ecology of a specific locality.[13] Differences in political strategies, degree of participation, and attitudes are reflections of such variables as life histories, settlement histories, and governmental policies and procedures.

Alejandro Portes and John Walton (1976: 70) postulate, and the literature demonstrates, that political responses of the urban poor are a "rational adaptation to the existing social situation":

By "rational," I mean a strategy of calculated pursuit of social and economic goals through available means. This strategy adapts to the existing situation by taking it as a given to be coped with and not as a contingency to be challenged. Patterns of political behavior exhibited by the urban poor in Latin America can more easily be characterized as deliberate manipulations of available channels for survival and mobility than as either careless abandon (subculture of poverty) or militant opposition (radical potential). [1976: 72.][14]

Food, water, shelter, temperature regulation, and safety are basic human biological needs. The ability to attain and maintain these needs constitute primary goals for the urban poor, as they do for all humans. Affiliated with but secondary to these goals for many of the impoverished are those of education and ensuing social advancement for their children, and improving economic and social status and material benefits for themselves and their children.[15]

One very important strategy of "calculated pursuit" of social goals is that of political demand making. Wayne Cornelius defines this behavior as "individual or collective activities aimed at extracting certain types of benefits from the political system by influencing the decisions of incumbent government officials" (Cornelius 1974: 1125). Thus, demand making is action to alleviate a perceived need by those who are experiencing the need. Cornelius identifies stages in the conversion of objectively defined needs into actual demands upon government:

Objective deprivations or problems must first be perceived by the individual as requiring some kind of solution or ameliorative action. Secondly, these felt needs must be viewed as needs particularly susceptible to satisfaction through governmental action. Finally, the potential demand maker must be able to perceive a strategy or channel through which to articulate the "politicized needs." [Cornelius 1974: 1127–8]

Cornelius conducted a study of politics, including political demand making, in six communities of poor urban migrants on the outskirts of Mexico City. He discovered that almost 50 percent of his respondents perceived economic concerns, increasing income, and steady work as their primary personal concerns. Education for self or children and tenure of land or home were primary concerns for 15.2 and 14.8 percent of the respondents, respectively. Better housing and attendant services such as electricity, piped water, and sewage disposal were the major concerns of 9.2 percent; and 7.7 percent were concerned with health. Community needs and problems were the primary concern of less than 1 percent of the respondents (Cornelius 1975: 171).

Although the major personal concerns of the majority of respondents in these communities were economic, these were barely reflected in the demand-making behavior directed to government officials. Only 3.1 percent of the contacts that had been made by individuals with government officials were on behalf of "personal or family related problems." The remaining contacts were concerned with community problems: 64.6 percent concerned land tenure for community residents. The remaining 32.3 percent of contacts were concerned with water, postal services, street paving, electricity, education, transportation, sewage, garbage, and others (Cornelius 1975: 180).

It is apparent that the residents in these six communities of urban migrant poor perceived that community needs were those most prone to be satisfied through governmental action.[16] It is also apparent that demand making is a request for tangible goods and services tied to a specific locality, not an attempt to address and petition on behalf of a larger segment of the population, and certainly not an attempt to institute a redistribution of national resources on behalf of a class, or a mass, of the urban poor.

It is not possible to enumerate and illustrate the diversities among these and other settlements. It is necessary, however, to emphasize that the histories of occupancy, governmental response to occupancy, development, and present status in regard to municipal services varies widely. Where squatters meet with steady opposition in securing land tenure and basic services, demand-making behavior, either by individuals alone or on behalf of a settlement organization, has been high, and a greater number of individuals have been involved in such behavior (Cornelius 1975: 188; see also Goldrich, Pratt, and Schuller 1970). In other words, where basic human needs have not been obtained, demand-making behavior has been high. Where basic human needs have been secured, it appears that the inhabitants have been more apt to accept the existing situation than to attempt to better it through governmental assistance.

If the government is to be perceived as a potential provider of needed goods and services, accessible channels must be available through which to communicate with it. In San Juan, Puerto Rico, Doña Felisa Rincón de Gautier held weekly sessions to which petitioners routinely brought both personal and community requests.[17] In such instances, demand making constitutes a direct interaction between the petitioner and the symbolic source of power over resources. This form of personalized political interaction (*personalismo*) achieves the immediate goal of the petitioner, but as Safa notes, it is a personal favor that is granted rather than an acknowledgement of the rights of a citizen (Safa 1974: 74–5). For the petitioner, such an interaction and transaction requires minimal political specialization and strategy decisions. Moreover, it results in minimal socialization for future participation in the political system at the local or supralocal level.

Demand making on behalf of the community is most often carried out through two channels: through a community association, such as the voluntary associations or the *mesas directivas* of the squatter settlements; or through a *cacique* (self-appointed political leader) and his or her organization. (There may be overlap in some cases.) Mangin states that barriada associations in Lima perform one of their most important functions by serving as "brokers between the barriadas and national ministries, city government, and international organizations such as the Peace Corps and the UN" (Mangin 1968: 416). The demands primarily concern land tenure and municipal services. Butterworth reports for colonias in Oaxaca, Mexico:

Most politics in the *colonias* revolve around acquisition and/or legislation of land titles and attempts to get community services. Three of the settlements . . . have a *mesa directiva* for this purpose. A *mesa directiva* is a form of local government that acts in a lobbying capacity as it represents the needs of a *colonia* in dealings with official government structures. Since the *colonias* must depend upon the city for water, electricity, and other services, the *mesa directiva* tries to apply pressure to obtain these amenities. [Butterworth 1973: 223]

A *cacique* is a political broker. His influence in the community is primarily a result of his derivative power and his importance as an effective demand maker on behalf of the community. Cornelius writes about a *cacique's* external resources:

The most important of these external resources are the cacique's relationships with political and governmental officials, professionals, such as lawyers, doctors, architects, or engineers, and other nonresident, high-status individuals who have skills or resources that can help to satisfy community needs. Such contacts are highly valued by the residents of low-income neighborhoods . . . They are viewed as enabling the cacique to deal effectively with external factors and to secure benefits beyond the reach of someone without access to higher levels of authority. And, in fact, numerous studies of both rural and urban communities in Mexico show that personal ties between local leaders and higher authorities are the key to success in petitioning for government benefits. [Cornelius 1975: 147]

Thus, voluntary organizations and brokers are recognized and utilized as effective channels between the inhabitants of a locality and the government in demand making. However, they appear to function as agents of political learning as well:

The cacique may also have a significant impact on the process of political learning among his followers in his role as political mobilizer. Through frequent public meetings to discuss community affairs, visits by delegations of community residents to the offices of politicians and government functionaries, voter-registration drives, and other group efforts, the cacique involves his followers in politically relevant activities. In doing so, he increases their awareness of the relevance of politics and political participation to the satisfaction of individual and community needs. [Cornelius 1975: 155]

As we look further at the barriada organizations, we see that they begin to take on functions of a local government, although they operate with formal sanction of the inhabitants only. The organizations originate as demand-making entities formed to acquire land for housing. They then take on the function of defense against authorities wishing to remove the squatters from their house sites, while continuing to perform their demand-making functions. In this capacity many of the same processes of political learning occur as described above for the followers of the *cacique.* A major difference exists in that the association leaders are chosen by the inhabitants of the settlement as their leaders and representatives. Association officials are elected at regular intervals, dues are collected to pay for the operations of the association, potential settlers are screened, land disputes negotiated, and self-help activities organized and administered. Contacts with the government proliferate through the activities of the association in their capacity as demand makers, and through the growth of interest and interaction in the association's election campaigns by members of national political parties. As the need for defense diminishes and the basic community needs are being met, the barriada association loses power. The community may increasingly become a part of the city. In Lima, older established barriadas have become joined together in new municipal districts with elected mayors and town councils (Mangin 1968: 413–17; see also Butterworth 1973).

While the histories of individual associations and their effectiveness vary from settlement to settlement, such associations serve as agents of political socialization from the moment of their origin.[18] They also offer evidence, contradictory as it sometimes appears, that the urban poor, particularly those living in squatments or self-built settlements, are not necessarily apolitical, disorganized, or lacking in concern for or experience in political activity at the local level.

Cornelius identifies nine structural characteristics that he says play a role in determining the development of norms leading to political involvement. Such norms are most likely to develop in small, densely populated communities with maximum opportunity for intensive face-to-face interaction in socioeconomically homogeneous communities whose inhabitants recognize the mutuality of their interests, in communities characterized by stability of residence, and in communities perceived of by the inhabitants as bounded or spatially separated from the rest of the city. The origin of the settlement – seized by the inhabitants or settled with the assent or aid of the government – is an important structural (or historical) considera- tion. In illegal settlements and settlements where the government has attempted to remove the settlers, the collective problem-solving institutions may develop. Relations with supralocal authority figures, which are characterized by negative sanctions on the community such as attempts to evict them, or by indifference to demand-making behavior, influence political participation. The former appears to have a positive effect; the latter may have a negative effect in that the inhabitants will perceive that they are ineffectual in relations with such authority figures. Community leadership that encourages high resident participation in community affairs may exert a positive effect, but leaders perceived to be serving their own interests or those of the supralocal authorities will not play "a constructive role in the development of participatory norms" (Cornelius 1975: 125–30).

Internal political cleavage and competition can be detrimental to the development of these "participatory norms." The personal costs of partici- pation under such conditions may become so high that the result is noninvolvement in political or community affairs. And finally, Cornelius lists development problems and needs as a structural characteristic highly conducive to the evolution of these norms. "In most low-income ur- ban communities, the key stimulus to political involvement is a set of community-related development problems and needs that must be met if living conditions in the neighborhood are to be improved significantly." Cornelius concludes that an additional factor of "differential opportunity structure" (the range and frequency of opportunities for political involve- ment to which people have access by virtue of their residence in specific communities) is of importance in explaining the process of politicization among low-income groups, and such opportunities are particularly avail- able in squatter settlements (1975: 131–4).

Janice Perlman, who studied two favelas and a *subúrbio* (which she defines as "outlying dormitory communities") in Rio de Janeiro, looked at both participation in favela associations and political involvement outside the favela. She found that both social and political associations are "of critical importance in understanding the politics of the favela. Both train members in the ritual of election of officers, rules of procedure, formation of charters, constitutions, and by-laws, and the process of collective decision-making" (Perlman 1976: 163). Looking at measure of political awareness, she concluded:

The amount of information the favelados have about international politics may not be great, nor is political discussion valued over other topics of conversation. However, the favelados are led by persons who are more keenly aware of politics and its ramifications than they are, and their attention is astutely selective, focusing on the local arena where their concern is more likely to produce results. [Perlman 1976: 169–70]

In summary, the major political activities of the urban poor consist of voting and political demand making. Portes and Walton (1976: 72) have pointed out that these activities constitute "a rational adaptation to the existing social situation." From the perspective of those outside these national political systems, governmental responses to such political de-mand making constitutes a means to co-opt the squatters. As a result, we might expect them to perceive themselves as pacified but not satisfied. The attitudes of impoverished urban agglomerations range from favorable to unfavorable assessments of the actions and efficacy of the government in meeting their needs and those of the country.[19]

We do not, however, see evidence of the anticipated and often highly feared radicalization of such settlements. Portes and Walton's (1976: 81) review of the evidence from Peru, Venezuela, Chile, and Brazil finds no signs of radicalism either at the polls through affiliation with leftist movements or through "strong political organizations acting indepen-dently of political parties and using either the electoral process or tactics of limited violence".[20] Scholars who have studied squatter settlements consider the inhabitants as both aware of the deficiencies of government and of the minimal input they have at the policy-making level. Nonethe-less, they see them as supportive of the system. They also see them as perceiving their needs as individual and local ones and their political strategies as aimed at serving the immediate needs of their community or associational cohorts.

Michael Whiteford (1974: 177) observed of the families he studied in Tulcán barrio, "Their concern is with themselves and their immediate families and not with implementing change on a large scale. While they might regard their situation as precarious, they are not revolutionaries: their feelings of neglect have not led them to violence." Perlman (1976: 243) states, "As for any signs of radical ideology, or propensity for revolutionary action, these are completely absent. Favelados are generally system supportive and see the government not as evil but as doing its best to understand and help people like themselves."

While the explanations for the lack of political radicalism are numerous and cannot be explored in detail here, Cornelius, Leeds, and Mangin identify some of the factors. Cornelius (1975: 233) notes deference to authority and realistic fears of government retribution as contributing to lack of radical activity. He also cites "a deeply held conviction that it is more productive to try to manipulate the system to satisfy needs than to confront it or overrun it." Leeds (1974: 82) offers a structural explanation: "The low-income settlement areas, examined collectively, are, to a marked extent, organizationally centrifugal and are separated from or divided against each other." Thus, there is little incentive or option for class consciousness or class action. Finally, Mangin (1967: 83) offers this insight:

My own impression from the studies cited and my experience in Lima is that a paternalistic ideology, combined with a "don't let them take it away" slogan, would be more appealing than a revolutionary "let's rise and kill the oligarchy" approach. Probably not many inhabitants of the squatter settlements would have regrets if someone else took the latter action, but they themselves are too busy.

9. International migration

The attention paid to migration within nations, particularly rural-to-urban migration, has resulted in a relative disregard by demographers, economists, and others of international population movements in Latin America and in other parts of the world as well (Tapinos 1974: 1–3). This is unfortunate, because many scholars believe that the distinction between internal and international migration is becoming increasingly artificial (Singer 1974a: 128; 1974b: 7–8). "The same 'push and pull' factors created by events in the international political economic system impel millions of these 'surplus' people not only to move within their own countries but to cross international boundaries" (Chaney 1979: 205).

International migration may be intercontinental, such as between European and South American countries; interregional, such as from Paraguay to Brazil; or what we might term "intracontinental," such as between Mexico and the United States.[1] Petersen (1975: 42–3) observes that statistics on international migration collected by national governments are not ordinarily accurate, complete, or comparable. He cites three main reasons for this:

1. The statistics collected are usually an adjunct to a border patrol that many try to evade. The neutral character of modern Western censuses and vital statistics – the fact that they are data collected for their own sake rather than as a step preparatory to unpopular state controls – is lacking in the statistics of international migration.

2. Migrants are not classified according to a uniform system in different countries. Among the total number entering and leaving a country – generally designated as arrivals and departures – the first subclassification is usually that of nationals and aliens. Each of these groups is then further subdivided into visitors and permanent migrants. All of these terms are in some degree ambivalent.

3. The relevance of the statistics available varies with the problem being studied. An analysis of a country's labor force, for instance, would obviously have to include incoming seasonal workers and daily commuters, although these would not necessarily have to be included in a study, say, of housing. But migration data are not ordinarily compiled so that one can take out just those statistics that are pertinent.

International migratory movements

Chaney suggests that recent large-scale movements of people across international boundaries, including the flow of Caribbean peoples to the United States, are directly related to the disparity in growth between developed and developing nations. These movements of people in search of greater economic opportunities occur not only because of push factors but also because of marked wage differentials between the developed and developing world. An irony in this situation, as Hendricks (1974: 79) notes in his study of Dominican migrants to New York, is that moderate improvements in economic opportunities in the sending country may accelerate the migratory movements, because more people can thus afford the journey. Chaney (1979: 204) observes that it is not surprising to find that many migrants are employed in their homelands in the period immediately prior to their departure, even though their employment histories are likely to include long periods of joblessness.

International migration has traditionally been considered as one of the most efficient methods of achieving economic progress (see Thomas 1958), another aspect of the equilibrium model discussed in Chapter 3. Thus, it has been maintained, the macro-objective of migration – correcting rural–urban imbalances and achieving equilibrium – was formerly served by international as well as by rural–urban migration within nations. However, some social scientists contend that international migration is currently much less significant as a source of relief for economically troubled countries (Spengler and Myers 1977: 19):

Indeed, the effects of emigration would seem to weaken countries when it drains away their superior manpower. Formerly, the job requirements for labor migrants were not technically very exacting, with the result that immigrants could find employment quite easily in receiving countries. This is no longer true today . . . Even in modern agriculture, the skill requirements have become so great that persons of limited skill are nearly as unemployable there as in urban settings . . . Emigrants from rural areas in underdeveloped countries are generally not equipped to meet most job requirements in advanced countries, with the result that the "new movement" tends to be selective of more skilled urban migrants. This is true also of migrants within advanced countries who originate in and move out of "culturally deprived" areas into more developed areas. In addition to general economic fluctuation (e.g., the recent oil crisis), problems associated with the admission of unskilled immigrants, together with the slowing down of natural population increase in immigrant-receiving countries and a consequent fear of qualitative dilution of their populations by inflows of less qualified immigrants, will increasingly make for the erection of barriers against immigrants from less-developed countries. [Spengler and Myers 1977: 19–20]

This statement represents a shift from an earlier position by Myers that "in spite of many problems produced by large-scale population movements, labor migration remains, on balance, a dynamic force for human betterment and economic prosperity" (Myers 1974: 16). The bulk of the evidence in international as well as in national migration, however, seems to be in favor of the position that equilibrium theory no longer has – if it ever did have – credibility as an explanatory or predictive device for analyzing population movements. We support Appleyard's conclusion that "international migration, once considered a potential major instrument for equating real incomes between countries, has achieved little in this direction since 1945 although, indirectly, remittances and the acquisition of skills which migrants later used in their homelands, have contributed to the latters' economic growth. Restriction has been the byword in all countries, developed and developing" (Appleyard 1977: 291).

Intercontinental migration

Insofar as intercontinental migration is concerned, movements between Latin America and non–Latin American countries have diminished since the beginning of this century, when they reached their maximum intensity. The countries with the greatest extracontinental immigration – Argentina, Brazil, and Uruguay – received the maximum number of immigrants in the decade prior to World War I and in the 1920s. Although many of these earlier migrants came to buy and work land in rural areas, it appears that many of them or their descendants found their way to urban centers, contributing to the rapid growth of cities.

Immediately after World War II there was a slight recovery in the migratory flow, especially to Venezuela. However, since 1950 the rate of these movements has noticeably decreased, and in the 1960s an inversion of earlier movements took place. The number of people returning to their countries of origin greatly exceeded the new migratory movements to Latin America (Morales-Vergara 1971: 2606).

Bastos de Avila's analysis of immigration to Brazil demonstrated that from the 1920s to the 1950s these movements followed a parabolic curve, the bottom of which coincided with the World War II years. There were two peaks, the first after World War I, the second after World War II. Although the number of Portuguese immigrants was as high in the 1950s as it was in the 1920s, German, Italian, and Spanish immigration fell from a peak in the 1920s only to recover slightly after World War II. For other nationalities the curves were similar, except for Japan, whose peak coincided with the trough for the other curves (Bastos de Avila 1958: 185–6).

The once heavy flow of immigrants from Europe and Japan had, by the 1960s, slowed to a trickle. By 1970 only 1.2 percent of the Brazilian population, including *jus sanguinis* citizens, had been born abroad (Weil 1975: 34). Immigrants to Brazil, who numbered some 120,000 in 1926, lessened to 85,000 in 1952 (Anuario Estatistico 1954: 59). By 1975 there was a total of only 11,566 permanent immigrants to Brazil (Anuario Estatistico 1977: 34).

Nations such as Argentina, Brazil and Uruguay (those with the highest percentage of immigration from overseas) were particularly affected by these population movements.[2] For example, Germani contends that contemporary Argentina cannot be understood without a thorough analysis of the role of immigration in its development, because immigration was a powerful factor in the process of modernization. Furthermore, the intensity and volume of immigration caused a substantial economic, social, and political realignment of the population.

In no other country did the proportion of adult foreigners reach the level that it did in Argentina, where for more than 60 years foreigners represented around 70 percent of the adult population in the capital city (which contained one-fifth to one-third of the total population of the country), and almost 50 percent in the provinces which were heavily populated and economically important. [Germani 1970: 289]

While the numbers differ, the situation in Uruguay and Brazil is analogous to that in Argentina. Other nations in Latin America have been less directly affected by immigration from abroad, but population movements brought about by civil or political strife, such as refugee migration, not infrequently produce unanticipated and perhaps unwanted effects upon a country or region.[3]

Interregional migration

There are few studies dealing with population movements between countries in Latin America. One estimate suggests that, as of 1975, continental migration in South America involved 5,000,000 migrants, of whom 3,000,000 were workers, 1,500,000 dependents, and 400,000 "frontier workers" (*Migration Today* 1975: 106). This estimate and most others of interregional migration are suspect. In those studies that are available, the resulting statistical data are often not reliable. De Villegas reports that eight or nine out of every ten migrants leaving one nation in the region for another (presumably to seek employment) are clandestine (de Villegas 1977: 61). To illustrate some of the difficulties in collecting data, Scott Whiteford and Richard N. Adams conducted a study of Bolivian migrant workers in northwest Argentina. They were mainly concerned with ethnicity and adaptation of the migrants. In one of the best studies of its kind we have come across, life histories of present and former agricultural migrant workers who work or have worked in the *zafra* (sugar harvest) formed the basis of their descriptive data. But as background information they cited the 1960 Argentinian census figure of 95,233 Bolivians in Argentina. In a footnote they remark that this figure underestimates the total Bolivian population in Argentina at that time, because it fails to take into account the large numbers of Bolivians without papers who would be reluctant to see census takers. The authors state that by 1969 there had been estimates ranging from 50,000 to 1,000,000 Bolivians in Argentina (S. Whiteford and Adams 1975: 180–1).

The problems of competent macrolevel population analysis under these conditions are obvious. Nevertheless, new demographic techniques developed by the United Nations, in conjunction with economic cooperation among certain Latin American nations, will doubtless improve the quality of data on migration within the region.[4]

The Centro Latinoamericano de Demografía has tried to organize the statistical information available on the total number of Latin American migrants in each country of the region. According to CELADE, the highest shares of migrants in the total population were 7.1 percent in Venezuela (1961), 6.2 percent in Panama (1950), and 1.0 percent in Honduras (1961). De Villegas states that these figures appear to be underestimations. ILO estimated that in South America alone there were some five million migrant workers in 1971. According to more recent estimates, the total number of foreign workers in the receiving countries would be: Argentina, 1,620,000; Venezuela, 820,000; Brazil, 140,000; Colombia, 120,000; Peru, 110,000; and Ecuador, 85,000. As for the emigrating countries, Bolivia would stand first with 715,000 emigrants, Paraguay has 690,000, Colombia 680,000, Chile 400,000, Brazil 180,000, and Ecuador and Uruguay 115,000 each (de Villegas 1977: 62).[5]

The number of emigrants from a given country should obviously be related to the total population of that nation. Thus, if Bolivia, with 5,110,000 inhabitants, is compared to Paraguay, with only 2,301,000, and both have 700,000 workers outside their borders, the situation is obviously different, and may be far more alarming for Paraguay. Conversely, the 680,000 emigrants from Colombia have little impact on Colombia, says de Villegas, as its total population is approximately 26,000,000 (de Villegas 1977: 62).

De Sierra and his associates have tried to place migration within the Southern Cone (Argentina, Bolivia, Chile, Paraguay and Uruguay) in relation to the so-called Mediterranean migrations (those that take place in Western Europe from the Mediterranean toward the countries of the north). The authors remark that at first sight migration in the Southern Cone appears to be a very similar phenomenon. "In fact," they say, "one is faced with a country (Argentina) which has a higher level of economic development; a higher rate of industrialization; a much larger and more developed internal market, and with a larger demand for labour force, receiving migrants from a number of less developed countries (Chile, Bolivia, Paraguay and Uruguay)" (De Sierra, Marcotti, and Rojan 1975: 55).

There are, however, important differences. Unlike countries of the Mediterranean basin, all the countries of the Southern Cone (including Argentina) are dependent on the capitalist system, which is largely centered outside of Latin America. The authors point out two characteristics of this phenomenon: First, the country of emigration is fundamentally more dependent upon other countries than that to which the migrants go; second, the receiving country, although it plays an intermediary role, is also dependent on the more advanced capitalist countries, and the growth of the receiving country suffers accordingly (1975: 55–6).

Nations bordering on Argentina have seen large fluctuations in their economies. Nevertheless, Argentina has always been more developed economically than the other Cone countries, so emigrants from Bolivia and Paraguay, as well as from Uruguay, head toward the agricultural or urban-industrial regions of Argentina in much larger numbers than they do toward the south or southeast of Brazil. In spite of the differences in the global level of development between Argentina and the other countries in question, gross national product growth is not especially rapid in Argentina. During the 1960s, a decade during which migration accelerated, growth was less in Argentina than in the neighboring countries, with the exception of Uruguay (De Sierra, Marcott, and Rojan 1975: 56).

These same authors note another aspect of interregional migration in the Southern Cone: because of the meager earnings of the emigrant laborers, any significant return of savings by the migrants to their countries of origin is almost impossible. De Sierra and collaborators are unaware of the existence of any precise studies on this point, but they contend that the near "miserable" standard of living of the migrants makes it almost impossible to save (1975: 61). Clearly, more reliable data and careful studies are necessary to understand the implications of these interregional population movements in Latin America.

Migration from Latin America to the United States

One of the most important migrations across borders is the movement of people from Latin America to the United States. Since 1820, some three million people have been admitted as legal immigrants to the United States from countries south of the border (U.S. Immigration and Naturalization Service, *Annual Report,* 1976). (These and other figures in this section exclude peoples from the Caribbean).[6] Table 3 illustrates the trends in immigration from Mexico and Central and South America to the United States during the past century.

The figures in Table 3 reflect both national and world trends. Figures for the period before the turn of this century should not be considered to be statistically accurate, because migration was largely uncontrolled at that time. No figures at all were kept on migration across the Mexican–U.S.

Table 3. *Immigration to the United States from Latin American countries (excluding the Caribbean)*

| Year | Country or region | | | |
	Mexico[a]	Central America	South America	Total
1881–90	1,913	404	2,304	4,621
1891–1900	971	549	1,075	2,595
1901–10	49,642	8,192	17,280	75,114
1911–20	219,004	17,159	41,899	278,062
1921–30	459,287	15,769	42,215	517,271
1931–40	22,319	15,502	7,803	45,624
1941–50	60,589	21,665	21,831	104,085
1951–60	308,515	44,561	76,562	429,638
1961–70	453,937	101,330	257,954	813,221
1971	50,103	8,626	20,700	79,429
1972	64,209	8,407	21,393	94,009
1973	70,411	9,125	22,423	101,959
1974	71,863	9,431	23,964	105,258
1975	62,552	9,800	24,183	96,535
1976	57,863	9,431	22,699	89,975
1977	44,079	15,554	32,954	92,587

[a] There were no records kept for immigration from Mexico from 1886 to 1893.
Source: U.S. Immigration and Naturalization Service: Annual Reports.

border from 1886 to 1893, and even the statistics for subsequent years are rough approximations. This was still the period of the American open-door immigration policy, modified only by some qualitative restrictions and a small head tax. Admission to the United States was arranged at the border, and no visa was required (Grebler et al. 1970: 63).[7]

Although the immigration statistics up to around 1920 may be suspect, the trend toward increased immigration is clear enough, despite the fact that the open door remained barely ajar. The entry of the United States into World War I attracted labor northward from Latin American nations, particularly Mexico, and the sharp decline in immigration during the 1930s was a direct result of the Great Depression. World War II and the Korean conflict acted as new pull factors that drew labor to a prosperous United States; political machinations and natural disasters in Latin countries afforded the push.

The sharp increase in the number of people born in Central and South American nations entering the United States during the period 1961–70 on temporary or permanent visas is particularly noteworthy (Table 3 shows only those admitted on permanent visas).[8] It reflects political turmoil in some Central and Southern Latin American nations as much as economic opportunity in the United States. Restrictionist sentiment was also an important factor in determining the makeup of the new immigrant population.

The Immigration and Nationality Act of 1952 (McCarren-Walter Act), following the lead of the National Origins Act of 1924, had established annual quotas based on national origins; the quotas applied to all countries except those in the western hemisphere. However, this act was amended in 1965, taking effect in mid-1968, to allow no more than 120,000 persons a year to enter from western hemisphere countries. Among the main arguments for the imposition of a quota was the sharp increase in total immigration from Central and South America and the Caribbean area. In the 1950s, 111,123 immigrants from Central and South America entered the U.S. on permanent visas. In the following decade, this number jumped to 359,284, an increase of more than 300 percent. In the decade 1951–60, legal immigrants from Mexico accounted for a little over 70 percent of the total from Latin America (again excluding the Caribbean). However, since that time (1961–77) that percentage has been reduced to less than 60 percent.

Mexico has thus been the leading supplier of immigrants to the United States. Argentina, Brazil, and Venezuela have contributed the highest number from South America, while (except for Belize), the Central American republics have contributed fairly equal numbers (not percentages of population) to the migratory flow in recent decades.

The amount of data on immigration from Latin America to the United States is vast. Except for the foregoing summary, we shall not attempt to deal with the topic in this volume. We limit ourselves to the most significant aspect of this subject, the movement of people from Mexico to the United States.[9]

Mexican migration to the United States

Introduction

Since the first national census was taken in Mexico in 1895, the population of that nation has increased five-fold, from about 12.5 million to over 65 million. Since 1930 its population has quadrupled; it has doubled in the past twenty years (México DGE 1940; 1950; 1960; 1970). Not very long ago it was feared that by the year 2000, Mexico would have 135 million people (El Colegio de México 1970: 19; *New York Times,* April 3, 1977, p. 1:5.) This assumed a continuing high birth rate and a continuing decrease in mortality. However, late as it may be, the Mexican government has at last taken an official position in favor of birth control (family planning). Its program appears to have made some progress in cutting birth rates: Between 1974 and 1976 the annual rate of growth fell from 3.5 percent to

3.2 percent and officials say it is now at 2.9 percent. Part of the drop in the birth rate is attributed to the relative ease of providing family planning services to poor urban women and to official propaganda (*New York Times,* Jan 9, 11, 1979, p. 1). But even if the new program is fully successful, the Mexican population will grow from its present size to 104 million by the year 2000 (loc. cit.). This has profound meaning in a country that is one-fourth the size of the United States and where much of the topography is hostile to agriculture and other forms of development. Population growth is the most important factor in the outcome of Mexico's efforts to reduce poverty, illiteracy, disease, and underproduction (Population Reference Bureau 1964: 173).

Frank Tannenbaum recognized the future repercussions of Mexican population growth thirty years ago. He wrote:

The very danger of overpopulation, which most Mexican economists refuse to recognize, is a byproduct of the forces set in motion to raise the standard of living of the Mexican people. In the process the older society is being undermined, not so much by the effects of the government program as by the increased population the program has stimulated. The increased population in its turn is hastening the threat of a seemingly inescapable doom hidden in the more and more rapid depletion of the soil. That is the contemporary Mexican dilemma. [Tannenbaum 1950: 180]

Until recently, Mexico has been able to absorb most of its population increase into its own economy. Industrialization and improved agricultural practices have been mainly responsible for the ability of the economy to handle huge population increases combined with rapid urbanization. Irrigation projects have brought new land into cultivation and improved seeds have been utilized; agricultural information services have been established by the government. The increased food production has allowed a declining proportion of the population to do the farming. Between 1950 and 1970 the proportion of the labor force employed in agriculture dropped dramatically. It was almost twice as great as the drop in agricultural employment between 1930 and 1950, and three times greater than the drop between 1910 and 1950. The men and women who shifted away from agricultural to nonagricultural employment have been principally absorbed by the manufacturing, commerce, and service sectors of the economy (services here include the government sector as part of the service sector). Together these three sectors increased their share of the labor force by nearly 15 percent, from 30.9 percent in 1950 to 45.8 percent in 1970. This was the first time in Mexican history that manufacturing absorbed a greater share of the increases in urban employment than services and commerce (Arroyo 1975: 426).

Despite its booming economy, given a new impetus by its newly discovered oil and natural gas deposits, Mexico already has a surplus population that it is unable to feed and house adequately and for which it is unable to provide full employment. Official figures mask the seriousness of this situation and thus contribute to the Pollyannish view taken by some planners and policy makers. One such masking device is the government's method of computing unemployment figures. The Mexican labor force is defined as including persons between the ages of twelve and sixty-five. Of the 11.3 million economically active Mexicans in 1960, 182,638 were listed as unemployed. The Mexican government was thereby able to report the phenomenally low unemployment rate of 1.6 percent (Population Reference Bureau, 1964: 191). However, these data obscure what many economic specialists consider to be Mexico's basic problem – underemployment rather than unemployment. A high number of workers are still employed in agriculture, the service sector is disproportionately large, and many of these employed Mexicans are working part-time and at the bottom of the wage scale. Further, many workers in nonagricultural industries are not employees of establishments, but are self-employed as everything from artisans to street vendors. More than one-third of the Mexican labor force is self-employed. "Such a high degree of individual endeavor suggests that, more often than not, the workers lacked more profitable alternatives" (Population Reference Bureau, 1964: 173).

Brandenburg (1964: 237–8) shows that:

Included in the [Mexican] labor force are at least 1.5 million individuals, and probably as many as 2.5 million, who find work only four or at best five months out of the year. The rest of their time is spent in scratching out a living as well as they can, often by migrating to other regions . . .

This situation can only worsen as more and more Mexicans enter the labor force. The growth in mean annual labor supply, which is already high, (more than 500,000 yearly from 1965 to 1970) will continue to swell at a fast pace, and by 1975–80 was expected to reach an annual average of over 830,000 persons (Banco Nacional de Comercio Exterior 1970: 34–8).

In spite of Mexico's impressive economic growth, the country has been unable to meet the needs of its growing economically active population. The number of landless agricultural workers had increased from approximately 2.3 million in 1950 to well over 3 million during the 1960s. Meanwhile, employment opportunities in agriculture had decreased (Arroyo, 1975: 426–7). This has resulted in large numbers of rural workers leaving the countryside to work in urban places. In addition, external migration to the United States has traditionally been a safety valve for Mexico's under- and unemployed millions; but this valve has been screwed tighter and tighter by U.S. legislation. An explosion of catastrophic proportions is not impossible.

Background to Mexican migration to the United States

Since the 1880s there has been a continual exodus of migrants from central Mexico to the United States. Improvements in transportation within

Mexico played a crucial role in this exodus. In particular, the construction of railroads spurred the flow of population movements northward from Mexico's central plateau (Gamio 1969: 163–9). Indeed, as Cornelius (1978: 14) pointed out, the railroads served as the only important means of transportation and the main source of employment for Mexican migrants to the United States in the late nineteenth and early twentieth centuries.

Mexican immigrant workers played a vital part in the development of a transportation network in the American Southwest. During the last two decades of the nineteenth century they helped lay the tracks of the Southern Pacific and Santa Fe railroads. Once the main lines had been completed, southwestern railroads continued to hire Mexicans in increasing numbers for the purpose of building auxiliary lines and maintaining track in good repair in some of the most arid and desolate areas of the United States (Reisler 1976: 3). "From that day to this," observed Carey McWilliams, "Mexicans have repaired and maintained Western rail lines. As watchmen of the rails, section hands must live near their work, while the extra crews literally live on the rails in boxcars which are shunted about the divisions. 'Their abode,' as one railroad executive tersely phrased it, 'is where these cars are placed.' Hundreds of Mexican families have spent their entire sojourn in the United States bouncing around the Southwest in boxcar homes" (McWilliams 1968: 167–8).

By 1916 Mexican workers were laying track in the Chicago area, and soon several hundred Mexicans were on the employment rolls of a Chicago iron company (Taylor 1970: 32–4). The large Mexican communities that are now found in such midwestern cities as Chicago, Detroit, Gary, and Kansas City began to form during this period as migrants left the railroad crews to seek employment in industry and the stockyards (Cornelius 1978: 14).

In the latter half of the nineteenth century, industrial and agricultural development in the American Southwest began to attract Mexicans to the United States. By 1888 the sugar-beet industry had begun to thrive in southern California and, because American laborers refused to do the backbreaking work that sugar-beet harvesting, thinning, and topping demanded, Japanese, Mexican, and Filipino workers streamed in to fill the labor vacuum that had been created by rejection by American labor and the exclusion of the Chinese (Martínez 1971: 2–3, 11).

Then came the cotton boom. Cotton had been raised in the American Southwest since pre-Colombian times, but it achieved its predominant position only after the Industrial Revolution permitted an enormous increase in the manufacture of textiles. The plant came to be known as King Cotton, "restlessly seeking new horizons, and new soil and climate that are favorable to it" (Cohn 1956: 171). Even before 1900, thousands of Mexicans crossed the border each year for the cotton harvest in Texas.

Later the crop moved westward across the mountains to New Mexico, Arizona, and California, where frontiers were opened to it in semi-arid lands. There men caused the onetime desert to blow white with cotton as they sank wells and pumped water through the dry land (Cohn 1956: 171).

As the crops moved, so did the farmworkers in their wake. They worked their way up the heart of the continent from northern Texas to the Dakotas and Canada, gathering wheat as it ripened successively in each state from south to north (Schwartz 1945: 12; McWilliams 1942: 91). Except in California, Mexicans predominated from the first as farm laborers in the border states. The Chinese were the first and largest source of foreign agricultural labor in California. Not until the Chinese were removed was it possible for other foreign labor to enter California. Japanese and Mexican workers were not employed to any extent in California until the anti-Chinese riots culminated in the Chinese Exclusion Act of 1882. Japanese agricultural workers were brought in by farmers ("slowly and silently") to replace their former Chinese coolies immediately following passage of the Exclusion Act (Martínez 1971: 11). The Chinese had been excluded largely because they were thought to lower labor standards, but the Japanese competed successfully with the very farmers who imported them. The Japanese farm worker was frugal, saved his earnings, and then bought farmland (Iyenaga and Sato 1921: 131). After 1900, American farmers began to resist Japanese immigration for two reasons: first, because the Asians bought up choice farmland and proved to be better farmers than their American competitors; second, because the Japanese tended to farm for themselves and were therefore not available as agricultural workers – the reason they were brought in in the first place (Martínez 1971: 12).

In an attempt to put a stop to the Japanese immigration, the United States and Japan made the "Gentleman's Agreement" of 1907, whereby Japan was to restrict voluntarily its nationals from emigrating to the U.S. It was in the decade after the Gentleman's Agreement – when the Japanese were in transition from farm workers to farm owners – that Mexicans entered California in considerable numbers. "Just as the farmers had sought the Japanese as substitutes for the Chinese coolie, in like manner, Mexicans were called in to replace the Japanese" (Martínez 1971: 12).

California's fruit, vegetable, cotton, and sugar-beet expansion in the period from about 1910 to 1917 would have drawn more Mexican labor to the field than it actually did but for the anti-Oriental campaign, which discouraged Mexicans from entering California. Although the Japanese and Chinese were the two groups against whom protests were made and actions taken, the Mexicans as an ethnic minority apparently felt the effects of discrimination. Mexicans therefore tended to enter Texas, Colorado, Utah, and Idaho. In the years between 1910 and 1917 they crossed the border at an average rate of ten thousand a year. The Mexican transient worker was the perfect answer to the Texas cotton grower's needs. During peak work periods, Mexicans were informed that they were needed and they obligingly entered the country by the tens of thousands. When harvests were over, they were expected to wander back across the border, rendering unnecessary the inefficient methods of sharecropping and tenant farming in the new cotton areas. Largely because of political instability in Mexico and cheap labor needs in the United States, approximately five hundred thousand Mexicans emigrated to the United States by 1917 (Martínez 1971: 14).

Trends in Mexican–U.S. migration

The Mexican revolutionary period beginning in 1910 spurred the first substantial permanent migration of Mexicans to the United States. Almost two hundred thousand permanent migrants entered the United States from Mexico between 1910 and 1919. The immigrants of that period seem to have had more differentiated backgrounds than those of the migrants who entered before and after this era. They included upper- and middle-class refugees who felt threatened by the Revolution as well as many others who simply want to escape from the protracted bloody conflict (Grebler et al. 1970: 63).

The Revolution also had a more important and durable indirect effect on movement to the United States. By liberating masses of people from social and geographical immobility, it served to activate a latent migration potential of vast dimensions (Grebler et al. 1970: 63). "For the first – and probably the last – time in U.S. history, tens of thousands of Mexicans were readily admitted to the United States during the 1911–15 period as *economic* refugees, whom the Commissioner General of Immigration chose to define as persons suffering from 'industrial depression and its attendant evils' ". (Cornelius 1978: 14–15).

With the advent of World War I, the push of the Mexican Revolution was reinforced by the pull of American labor requirements. The shortage of domestic workers in the South and Southwest – brought on both by military service duties and migrations of poor whites and blacks to the North – meant that growers could make a good case for opening the southern border. Mexicans were close at hand, and we have seen how they poured over the border in droves.

Immigration from Mexico reached a peak in the 1920s. Close to five hundred thousand Mexicans were reported as entering on permanent visas during this time. Mexican immigrants accounted for 9 percent of all immigrants to this country in the first half of the decade, and nearly 16 percent of the total in the second half when the quota system, European prosperity, and emigration restrictions in fascist Italy and communist

Russia reduced the movement of people from Europe. In the 1920s, too, migration from Mexico to the United States reached a peak relative to Mexico's own population. Mexican literature of this period began to express fears that Mexico was losing too many of her energetic, skilled, and ambitious people to its neighbor to the north – a harbinger of today's brain drain dilemma. On the other hand, apprehensions in the United States about the volume and composition of Mexican immigration led to vigorous Congressional debates over the extension of the quota system to Mexicans. Stricter administration controls were imposed in the 1920s (Grebler et al., 1970: 65).

World War I was followed by an economic recession, and with it came the first of the mass repatriation campaigns aimed primarily at Mexican migrants. Urged on by politicians and labor leaders, mobs of native-born Americans in Texas, Oklahoma, and other states launched attacks on Mexicans in their work places, while vigilante groups terrorized them in their homes and destroyed their property. During 1920 and 1921, nearly one hundred thousand Mexicans left the U.S. under varying degrees of coercion (Cornelius 1978; 15).

The late 1920s brought a new wave of Mexican migrants from the central plateau region, which had been spared the worst ravages of the Revolution. However, new restrictive measures were soon to come. The Border Patrol was established in 1924. Congressional passage of the Immigration Act of 1924 sharply reduced immigration from southern and eastern Europe and Asia, and advocates of an even more restrictive immigration policy clamored for further action to curtail immigration from the western hemisphere, which had been exempted from the 1924 Act (Cornelius 1978: 15). Mexico was the main target of the restrictionist forces:

All along, Americans had viewed the Mexican in terms of a racially inferior labor commodity. Employers who had recruited the immigrant from below the Rio Grande and had continually worked to keep the border open agreed that the Mexican's "biologically determined attributes" made him perfectly suited as a manageable farm, construction, or railroad maintenance laborer in desert regions. Most importantly, from their point of view, a large supply of fresh Mexican immigrants would keep wages low in the Southwest. Thus, employers were willing to risk the presence of a racially undesirable people to protect and fatten their profits. Restrictionists, on the other hand, saw the Mexican as an inherently unequal peon who would reproduce without limit and undermine the idealized economic standards of the American worker and farmer. They believed that the continuation of boundless Mexican immigration would negate all they had accomplished in excluding undesirable Europeans, as peons constituted a far greater racial menace. The federal government, caught between these conflicting pressures, generally bowed to the appeals of growers for plentiful labor. [Reisler 1976: 261]

With the onset of the Great Depression in 1928–9, further restrictionist agitation in the U.S. Congress became unnecessary. Another mass repatriation campaign was launched against Mexican migrants – this time a much larger effort than the one of 1920–1. Perhaps more than 415,000 Mexicans were forcibly expelled from the United States between 1929 and 1935; some 85,000 more left "voluntarily," usually under intense pressure from local officials (Cornelius 1978: 16). The United States–born children of these Mexicans were deported along with their parents. The deportation of Mexican Americans – United States citizens – was not uncommon, because the Texas Rangers, the U.S. Border Patrol, and the U.S. Immigration Service frequently saw little or no difference between Mexican Americans and Mexican nationals; they were all simply "Mexican" (Alvarez 1973: 931).

During and after the repatriation campaign, Mexican migration to the United States dropped to a trickle. Throughout the Depression far more Mexicans returned to their homeland than left for the United States (Cornelius 1978: 17). As the Depression took its toll and soil erosion in the Dust Bowl displaced farmers, rural tenants, and workers, American agriculture found a new source of low-wage labor supply in the "Okies" and the urban unemployed who sought refuge in temporary farm work. During the 1930s only 27,900 Mexicans entered on permanent visas. The share of Mexicans in total immigration was less than 4 percent as compared with more than 11 percent in the previous decades (Grebler et al. 1970: 66).

The manpower emergency of World War II made the Mexicans welcome again. This time, however, legal immigrants from Mexico were slow in responding. Mexico was enjoying a new prosperity, and, as world demand for some of its export products rose, that nation needed its own workers. Besides, immigrants to the United States faced the prospect of service in the armed forces, and some of Mexico's manpower was drawn into its own army when it declared war against the Axis nations in 1942. But the small figures for visa immigrants during World War II tell only part of the story, for this was when the bracero program was born. The program provided for the government-regulated recruitment of temporary workers. Conceived as a war-emergency measure, it was to be twenty-two years before the agreement was terminated (Grebler et al. 1970: 66–7).

The bracero program employed over four hundred thousand Mexican workers per year at its peak. During the first ten years of the program, however, the number of employment opportunities available under the program was far more limited – usually well under one hundred thousand per year. The demand for bracero contracts greatly exceeded the supply during this period, and many of those Mexican workers who failed to get on the hiring list went to the U.S. anyway, as illegal migrants (Cornelius 1978: 17).

Immigration on permanent visas began to accelerate in the early 1950s, increasing steadily from 6,372 immigrants in 1951 to over 65,000 in 1956. Nearly 293,500 were recorded in the decade as a whole, and the share of Mexicans in total immigration exceeded 15 percent in the second half of the 1950s. This increased volume did not reflect a relaxation of the law or its administration. The Immigration and Nationality Act of 1952 recodified existing statutes and introduced changes that primarily affected Europeans, but the Act left the position of Mexican immigrants essentially unchanged. Temporary migrations, too, increased markedly during the 1950s. The bracero program was inoperative for a time after World War II, but American growers made such a persuasive case for its resumption that Congress enacted Public Law 78 in 1951, which replicated the earlier bracero agreement (Grebler et al. 1970: 67).

Rising unemployment rates after the end of the Korean conflict generated pressures for a new crackdown on Mexicans; Operation Wetback was mounted in 1953–4. However, between 1953 and 1956 the bracero contract labor program had more than doubled in size, and many of those returned to Mexico by Operation Wetback were soon able to return to the United States as braceros (Cornelius 1978: 17).

Although the bracero program offered a legal alternative to men sneaking across the border for temporary work, there was a limit on the number of Mexicans who could participate. Furthermore, through illegal employment both Mexican laborers and American ranchers could save money, time, and inconvenience – and avoid regulation. "In the early postwar years, the situation became so confused that an administrative solution was devised by transporting the illegal migratory workers back across the border and then readmitting them as 'legally contracted.' The process was, perhaps inevitably, called the 'drying-out' of wetbacks" (Grebler et al. 1970: 67–8).

By the late 1950s and early 1960s the border was closing once again. The U.S. Department of Labor, acting in response to rising opposition to the bracero program from organized labor (and, allegedly, from some religious groups) issued increasingly restrictive regulations for the hiring of contract laborers. Combined with rapid mechanization of cotton harvesting, these administrative restrictions sharply reduced bracero contracting. In 1964 the program was terminated. As the number of bracero contracts available to them dropped, there was a corresponding increase in the number of Mexican farmworkers seeking U.S. permanent resident visas. By the late 1960s, however, these visas had become difficult to obtain, so, not surprisingly, the volume of illegal migration from Mexico to the United States began to increase rapidly (Cornelius, 1978: 17).

The Mexican government was not unaware of the problems that could result from the termination of the bracero program. Then ambassador to the United States Carillo Flores made this statement to the U.S. Congress:

It should be considered that on various occasions when at international meetings on migrant worker problems representatives of the Government of the United States have indicated their purpose of decreasing the contracting until the elimination point is reached, the Mexican representatives have requested that an attempt be made to make the decrease gradually, in order to give Mexico an opportunity to reabsorb the workers who have habitually been working in the United States and thus stave off the sudden crisis that would come from an increase in national unemployment. The stoppage of the contracts at the start of 1964 would leave approximately 200,000 persons out of work. [U.S. Congressional Record, 109, 14389]

Richard B. Craig, who cited Ambassador Flores's remarks in his excellent documentation of the bracero program, noted that "what the ambassador did not say, but what was understood by all students of the bracero program, was that each bracero supported an average of four persons. An end to recruitment would mean that 800,000 Mexicans would be faced with the prospect of going hungry" (Craig 1971: 187).

Bustamante (1978: 183) recorded that rural unemployment was high when the bracero program was terminated; those who had gone to the United States initially as braceros continued to go, but now illegally. "In this sense the bracero program never really ended, it simply went underground" (Cornelius 1978: 18).

The demand for U.S. visas by Mexicans is considerably higher now than in any previous period; but the supply of visas available to Mexican nationals has been reduced by a series of amendments to the Immigration and Nationality Act. The amendments passed by Congress in 1965 have made it extremely difficult for any Mexican who is not an immediate relative of a U.S. citizen or legal permanent resident to migrate legally to the United Sates. All others are required to have a prearranged job offer from a U.S. employer, and the employer is required to obtain a certification from the U.S. Department of Labor to the effect that there are no domestic workers available to fill the job and that the employment of an immigrant in the job will not have an adverse impact of local wages or working conditions (Cornelius 1978: 18).

The Immigration and Nationality Act Amendments of 1976 represent one more turn of the screw. By imposing a ceiling of 20,000 immigrant visas per year on each western hemisphere country, these amendments have had the effect of reducing legal immigration from Mexico from over 60,000 to 40,000 per year. "The 1976 amendments essentially completed the process of restricting legal immigration opportunities to a very small, elite group of Mexicans who can afford the long delays and expenses involved in obtaining a visa. This closure of the legal entry option for most Mexicans seeking to go to the U.S. has itself been an important factor encouraging illegal migration in recent years" (Cornelius 1978: 18).

Illegal migration from Mexico to the United States

The problem of illegal immigrants from Mexico – in diplomatic terms, "undocumented aliens"; in colloquial English, "wetbacks" – is easily the touchiest subject between the United States and its neighbor to the south. "Both in terms of the sheer number of people involved, and of the social, economic, and political consequences of the phenomenon for both the sending and receiving nations, illegal Mexican migration to the U.S. should be regarded as the most critical issue currently affecting relations between the U.S. and Mexico. It is of considerably greater importance than illicit drug traffic, prisoner exchange, Colorado River salinity, and other issues which have dominated discussions between the two countries for more than a decade" (Cornelius 1977: 1). The literature on the subject is almost as vast as the number of wetbacks. We shall limit ourselves here to a brief review of the most salient aspects of the problem. For more detailed reports, the reader is referred, as a starting point, to the sources listed in the bibliography to this volume.[10]

Estimates of the total number of illegal aliens of all nationalities present in the United States range from 4 to 12 million. The most widely publicized estimate, provided for the Immigration and Naturalization Service (INS) by Lesko Associates in 1975, is 8.2 million undocumented (illegal) aliens, of whom 5.2 million are estimated to be Mexicans. Cornelius and other experts regard the Lesko figures as excessively high by several million, and, they say, the assumptions and methodology employed in these calculations are scientifically indefensible. Because of the clandestine nature of the population and its geographical dispersion throughout the United States, it is impossible to estimate the size of the total illegal population with any degree of precision (Cornelius 1977: 1; Keely 1977: 473–81).[11]

The number of illegal Mexican aliens detected in the United States increased from 48,948 to about 773,000 in 1976. Most experts agree that the INS apprehends only about one out of three or four illegal entrees. The concentration of INS enforcement activities in those portions of the country where Mexican illegals are clustered makes it impossible to estimate the true proportion of Mexicans among the country's illegal alien population from apprehension statistics (most experts believe the actual figure to be about 60 percent), but it is clear that Mexico is by far the most important source country for illegal aliens (Cornelius 1977: 1–2).

All studies stress the strongly economic motivation of Mexican wetbacks. The huge wage differentials (often three to four times, for comparable work) between the United States and Mexico are more important than outright unemployment in Mexico in promoting migration. The importance of unemployment and underemployment in Mexico should not be underestimated; however, indications are that it is not just the lack of jobs, but of reasonably well-paid jobs, that spurs migration to the United States. Enforcement of official minimum wage levels is extremely lax in rural Mexico, in particular, and since 1971 the real incomes of poor Mexican families have been seriously eroded by a sharply increased rate of inflation. Another inflationary spiral has resulted from the nearly 100 percent currency devaluation in Mexico during 1976. With U.S. dollars now worth twice as much in Mexico as previously, the devaluation can be expected to produce a substantial increase in illegal migration to the United States. The general point is that the flow of illegal migrants from Mexico seems far more responsive to economic conditions within Mexico than to conditions in the United States, including the U.S. level of unemployment and the level of apprehension efforts by the INS (Cornelius 1977: 3–4; see also Briggs 1975a; Briggs 1975b; Bustamante 1976; Evans and James 1979; Jenkins 1977; Jenkins 1978; Portes 1978a, 1978b).

Mexico's poor are aware of the increasing difficulty of finding employment in the United States, given the current state of the economy and the saturation of some labor markets by illegal aliens. They are also aware of the considerable expense involved in making the trip and the danger of apprehension by the INS. Even under such circumstances, however, the decision to go to the United States is often eminently rational. Cornelius's investigations show that the peasant usually estimates that the risk of not finding a job, or of being caught and expelled by the INS, is substantially lower than the risk of being unemployed or having an inadequate income if he remains in his home community. Among the illegal migrants interviewed in Cornelius's study, 62 percent had found a job in ten days or less after crossing the border during their first trip to the U.S. (1977: 4–5).

The most favored destinations for wetbacks are California (especially the southern part of the state), the Chicago area, and the state of Texas, in that order. For those migrating without enough resources to support themselves during a prolonged period of job seeking, California offers the best possibilities, because agricultural jobs are plentiful there and are less time-consuming to obtain. Texas is least favored because of the low wage scales prevailing there. The Chicago area, offering higher-paid jobs in both industrial and agricultural enterprises, is preferred by those having sufficient time, money, and personal contacts to facilitate job seeking (Cornelius 1977: 6–7).

All experts agree that the principal impact of Mexican and other illegal aliens within the United States is experienced in the labor market. However, there is considerable disagreement about the nature of this impact. Most of the concern about the influx of illegals from Mexico among U.S. labor union leaders stems from the fact that illegal aliens tend to be concentrated in the low-wage, low-skill sector of the labor market, where they presumably compete directly with or displace disadvantaged native Americans, especially blacks and Chicanos. There is, however, no direct evidence of displacement of native Americans by illegal Mexican workers, at least in those sectors of the job market in which the Mexicans typically seek employment. The principal impact of illegal migration may be to depress wage scales – or maintain the status quo – for certain types of unskilled jobs, rather than to displace native Americans from them. As Cornelius points out, workers cannot be displaced if they are not there, and there is no evidence that disadvantaged native Americans have ever held, at least in recent decades, a significant proportion of the jobs for which illegals are usually hired, especially in the agricultural sector. Most of the jobs in question are the least desirable in the U.S. labor market: they involve dirty, physically punishing tasks, low wages, long hours, generally poor working conditions, low job security, and little chance for advancement (Cornelius 1977: 8–9).

The reassessment of U.S. immigration policy that is now underway must eventually confront one basic question. In a few years the INS will no doubt possess sufficient manpower and hardware to reduce sharply the influx of illegal migrants from Mexico, although certainly not to halt it. But, asks Cornelius, at what cost to the economies and societies of the U.S. and Mexico? While our knowledge of the impact of illegal migration on the two countries is still limited, the available evidence does point to one general conclusion: that stopping or severely reducing the migration would not be cost-free for the United States. The probable costs would include:

1. Loss of jobs for American workers in firms that mechanize or relocate in a foreign country or shut down entirely in response to a sharp reduction in the supply of migrant labor.

2. Loss of jobs for American workers due to reduced consumer spending, both in those areas of the United States where the migrants have been concentrated and in Mexico, where the demand for American-made imports would fall off.

3. A higher rate of inflation in the United States, because of the higher prices that consumers would pay for goods currently produced with migrant labor, and because of upward pressure on the wage structure.

4. A lower rate of future economic growth and more limited mobility for disadvantaged Americans as the U.S. population growth declines and the population ages.

5. Increased public hostility and discrimination in hiring against all Spanish-speaking people in the United States, regardless of immigration status.

6. A sharp deterioration in our bilateral relations with Mexico, and, if the migration is reduced too rapidly, the possibility of economic and political disruptions within Mexico that would eventually threaten U.S. interests (Cornelius 1978: 93–4).

One other question remains. Who will benefit from a more restrictive migration policy? The benefits of a restrictive immigration policy to its alleged main beneficiaries – the already disadvantaged workers (blacks, Hispanics, women, teenagers, the handicapped, low-skilled legal immigrants) – seem to have been vastly overestimated. Do the conceivable benefits of a restrictive policy to the U.S. outweigh the probable costs? Cornelius says the answer is very likely to be "no." The long-term interests of Mexico would probably be best served by a reduction of the flow of immigrants, but only if that reduction is gradual, and if alternative income-earning opportunities can be created at a commensurate rate within Mexico (Cornelius 1978: 94).

The Mexican–United States border region

Clearly, most entry by illegal Mexican aliens occurs across the 2000-mile border that separates Mexico and the United States. Since the 1940s, there have been two main streams of migration within Mexico: one to the capital and another to the northern border region. Rural-to-urban migration has, as we have seen, been heavy in Mexico during this period, particularly to Mexico City, but the rate is substantially lower than it would have been in the absence of temporary (or permanent) migration to the United States. Landless agricultural workers – peones, *jornaleros* (day laborers), and *medieros* (sharecroppers) – are by far the most migration-prone groups (Cornelius 1976: 23).

The initial consequence of migration to the north by Mexicans has been the formation of a veritable human log jam in the border region. Since 1940, the northern border has had the highest population growth rate of any major region in Mexico. From 1940 to 1950 the population of the northern border states of Mexico increased by 44 percent; in the following decade it rose by 47 percent. The eight major municipalities of the Mexican border – Tijuana, Mexicali, Nogales, Ciudad Juárez, Piedras Negras, Nuevo Laredo, Reynosa, and Matamoros – increased by 83 percent between 1950 and 1960, from less than 900,000 to 1.5 million (these figures include Ensenada). By 1970 the population had reached a total of 2.3 million persons, or about 5 percent of the total population of Mexico.

Between 1960 and 1969 the population in the northern border states (Baja California, Sonora, Chihuahua, Coahuila, Nuevo León, and Tamaulipas) grew by 43 percent, in contrast with a figure of 31 percent for the nation as a whole. During the 1950s the rates of growth of the largest cities on the border surpassed that of the Federal District, and the growth continues unabated today (Fernández 1977: 113–15). Thus, with an average annual growth rate of nearly 5 percent, northern Mexico is probably the fastest-growing region of its size in the world today (Price n.d.).

Population projections by demographers point to a continuing growth in the Mexican borderlands. In 1970 the six Mexican border states had almost 8 million inhabitants (México DGE 1970). Some projections indicate a population of some 13 million in the region by 1980, but this estimate is excessive, because two border states, Chihuahua and Tamaulipas, experienced negative migration in the intercensal period 1960–70 (Weaver and Downing 1976: 47).

The rate of growth of most border cities in Mexico has been extraordinary. Between 1930 and 1950 Mexicali increased from 6,782 to 171,648 people. In the following decade this figure jumped by a startling 136 percent and doubled in the next fifteen years. Tijuana had 16,486 inhabitants in 1940 and 148,867 in 1960. By 1976 there were 411,643 people living in the city proper and 535,535 in the urban agglomeration. Ciudad Juárez, which counted 544,900 residents in 1976, had reported only 39,669 four decades earlier. Many of these communities and their immediate hinterlands attained a rate of growth between 1940 and 1960 in excess of 400 percent, with Tijuana probably holding the record at 750 percent (United Nations 1977: 235; Galarza et al. 1969: 12; Price [n.d.]). And there is no end in sight, especially considering the impact of the Mexican peso devaluation of 1976.

Some writers have referred to the Mexican border cities as terminal points of migratory routes to which the congested cities and the impoverished villages of central Mexico are tributary. More accurately, they should be looked upon as serving an Ellis Island function, serving as temporary asylums for Mexicans seeking admission – often on a daily basis – to the United States. Galarza and his colleagues (1969: 13) have made this clear:

That the teeming, congested *barrios* of the Mexican border cities are not truly terminal for the hopes of those who live in them is shown by one striking characteristic of economic life – the border crossings. In 1965 nearly 65,500,000 individual crossings of Mexican citizens under day permits were recorded. They crossed the international boundary to shop and to work. This figure does not include the many thousands of men and women who cross illegally to work on the American side.

The question of illegal entries was discussed earlier in this chapter. The day permits referred to by Galarza concern commuters.

A special issue that affects border conditions and sentiment is the problem of commuters who live in Mexico and work in the United States. Commuters may be Mexican (or other) nationals, or they may be United States citizens (including naturalized Mexican-Americans) who live south of the border. If they are aliens they are usually green-card holders; that is, at each crossing they present an alien registration card that shows that they are legally admitted immigrants and can therefore work and live in the United States. Some of the commuters are blue-card holders, who are permitted to cross the border for periods not to exceed seventy-two hours (Grebler et al. 1970: 73).

No one knows how many regular commuters there are. Statistics kept by the Immigration and Naturalization Service cover all legal border crossings – shoppers, entertainment seekers, people visiting their relatives, and those on business trips, as well as workers. Each entry, no matter what the purpose, is counted separately; no notation is made of repeated crossings by the same individual. Thus, United States officials have yet to produce any continuous, reliable data on the number of Mexicans who commute to work in the United States. "It is astonishing to find that this statistics-minded nation has failed to develop measurements of important border transactions that could be easily supplied by means of modern data gathering and data-processing techniques" (Grebler et al. 1970: 73). In the absence of reliable data, observers and analysts have made varying guesses on the number of commuters who cross the border regularly to work – from 20,000 to 120,000 – depending on the purpose of the guess and the definition used of the word "regularly."

In any case, the policy issues posed by this movement are highly complex, and the commuter problem has accordingly received Congressional and other public attention. A drastic curtailment of commuting would have serious repercussions on the economic base of some American border cities. For example, in the absence of the low-wage workers who commute from Mexico, El Paso and Brownsville, Texas would probably not be logical locations for garment factories. If such businesses closed, as some of them have recently, the adverse effects on the entire local economy could be considerable. Moreover, commuters are important customers of retail stores on the American side of the border. If commuting were blocked, the Mexican government might make it more difficult for Mexican nationals to cross the border for shopping. "Thus, on balance, the local economy might be stronger with than without the commuting system even if it involved spending more tax money to support unemployed domestic workers and their families" (Grebler et al. 1970: 73–4).

Expenditures by Mexican nationals on the U.S. side of the border are not limited to local shoppers. The wholesale and retail establishments in these American border towns cater to a market that extends deep into Mexico. The town of Laredo on the Rio Grande, which is also on a major highway that connects to the interior of Mexico, is one example of this far-reaching trade. Mexicans from Monterrey and even beyond come to Laredo to make special purchases, mostly in the clothing stores of that city (Fernández 1977: 121). Recent tightening of customs procedures in Nuevo

Laredo (on the Mexican side of the border) has put a crimp in the trade of merchants on the U.S. side. But the seemingly insatiable appetite of Mexicans for brand-name items led to nearly $500 million in Laredo sales in 1978 (*Financial Trend,* January 15–21, 1979, 1–2).

Thus, while the flow of labor resources northward is the principal element in what has been termed the "border equation," other elements are also important. We have noted the flow of Mexican workers' wages into retail establishments on the U.S. side of the border and the dependence of this retail trade on a wider Mexican region. Also important are the flow of agricultural production from Mexican border states into the United States, the contribution of tourist dollars to the trade economy of Mexican border towns, the direct technological dependence of Mexican industry upon U.S. industry, and a host of illegal activities and enterprise (Fernández 1977: 119).

Raúl Fernández, a political economist, contends that current thinking about the economic lessons of the postwar period for Latin America (and the rest of the backward nations) is taking the direction of a "new orthodoxy":

The new orthodoxy which is slowly emerging presents the following prescriptions to remedy Latin America's ills: a) import substitution to be abandoned in favor of policies that promote the export of manufactured goods; b) planning and restrictions are to be deemphasized in favor of freer utilization of the "market mechanisms" for national development; and c) foreign capital is welcome, but it will be subject to restrictions designed to "guide" its route so that its introduction will benefit the host nation. [Fernández 1977: 133]

One manifestation of this "new orthodoxy" may be the Border Industrial Program.

The Border Industrial Program

The seeds of the Border Industrial Program (BIP) may be found in legislation by the Mexican and U.S. governments some twenty years ago. By the end of the 1950s it was clear that the northern border zone of Mexico faced complex urban problems requiring intervention by the Mexican federal government. The *Programa Nacional Fronterizo* (PRONAF) represents an effort by the republic since 1961 to strengthen the integration of its border regions, especially the north, within the national economy, particularly the major municipalities. From Tijuana to Matamoros, United States twin cities face their Mexican counterparts across the international boundary, and except at Tijuana, the U.S. city in each pair is smaller. A history of relatively free exchange between each pair of twin cities has made them not individual entities but divided cities that must be viewed inseparably (Dillman 1970: 48).

The rising trend in commuter traffic into the more advanced economy of the U.S. border zone spurred passage of Senate Bill 2790, allowing entry of permanent resident aliens only to districts whose wages and working conditions were not adversely affected by Mexican commuters. By the mid-1960s, the Mexican government foresaw progressive tightening of entrance requirements and consequent inability of the Mexican centers to provide added jobs in a region with 25 to 30 percent unemployment. As a result, the Border Development Program was established within the broader scope of PRONAF in 1965. It went into full operation in 1967 (Dillman 1970: 49).

The purpose of the program was to attract U.S. industries to border cities, each having free-zone status, to which machinery and raw materials could be imported duty free. Under the program, entirely owned subsidiaries of foreign companies could lease property within sixty miles of the border. To qualify for tax exemptions, participating firms had to export processed or manufactured items without duty, except that on value added to goods finished by Mexican labor. All goods brought into the border zone were classified as part of Mexico's tourist expenditures abroad rather than as imports. Goods taken from the zone to the United States were not designated as exports but regarded as tourist revenue for Mexico (Dillman 1970: 49).

The advantages of the BIP for Mexico were officially seen as: (1) the appearance of new jobs and larger incomes; (2) the introduction of modern methods of manufacturing; and (3) the increase in consumption of Mexican raw materials (Fernández 1977: 134). At the start of the program there were 72 authorized American-owned plants (*maquiladoras*) operating in Mexico. By the mid-1970s over 470 border plants were in existence, with a total investment estimated at close to $1 billion (American billion) (Van der Spek 1975: 33).

The BIP ceased to be a border program when the Mexican government extended it to a twenty-kilometer-wide coastal strip in 1971 and to the whole country in November 1972 (the so-called in-bond industries). In 1973, exports were estimated at approximately $400 million. The vast majority of the plants are located on the area bordering the United States (Fernández 1977: 134–5).

Van der Spek concluded that "Mexico's in-bond program has proven to be advantageous, not only to Mexico and to many of the U.S. plants that have been established along the border, but also to the zone on the U.S. side of the border. Proof of benefits is the widening of the scope of the program by the Mexican government, the rapid growth of the number of plants, the successive expansion of many plants, and the promotion of the program by U.S. border cities" (Van der Spek 1975: 47).

Yet apparently all is not well. Baerresen (1975: 82–3) states that the advantages associated with the proximity to the United States of Mexico's border cities are more than offset for many companies by lower wage rates in other countries competing with Mexico for this type of investment. Wages in Mexico have risen dramatically. The effect of these increases on border industrialization has been a shift of investment from the higher wage-rate areas of the border to lower wage-rate areas of the interior, delay or curtailment of new investment in the program, increase of investment in other countries, retention in the United States of investment that was destined for Mexico, and withdrawal of investment from Mexico.

Baerresen thus sees the Mexican government facing a serious dilemma: When it raises wage rates in order to dampen domestic dissatisfaction it also depresses job opportunities that are required to lessen that dissatisfaction:

Not only is the Border Industrialization Program influenced by changing conditions within Mexico, but also by developments north of the border. Part of Mexico's inflation results from inflation in the United States through purchase there of approximately 60 percent of Mexico's imports. The current economic recession in the United States has led to sharp declines in demand for some products assembled in border industry plants, and there have resulted layoffs of many workers. Moreover, the viability of the Program is largely dependent upon certain United States import policies. [1975: 83]

The extent to which organized labor in the United States can exert enough pressure to limit and control the expansion of the BIP is limited by the extent to which organized U.S. labor can be partner to U.S. government interests. To some it appears that the unspoiled workforce that lured companies to the border fifteen years ago has undergone some changes. Thus, North American companies in Mexico feel that Mexican labor today – like U.S. labor a few years ago – is killing the goose that laid the golden egg of border manufacturing. "In fact," says Fernández, "many feel that the goose is already dead and that it is only a matter of time before the border cities become ghost towns. Thus, between October 1974 and April 1975, thirty-nine U.S.-owned assembly plants closed down operations along the Mexican border, while many others cut their work force by as much as 50 percent. More than 23,000 workers were laid off in less than 10 months with employment down by 30 percent in Tijuana and Mexicali" (1977: 148).

This pessimism may be premature. Companies from the Far East are showing heightened interest in twin-plant operations along the Mexican–U.S. border, although it is too early to call this a trend (*Financial Trend,* November 13–19, 1978: 1). Several European companies with established U.S. distribution points have set up operations in the Juárez Industrial Park, just across from El Paso. A Polish company has been negotiating to manufacture boats in Ensenada, a Spanish firm wants to make champagne in Baja California, and some Asian firms are investigating possible locations for electronic plants along the border. In mid-1978 a group of South Korean businessmen toured the border, collecting information about Mexican manufacturing operations and the BIP policy of allowing businesses to import components without paying duties, assemble them into completed products, and ship them to customers on the U.S. side of the border. By the end of 1978, eighty-five U.S. companies were asking Mexico's permission to launch twin-plant operations that would employ twelve thousand new workers. Not all Mexican industrialists welcome the plants, finding it difficult to compete with foreign companies for labor. However, President José López Portillo has extended the program through 1985 (*Financial Trend,* loc. cit.).

Assimilation and acculturation of Mexican Americans

The idea of a melting pot, state Nathan Glazer and Daniel Patrick Moynihan (1963: 288), is as old as the American republic.[12] They quote Michel-Guillaume Jean de Crèvecoeur, who, in *Letters from an American Farmer* (1782), wrote, "I could point out to you a family whose grandfather was an Englishman, whose wife was Dutch, whose son married a French woman, and whose present four sons have now four wives of different nations. *He* is an American, who leaving behind him all his ancient prejudices and manners, receives new ones from the new mode of life he has embraced . . . Here individuals of all nations are melted into a new race of men."

The melting pot was an idea dear to the hearts of Americans, but as a century passed and the number of individuals and nationalities grew, the confidence that they could be fused together lessened, as did the conviction that it would be a good thing if they did. We noted the passage of the Chinese Exclusion Act in 1882 and the subsequent raising of barriers until, with the National Origins Act of 1924, the nation formally adopted a policy of using immigration to reinforce rather than dilute the racial stock of America (Glazer and Moynihan 1963: 288–9).

The term "melting pot" originated, or at least became popularized, in a play by Israel Zangwill, *The Melting Pot,* first performed in 1908. The process of restrictionism was well underway by that date. Glazer and Moynihan speculate that the success of the play, which exulted the glory of America, "God's Crucible, the great Melting Pot, where all the races of Europe are melting and reforming!" was as much a reaction of relief as of affirmation – more a reassurance that what had already taken place would turn out all right than encouragement to carry on in the same direction (1963: 289).

The melting pot was an apocalyptic vision of a real America homogenized by the full assimilation of its foreign stock. Wrote Zangwill:

Here you stand, good folk, think I, when I see them at Ellis Island, here you stand in your fifty groups with your fifty languages and histories, and your fifty blood hatreds and rivalries, but you won't be long like that brothers, for these are the fires of God you've come to – these are the fires of God. A fig for your feuds and vendettas! German and Frenchman, Irishman and Englishman, Jews and Russians – into the Crucible with you all! God is making the American ... The real American has not yet arrived. He is only in the Crucible, I tell you – he will be the fusion of all the races, the coming superman. [Zangwill 1913: 37–8]

The "real American" would presumably be free of ethnic labels. Glazer and Moynihan observed that perhaps these labels and their meaning will yet be erased in America, but this has not yet occurred. It may be true that distinctive language and culture are largely lost in the first and second generations, and this makes the dream of cultural pluralism as unlikely as the hope of a melting pot:

As groups were transformed by influences in American society, stripped of their original attributes, they were recreated as something new, but still as identifiable groups. Concretely, persons think of themselves as members of that group, with that name; they are thought of by others as members of that group, with that name; and most significantly, they are linked to other members of the group by new attributes that the original immigrants would never have recognized as identifying their group, but which nevertheless serve to mark them off, by more than simply name and association, in the third generation and even beyond. The assimilating power of American society and culture operated on immigrant groups in different ways, to make them, it is true, something they had not been, but still something distinct and identifiable ... *The ethnic group in American society became not a survival from the age of mass immigration but a new social form.* [Glazer and Moynihan 1963: 13–16; their emphasis]

Attempting to fit Mexican Americans into a scheme that assumes ultimate full assimilation is no more profitable than to force them into a pattern that assumes no assimilation whatever: The classification of an ethnic group as a collective entity serves the limited purpose of enabling one to see the group's problems in the perspective of the problems of other groups; such an approach is especially useful in the case of a little-known minority (Grebler et al. 1970: 577).[13]

The studies by Grebler and his colleagues give the following portrait of acculturation or assimilation of Mexican Americans, putting them into perspective with other ethnic groups over time. They share with blacks the disadvantages of poverty, economic insecurity, and discrimination. Problems of adaptation, especially the difficulty of acquiring an adequate command of English, were experienced by many other immigrant groups to the United States. Like all other poor and uneducated people, Mexican Americans have the frustrations of coping with bureaucracy – even of the benevolent kind – especially in the modern world of impersonal government forms, documents, and computers. Their status as an ethnic minority has been compounded by religious-minority status, as was that of Catholic immigrants from Italy and Ireland. Like other subordinated groups, past and present, they have experienced obstacles to attaining influence at all levels of government (Grebler et al. 1970: 577). The authors could have added that, in addition to language, religion, and education, Mexican Americans, Puerto Ricans, and others of non-European stock have had to bear the stigma of dark skin, which further hinders assimilation or acculturation.[14]

In many cases, Grebler's analysis was able to measure the severity of the Mexican Americans' problems in comparison with those of other identifiable subpopulations. One example cited is housing. Throughout the major Southwestern cities, Mexican housing segregation from Anglos is significantly less extreme than the segregation of blacks from whites. Since residential location is considered a fairly reliable indicator of general social segregation, this finding is important in defining the place of Mexican Americans in U.S. society. On the other hand, Mexicans fall well below other minorities on certain measures of acculturation: there is a high proportion of first- and second-generation persons in the population, and the naturalization rate among the foreign-born is low. Except for Puerto Ricans, Mexican Americans purportedly retain their native language more persistently than any other major ethnic population on the United States mainland. Their average school attainment is substantially poorer than that of blacks and well below that of Asians (1970: 577).

Mexican American incomes tend to be higher than nonwhite or black incomes. Their occupational structure is also less depressed than that of blacks. But Mexicans are plagued by all the problems of a population with a large proportion of low-skilled workers: a high rate of under- and unemployment and declining income with advancing age. Their per capita income is far lower than that of nonwhites or blacks – "a consequence of one of the most distinctive characteristics of this population: exceedingly high fertility (and, by implication, a high birth rate) and the prevalence of unusually large families. Low income per person in the family, in turn, accounts for an extremely high incidence of poor, overcrowded housing and probably a great many other serious consumption deficiencies (which we were unable to identify and measure)" (Grebler et al. 1970: 577).

The authors point out that, in comparison with other immigrants, even the southern and eastern European immigrants of the late nineteenth and early twentieth centuries, Mexican Americans have had little time for acculturation. This contention is at least debatable; however, the point is well taken that the initial concentration of Mexicans in rural areas and agricultural work contrasts sharply with the earlier immigrants' direct movement to the cities and urban employment. Rural concentration limited the opportunities for Mexicans and, as Grebler and associates maintain, "limited their opportunities to become acculturated. Rural settlement retarded the education of their children, made it far more difficult for them to consolidate their position through labor organization, restricted their job mobility, and kept them from attaining political influence." (1970: 578).

Contrary to the widely held stereotype of the Mexican American enmeshed in a continuous migratory trek from Texas to regions north and westward – rootless, returning to his home briefly only to prepare for next season's sojourn – the Mexican American is becoming increasingly a sedentary city dweller. True, many Mexican laborers are forced, or voluntarily choose, to follow the traditional migratory paths, but in the past quarter century Mexican Americans have become urbanized more rapidly than Anglos or blacks. That is, a larger percentage of their population has been moving to urban centers. As Grebler and his associates stated:

A population once dependent largely on agriculture is now so greatly linked with city life that many of its problems mirror the problems of urban America. And although on balance the group has benefited from the rural–urban shift, the transition has been associated with the usual personal stresses of adjustment to the city, and compounded by the problems of minority status and often by language handicaps. Formal and impersonal controls enforced by an anonymous urban officialdom have replaced the informal and person-to-person contacts with authority in rural areas. There is a world of perplexing and ego-wounding forms and documents. City living compounds the problems of transportation and schooling. The new urban milieu often has a disruptive influence on family life. [Grebler et al. 1970: 112]

Conclusion

In this book we have been primarily concerned with the process of Latin American urbanization in its several dimensions, including the demographic, sociocultural, economic, and political. It would be a mistake to conclude, however, that the city and the forces that shape it can be understood in isolation. In the final analysis, urbanization blends into processes of national change and development and international dependency, and Latin American cities must be viewed in their broader societal contexts. A thorough examination of the relationships between urbanization and other processes of change affecting Latin American nations today lies beyond the scope of this volume. In closing, however, we wish to indicate the general ways in which social scientists have conceived of these relationships. The knowledge we possess about urban Latin America is directly linked to the methods and theories (and the values that underlie them) that investigators have brought to the research task. And like the city itself, these methods and theories are changing rapidly.

The Argentinian city planner Oscar Yujnovsky (1976: 18–22) argues that the principal orientations in Latin American urban studies have been heavily influenced by socioeconomic and political changes in the region. The pioneering studies of the 1950s were grounded in concepts of economic development. Emphasis at that time was placed on the problems and supposed pathologies brought about by urbanization, such as unemployment, lack of housing and public services, anomie, family disorganization, and delinquency. Empirical studies of these and other topics, however, soon showed that urban Latin Americans were not nearly as pessimistic about city life as were the investigators. The problems were and are real enough, but so are a healthy variety of creative solutions of the grassroots sort, and the preoccupation with social pathologies began to show signs of ethnocentrism.

The 1960s ushered in a new wave of optimism regarding the urbanization process. Widespread faith in the eventual triumph of "modernization" in Latin America and the rest of the Third World transformed the old urban problems into temporary maladjustments that would soon be straightened out. Instead of a dependent variable of development, the city was now viewed as an independent variable – a prime catalyst of change in the modernization process. Rapid urbanization was both necessary and beneficial, it was argued, since only the large metropolitan centers could accommodate the people, the economic infrastructure, and the industrial plant required for modernization to proceed.

The 1970s ushered in a time of uncertainty during which many urbanists critically reexamined many of the basic tools of their trade. By now it has become painfully clear that urbanization is not coterminous with national development but may often generate new forms of underdevelopment and inequality. The optimism of the 1960s faded with the realization that in their haste to analyze the change wrought by urbanization social scientists had overlooked the persistence of many forms of inequality, hierarchy, and domination. If the terms "problems of development" and "modernization" best describe the ideological orientations of the 1950s and 1960s, the concept of "dependency" is the emerging frontier in Latin American urban research today.

Dependency theory is a neo-Marxist point of view that purports to explain the lack of economic growth in the underdeveloped world (see Frank 1966; Frank 1969; Sunkel and Paz 1970; Chilcote and Edelstein 1974). Latin American scholars have been instrumental in demonstrating that the prophecies of the optimistic modernization paradigm have gone unfulfilled. Many of the problems (if not the supposed pathologies) of urbanization not only persist but have been exacerbated by adverse international political and economic trends and the failure of development schemes. The intensification of social conflicts in many countries, the strengthening of the Cuban Revolution, and the swift rise and fall of Allende's Chile have also played a part in stimulating the search for an alternative to orthodox theories of development.

Although dependency theory now assumes many guises, its basic premise is that underdevelopment in Latin America is itself a particular type of capitalist development. Underdevelopment stems from an international division of labor, articulated by the world capitalist market, that encourages economic growth in some countries and discourages it in others. The process began with the centuries-long exploitation of Latin America by the Iberian colonial powers and continues today through dominance by neocolonial industrial powers, especially the United States. As a result, much of Latin America is dependent on crucial economic and political decisions that are made far beyond its borders in cities such as London, New York, Washington, Paris, Moscow, and Tokyo. Foreign investors and multinational corporations have siphoned off a large portion of the profits generated in the Latin American economies, leaving the countries themselves with an insufficient supply of capital, technology, and skilled personnel. Historically, developed Western nations have been most interested in the raw materials and agricultural products that could be extracted from Latin America's mines and plantations.

Consequently, most nations in the region continue to rely heavily on exports of a small number of extractive commodities. This has had two results: (1) Latin American nations are dependent for their foreign earnings on goods whose prices are notoriously unstable; and (2) the overall terms of trade have moved against their interests, for while the prices of raw commodities fluctuate both upward and downward, the prices of the manufactured products for which they are exchanged have been moving in only one direction – up (Wolf and Hansen 1973: 6). The central point of dependency theory is therefore that continued development in the already industrialized capitalist nations – especially the United States – tends to perpetuate underdevelopment and inequality within the Latin American nations. It follows from this premise that no Latin American city can be fully understood unless the nature of its dependence on the world capitalist system is investigated.

The implications of this perspective for the study of urbanization have only begun to be explored, but the approach may be said to rest on two fundamental postulates: (1) urbanization in Latin America must be regarded as a dependent social formation within the capitalistic world system; and (2) the appropriate units of analysis are not geographical entities such as cities or villages, but processes that link together a hierarchy of core–periphery relationships stretching from the international level down to the rural hinterlands of the smallest provincial cities. Dependency theory thus bids us to examine cities as "nodes in a process of surplus extraction, expropriating resources from their hinterlands for purposes of packaging and subsequent transmission" (Walton 1975: 47). In this hierarchy of dominance, provincial urban centers exploit their hinterlands, the primate cities of the region in turn dominate these provincial cities, and the far-off industrial capitals of the world exercise a degree of control that limits the autonomy of both by means of a kind of chain reaction. John Walton (1975: 47–8) summarizes the results:

Urban social structures, at least in Latin America, tend to amplify the differences between social classes. Marginal service sectors and the working class expand while industrial and export elites draw away from a reduced middle class under the support of transnational enterprise. On the physical side, land prices skyrocket from upper class speculation resulting in further overcrowding against which calculated land invasions at certain vulnerable points become the only recourse for the homeless. And all of this has less to do with competition in the marketplace than with monopolization and power.

Although it is still only in its infancy as far as urban studies are concerned, dependency theory helps us to understand the highly uneven pattern of development in Latin America. It helps explain why urban hierarchies, instead of promoting stability, social integration, and national unity, seem instead to be a major polarizing influence in the early 1980s. In a very real sense, urban development in Latin America has occurred partially at the expense of rural areas. As cities have expanded during the last several decades, large portions of the countryside have stagnated, much of their resources and many of their most talented people being funneled into the urban centers. The same pattern of dominance and dependency is replicated at the national level, where until very recently the large primate cities have developed at a much faster pace than the smaller provincial towns that exist in their shadows. To understand why this is so we must think not in terms of discrete units such as the nation or city, but of hierarchical relationships where each node in the chain can thrive (or maintain itself) only by dominating those below it to some degree. Hence, we find that in Latin America, "the elitist character of urban social structure has remained, despite major processes of differentiation and growth" (Portes and Walton 1976: 170). Large-scale migration and industrialization have not subverted the tight elitist control over political and economic structures. This control continues in part because the urban elites themselves are dependent on external sources of support. Dependency theorists have cogently argued that no really fundamental change can occur at the upper levels of national urban hierarchies in Latin America unless there are real changes at the international level. Only by decreasing their dependence on external capital and technology can these cities begin to gain control of their own destinies.

The situation of many of the smaller provincial towns and cities may be different, however. Little systematic research has been carried out in this area, but Bryan Roberts's (1976) recent work in the small Peruvian city of Huancayo may serve as a model for future studies. In this case, Roberts found considerable evidence of local urban autonomy and warns that we must beware of applying dependency concepts in too top-heavy a fashion. Roberts believes that Huancayo exemplifies a class of small, commercially oriented cities in Latin America that are not well integrated into their respective national economies and therefore are only loosely articulated with the hierarchy of dependency. The small-scale, labor-intensive, and heavily personalized nature of economic relationships in such towns creates a kind of informal structure that in turn helps maintain a degree of independence from the dominant national urban hierarchy. The case of Huancayo suggests the hypothesis that the degree of relative urban autonomy at the local level will vary in accord with each country's degree of incorporation into the world capitalist system. Generalizing for Latin America as a whole, Roberts (1976: 100–1) concludes that:

the economic and social transformation entailed by capitalist development is not only more restricted in its scope but also less hierarchically organized than was perhaps the case in the countries of Europe in their period of urbanization. Consequently, the strength and permanence of unanticipated responses to current urbanization may be greater than has been supposed.

In any case, it is clear that the future of the Latin American city will be decidedly different from that of its modern Euro-American counterpart. In the developed Western nations, urbanization has historically been to a large degree a correlate of industrialization. But the Latin American experience is different: Here the process of urban growth is less a result of nascent industrialism than of stagnant agriculture. Latin American urbanization is symptomatic not of forward-looking national integration but of growing imbalances, excessive centralization, and inequality (Portes and Walton 1976: 169). The Latin American city – and many cities in Asia and parts of Africa – is an "underdeveloped city," to use the phrase of Mexican demographer Victor L. Urquidi (1975), although the terms "colonial city" or "dependent city" would serve just as well.

Dependent capitalism, high rates of population growth, and massive movements of people from rural to urban areas have fostered a pattern of urban growth *without* development, "if the latter term is taken to mean an organic, purposeful pattern of change that may contribute to solid economic advance and greater well-being without creating painful imbalances or producing new forms of social ills" (Urquidi 1975: 340). This observation is even more compelling when we consider Urquidi's projections that the Latin American urban population as a whole is bound to double every fifteen years, and that by the year 2000 nearly half of the total population may be living in cities of five hundred thousand or more, which would be about twice the ratio for the world as a whole.

It goes without saying that strategies for urban planning and development must take these factors into account, for they are not likely to change for some time. It is not our purpose to address policy issues in this book, and it would be premature to make specific predictions about the future. But we do believe that the important solutions to the problems of Latin American urbanization in the years to come will be social rather than technological. Such changes will not happen automatically according to some preordained plan of urban evolution, nor will they all fall within the jurisdiction of municipal governments. They will require careful deliberation, planning, and sacrifice at the local, regional, national, and international levels.

Notes

Preface

1   William Mangin (1970) speaks of "peasants in cities." McGee and others
    have questioned Mangin's usage of this term. McGee says that Mangin
    appears to challenge conventional interpretation of peasants as rural people:
    "Hence the paradox – for if in truth peasants are rural people, how can they
    be urban?" He believes that "Mangin's arguments are simply a masquerade
    of the increasingly criticized Redfield–Tönnies approach" (McGee 1973:
    136)
2   Luis Alberto Sánchez has given us an example of the "city as den of iniquity"
    approach: The old agrarian tradition of Latin American is being broken "by
    the absorbing attraction of the large cities that bewitches countrymen,
    drawing them out of their natural environment without offering the compen-
    sations that industry creates. Such historical development is taking place
    before everyone's eyes and is meeting with everyone's indifference. In reality,
    the preeminence given to agrarian reform is justified, inasmuch as it tackles a
    permanent condition, an endemia; but nonetheless, the crisis of urban growth
    must be give higher priority because it constitutes a mortal growth, an
    epidemic. Following medical terms and procedures, we must attack the
    epidemics aggressively and at the same time treat the endemias systematical-
    ly" (Sánchez 1967: 30).

1. The city in history

1   The interested reader is referred to Jorge Hardoy's comprehensive *Pre-
    Columbian cities* (1973).
2   Jorge Hardoy (1975) has also presented a model of six "stages" of Latin
    American urbanization from pre-Hispanic times to the present, emphasizing
    their size and general functions.
3   Richard Morse (1975b) discusses various sorts of dichotomies for the analysis
    of Latin American urbanization, but only the industrial–preindustrial will be
    mentioned here. We favor the approach of Richard Fox (1977) – see note 4.
4   Richard G. Fox (1977) has recently presented a fivefold typology of urban
    social organization that improves considerably upon the dichotomous schemes
    of Sjoberg and Redfield and Singer. Fox distinguishes among regal-ritual,
    administrative, mercantile, colonial, and industrial cities.
5   The best introduction to the role of capitalism in the formation of Mexican
    colonial society remains Eric Wolf's *Sons of the shaking earth* (1959).
6   Developing a line of thought from the earlier paper, Morse (1973: 4–26)
    outlines some points of departure for a comparative analysis of urbanization in
    Latin America during the nineteenth century. In companion papers in the
    same volume, Moreno Toscano and Aguirre Anaya examine migration to
    Mexico City in the nineteenth century, and Cowell examines cityward

migration to Recife, Brazil, in the same century. Conniff (1975: 65–81) attempts a new approach to urban social dynamics in his study of voluntary associations in Rio from 1870 to 1945, and Stann (1975: 82–100) examines the problem of urbanization in Caracas from 1891 to 1936. Hardoy and Langdon (1978: 115–74) undertake an ambitious statistical analysis of urbanization in Latin America between 1850 and 1930. Their article is particularly recommended for its list of sources on population statistics.

7   These data were complied from viceregal, national, and regional censuses, estimates of travelers and residents, and from data published in government tracts. The authors note that statistics for nineteenth-century Latin America are notoriously inaccurate.

8   A "primate city" is one that towers above the other groups of cities within a country (see Morse 1965: 47–8 for a more detailed explication). Morse notes that, except for Brazil, neither the size of a country nor the size of its "urban system" has any systematic influence on its urban pattern.

9   Sources differ on these as well as most other figures. A city's population, for example, may be cited as those people living within the "city proper"or in the "urban agglomeration" (the "greater metropolitan area").

10 There is no accepted definition or usage of the terms "urban" and "rural," universally throughout Latin America. In Mexico, "urban" refers to localities of twenty-five hundred or more inhabitants. In Brazil, the term is employed for administrative centers of *municipios* and districts. Capitals of districts are classified as urban in Peru, as well as populated centers with such characteristics as streets, plazas, water supply systems, electric lights. (See United Nations 1974: 126 for designations employed by other nations in Latin America.)

The Department of Economic and Social Affairs of the United Nations warns readers of its *Demographic Yearbook* that the designation of areas as urban or rural is so closely bound up with historical, political, cultural, and administrative considerations that the process of developing uniform definitions and procedures moves very slowly. Not only do the definitions differ one from the other, but, in actual fact, they may no longer reflect the original intention of distinguishing urban from rural. The criteria once established on the basis of administrative subdivisions (as most of them are) become fixed and resistant to change. For this reason, comparisons of data over time may be invalidated by the inapplicability of the definition to current circumstances. Special care must be taken in comparing data from censuses with those from sample surveys because of the likelihood that the definitions of "urban" or "rural" are not comparable (United Nations 1974: 21).

In a curiously ambiguous afternote, the publication states that "no matter how they are defined, *urban* is likely to include a heavy concentration of clearly urban population, while *rural* will be heavily weighted towards village or clearly rural areas. Thus, the differences between urban and rural characteristics of the population, though not precisely measured, will tend to be reflected in the statistics" (21). One is almost tempted to take seriously Mangin's comment that "a city is a place that when you are in it you know, especially if you are downtown" (Mangin 1970: xiv), but he admits that such a definition may be too frivolous. Nevertheless, there is growing agreement that the term "urban" should refer to agglomerations of twenty thousand people or more.

2. Why people move

1 Among those consulted are Arias and Alcalá 1973: 3; Bradfield 1973: 360–1; Browning and Feindt 1971: 49; Butterworth 1962: 260–1; Butterworth 1969: passim; Campiglia 1967: 66; Chen 1968: 167; Cornelius 1976b: 3; Doughty 1963: 115; Elizaga 1966: 352; Elizaga 1970: 88; Feindt and Browning 1972: 49; Flinn 1966: 8; Germani 1961: 212; Herrick 1965: 42; Kemper 1975: 228; Kemper 1977: 51, Lomnitz 1973: 60, López 1968: 83; Margulis 1967: 78; Margulis 1968: 101; Matos Mar 1961: 183; Métraux 1956: 392; Molina 1965: 12–13; Perlman 1976: 67–8; Preston 1969: 282; Recaséns Siches 1955: 365; Rivarola 1967: 10–13; Romero and Flinn 1976: 37; Solari 1958: 526; Usandizaga and Havens 1966: 42; Van Es and Flinn 1973: 16; Viale 1960: 141–8, M. Whiteford 1976b: 15; and Wilkening 1968: 692. A cross-cultural review of the literature is contained in Connell et al. 1976.

2 In this connection, see the articles in the volume on internal migration in Brazil edited by Manoel Augusto Costa (1971). Of special interest is the contribution in that volume by Douglas Graham, "Algunas considerações econômicas para a policítica migratória no meio brasileiro," (13–43).

3 Shaw (1974: 123–8) has attempted an empirical test of a model relating land tenure to migration in Latin America. Briefly, the model applies to Latin American economies with a high rate of rural natural increase, a large proportion of the rural agricultural population in minifundia or landless employee class, and a large share of the agricultural land held by latifundistas. A basic premise is that the nature of productive organization on latifundias has conditioned the cost, use, availability, and development of land to the extent that social and economic opportunities for the majority of the rural agricultural population have been stifled. Accordingly, a large proportion of rural agricultural laborers likely to be subjected to limited employment opportunities owing to the institutional system of land tenure, and, in combination with rapid population growth, conditions of economic stress are likely to evolve, followed by high rates of rural emigration.

   Based mainly on statistical analysis at the rural provincial level for Chile, Peru, and Costa Rica from periods from the 1940s to the 1960s, Shaw found that Chile and Peru had an extremely unequal distribution of labor to land resources. Costa Rica had one of the most even. Therefore, one would expect much higher rates of rural emigration in Chile and Peru than in Costa Rica. The empirical results generally accorded with this expectation.

4 See Rojos and de la Cruz 1978: 49–66.

3. Who moves from where

1 Mangalam and Schwarzweller (1969: 7) note that an important development in the study of migration is the greater diversity of variables used in research dealing with this complex phenomenon. They add that this is especially true in studies on the selectivity of migration. In addition to such "traditional" (i.e., demographically relevant) variables as age, sex, distance travelled, ethnicity, education, occupation, and income, recent studies reveal an expansion of interest in attitudes, aspirations, motivations, values, community identification, institutional influences, and other social and sociopsychological factors intrinsic to an adequate explanation of migration. Unfortunately, this trend is still in its infancy in Latin American studies.

2 Bogue (1963: 405) observes that it is essential to differentiate between rate of migration (volume of movement)and differentials in migration (selectivity of movement).

3 Bogue reported: "It is widely appreciated that migration is highly selective of younger persons. This arises because each oncoming generation must adapt to the social and economic changes that are taking place. This is the price that neophytes must pay to get an acceptable and secure 'niche' in the social organization. When these changes require a shift of population, it is the younger, more flexible, and less burdened members who re-examine the distributional imbalance and make the needed improvements. As a corollary of this, if marital status is determined before migration, it is found that migrants tend to be single, widowed, or divorced persons rather than married" (Bogue 1963: 410). This dictum is based mainly on U.S. data. Its mechanistic equilibrium bias was criticized in Chapter 2.

4 According to a study by Margulis (1968: 144), 86.4 percent of migrants to Buenos Aires from La Rioja Province were 30 years of age or under. Drawing upon various Colombian sources, McGreevey (1968: 218) observed that the great majority of people heading toward cities in that nation are in the 15-to-34 age bracket. Michael Whiteford's comparison of two barrios in Popayán, Colombia, showed that the arrivals tend to be young adults, averaging about 22 years in one of the barrios (Tulcán) and 25 years in the other (Alberto Lleras) (M. Whiteford 1976a: 98–9). Flinn's analysis of his Bogotá data (1966: 30) is in agreement with these trends in Colombia, as are those of Simmons and Cardona (1968: 7) and Martine (1975: 193). Schultz (1971: 157) also found that migration was age-selective in Colombia. Women appear to leave the rural areas and arrive in the cities at a somewhat younger age than men, but their net departure rate from towns is later than that for men. (The distinction in the literature between city and town, and town and village, is as blurred as that between rural and urban. It becomes more of a problem when translating from the Spanish – *pueblo* can be translated as "village," "town," or, more broadly, "community." The problem is compounded by the circumstance that in British usage, "town" is often equivalent to "city," while in American English, it more often means "village.")

Escobar and Magrassi (1969: 35) report that the highest tendency to migrate from Villa María, Córdoba, is among young single women. Recchini de Lattes (1972: 590) showed that previous to 1915, migrants to Buenos Aires were mostly male, but after 1935 mostly female. Positive selection of women in migration to urban centers has also been reported for Colombia (Flinn 1966: 30; McGreevey 1968: 218; Martine 1975: 193; Schultz 1971: 151–63; and Cardona 1968: 7). For Chile see Elizaga 1966: 353; Elizaga 1970: 487; Herrick 1965: 73. For Brazil see Hutchinson 1963: 50. For Venezuela, Chen 1968: 135; and López Eliseo 1968: 156. For Uruguay, Solari 1958: 532. For Costa Rica, Carvajal and Geithman 1974: 106–7. For El Salvador, Ducoff 1962: 131. For Guatemala, Arias 1963: 403; and Roberts 1973: 66. For Mexico, Butterworth 1975a: 278; Cabrera 1972: 516; Cornelius 1976b: 8; and Kemper 1977: 60–1. For Peru, see Macisco 1975: 103–21. Hammel (1964: 351) reported that a slum in the city of Ica, Peru, had more males (largely in-migrants) than females, although data on other Lima slums show the predicted excess of females in the younger age groups. Men continue to migrate to the cities at later ages, whereas the rate for women drops sharply with age.

In one of the few studies of the place of origin of migrants rather than destination, Escobar and Magrassi (1969: 36), who worked with youth in the small city of Villa María, Córdoba, Argentina, documented that potential migrants from that center, which is both a receiver of migrants and site of departure, were young and mainly single (marital status of migrants is discussed elsewhere in Chapter 3).

Herrick (1965: 73) found that in Chile almost one-third of the migrants to Santiago arrived during their late teens, and more than six of ten were present in that city before their twenty-sixth birthday. Elizaga and his colleagues from the Centro Latinoamericano de Demografía (CELADE) have come to similar conclusions (see Elizaga 1965, 1966, 1969, 1970, 1972a, 1972b, 1972c). Reviewing CELADE studies in Santiago and in Lima, Peru, Elizaga demonstrated that there was a preponderance of young adults migrating to these cities. Between 45 and 50 percent of the migrants were 15 to 29 years of age. However, in the younger and older age groups there were disparities in the studies. For example, the proportion of women migrants under 15 years was 26 percent in Santiago and 38 percent in Lima. Earlier, Elizaga (1965: 149) compared the above two cities with Panama City for age and sex differentials. In the three nuclei considered, the highest percentage of in-migrants was of females between 15 and 29 years of age, with greatest intensity in Panama City and Greater Santiago in that category. Next in order of importance was the group between 20 and 24 years of age, in which the highest proportion of male in-migrants was found.

Campiglia (1967: 28) noted that almost 34 percent of the in-migrants to Montevideo, Uruguay, arrived when they were between 19 and 28 years of age. Population movements in Paraguay seem to correlate with the youthful demographic structure of that country (Rivarola 1967: 18–19).

Brazilian and Peruvian data also conform to the general age pattern. Brandão Lopes (1961: 237) reported that *nordestinos* in Brazil usually come south to São Paulo while in their late teens or early twenties. Garayar (1963: 30–3) noted that Peruvian migrants to cities are generally young. Hammel (1964: 351) found the same phenomenon in his study of a Peruvian slum. Stillman Bradfield looked at pairs of brothers originating in Huaylas, Peru. In each pair, one brother had migrated to either Chimbote or Lima, and the other was still resident in Huaylas. He found that the average age for men from Huaylas in Lima at the time of the survey was 40.9 and in Chimbote 39.2 (Bradfield 1973: 353–62). However, the study was limited to males and largely left uncontrolled for age; it does not tell us at what age the men left Huaylas.

Carvajal and Geithman (1974: 111–12) reported that the average age of recent migrants in Costa Rica (not necessarily people going from rural to urban regions) was significantly lower than the average age of the rest of the population. The authors put forth economic reasons for this, citing the length of the "pay-off period": younger people have more time to reach their goals.

5   This holds true for emigration from Latin America to the United States as well, if we can generalize from the findings of Wayne Cornelius. Cornelius undertook an intensive comparative study of nine rural communities in the Los Altos region of Jalisco, Mexico. The region is characterized by heavy

out-migration, and although it was selected initially because of its contribution to rural–urban population movements in Mexico, it was later found to
make a large contribution to Mexican migration to the United States. The
destinations of migrants, both within and outside of Mexico, were overwhelmingly urban, with large cities predominating, especially Guadalajara, Mexico
City, León, Los Angeles (California), and Chicago (Illinois). More than 41
percent of individual migrants leaving between January 1975 and January
1976 went to the United States. In fact, Cornelius points out, only Guadalajara exceeded Los Angeles as a destination. Most migration across the border
was temporary and involved only one or two members of a household. Only a
handful of families left for the United States. When whole families migrated,
the move tended to be permanent, regardless of destination. Both families and
individuals migrating permanently showed strong preference for large cities,
avoiding smaller ones in the same region (Cornelius 1976b: 1–11).

6   Noting criticisms of the earlier IE employment survey, Herrick's question-
naire carefully asked for residential histories. Herrick explains: "Some objec-
tions, probably justified, had been registered against the use of place-of-birth
data from the Institute's employment survey. The respondents were asked for
thier *lugar de nacimiento* (place of birth). Some observers, skeptical of the
quality of the answers, have said that respondents would tend to give the name
of the nearest big town to their birthplace or that the interviewer would tend
to repeat the question until the respondent named a town of sufficient size to
be familiar to him. To the extent that this occured, it would naturally bias the
results, making migrants' origins seem more urban than they really were"
(Herrick 1965: 52).

7   "The many instances of internal colonization in the modern world provide a
fruitful and hitherto largely neglected subject for anthropological study"
(Casagrande et al. 1964: 320).

8   Except where otherwise noted, personal names used in this volume are
pseudonyms.

4. Return migration, brokerage, and effects on the community

1   For a fascinating firsthand account of a Mexican peasant who fought for the
Zapatistas in the Revolution, the reader is referred to Oscar Lewis's *Pedro
Martínez: a Mexican peasant and his family* (1964).

2   Some student migrants return after completing basic or higher education
elsewhere. Connell et al. (1976: 126) note that student return migrants are
prone to out-migrate again, because they cannot easily find suitable uses of
their acquired skills in the village and because the wage differential between
city and village is generally quite high for them.

3   In December, 1951, by virtue of an agreement between the Peruvian Indian
Institute and Cornell Universtiy, the Peru-Cornell Project was created. Its
purpose was to conduct a program of community development and social
studies in Vicos Hacienda. With a grant from the Carnegie Institution,
Cornell and the Indian Institute leased the hacienda for five years "and began
an experiment in applied social science that has achieved world renown" (G.
Foster 1969: 29). Foster observes that project results, while perhaps not as
successful as originally planned, are impressive in comparison to community
development programs in other parts of the world (G. Foster 1969: 30). He
concludes, "Vicos is justly famous, and the Cornell Peru Vicos Project will

rank as a milestone in the development of applied social science" (Foster: 33–4).

4   A still-pertinent evaluation of this problem was presented by the International Labour Office in its report on *Why labour leaves the land* (1960).

5   One of the earliest and best studies of remittances to Mexico from the United States was conducted by Mexican anthropologist Manuel Gamio. Based on his analysis of postal money orders, Gamio estimated that since 1910 at least ten million pesos a year have been remitted by migrant workers (Gamio 1969: 30).

6. The urban class structure

1   The ethnographic studies include Hammel 1969; Hawthorne and Hawthorne 1948; Higgins 1971; Reina 1973; Royce 1975; Thompson 1974; A. Whiteford 1964; A. Whiteford 1977; Whitten 1965. For more statistically oriented analyses see González Casanova 1968; González Cosío 1961; Iturriaga 1951; Kahl 1965; Reyna, Villa, and Albrechtsen 1967; Stern and Kahl 1968; Tumin and Feldman 1971.

7. Voluntary associations

1   Kerri (1974; 1976) has brought up the "ever present problem" of finding a definition of "voluntary association" that will include the diverse ways in which research workers have viewed it. Kerri (1972: 44) earlier adopted a definition of voluntary association as "any private group voluntarily and more or less formally organized, joined and maintained by members pursuing a common interest, usually by means of part-time, unpaid activities." Anderson (1964: 175–6) has also addressed himself to this problem:

> In dealing with voluntary associations the social scientist finds himself confronted with ambiguities of definition. Some investigators do not include churches and unions while others do (Babchuk and Thompson 1962: 648). Some consider voluntary associations to be only those groups with completely voluntary membership participation and absolute independence of formal governmental control (Rose 1954: 52, 70; Axelrod 1957: 723). Others note that volition is a relative concept which cannot distinguish associations from other institutions in any consistent way (Piddington 1950: 206; Norbeck 1962: 76). Norbeck attempts to avoid these definitional obstructions by taking "common interest association" as his subject. [Norbeck 1967]

Gordon and Babchuk (1957) developed a typology of voluntary associations employing and interrelating the degree of accessibility of membership, the status-conferring capacity, and the classification of groups as "instrumental," "instrumental-expressive," and "expressive," as these relate to the functions of organizations. The Ku Klux Klan, for example, would have low status, high accessibility, and be "instrumental" in function, in that its primary purpose of existence is to carry out social change or create a normative condition.

Amis and Stern (1974: 91–9) have presented a critical examination of theory and functions of voluntary associations. They focus particular attention on the functionalist orientation, attempting to synthesize a wide range of functions attributed to voluntary associations into categories representing a limited number of central issues. The fault of this and other similar attempts at synthesizing and generalizing about these organizations lies in the lack of coverage of many geographical areas, particularly Latin America.

2   Although Kerri admits that his coverage of voluntary associations is biased in favor of certain areas of the world, it is odd that he omits most of the literature on these associations in the New World. As Dobyns (1976: 36) commented, "Latin American research offers abundant cases of transitions from kinship- and territorially based social organizations." Edward M. Bruner, writing of the Batak of Indonesia but generalizing for other regions, says that "those simplistic overgeneralized schemes which dichotomize the population into two 'groups,' of traditional vs. modern, or older generation vs. younger generation, or village-oriented vs. city-oriented, are totally inadequate as explanations" (Bruner 1973: 385). Kenneth Little, whose pionerring work on voluntary associations in West Africa has been a dominant influence in the anthropolog- ical study of associations for thirty years, has discussed the "paradoxical function" of voluntary associations (Little 1973: 407–24). For a background to his remarks, the reader is referred to Little 1949; 1959; 1964; 1965; and 1967.

3   The Mixteca is located in the eastern part of the Southern Pacific Zone of Mexico, largely in Western Oaxaca, but extending into portions of the states of Guerrero and Puebla.

4   The names of the Coalición and its president are real.

5   A member may represent either an entire community or a subdivison thereof. The basic political division in Mexico is the municipio. Within or attached to the municipio may be political categories listed as *rancherías, ranchos, congregaciones*, or *agencias*. The Mexican census has listed about 100 of these political categories (see Whetten 1948: 40–1). Any one of these categories may elect its own representative to the CPMO.

6   In his 1962 article, Butterworth mentioned that "one of the most striking aspects of the group of Tilantongueños now living in Mexico City is the complete absence of any formal or informal participation in organizations. Although Tilantongo has probably one of the largest migrant populations from the Mixteca in Mexico City, it is not an official member of the *Coalición de Pueblos Mixtecos Oaxaqueños* . . ." Some years later, Tilantongo did join the Coalición and became an influential member of the organization.

8. Housing, poverty, and politics

1   Nomenclature for squatter settlements varies from country to country: *favelas* in Brazil, *callampas* in Chile, *barriadas* or *ranchos jóvenes* in Peru, *colonias proletarias* or *colonias paracaidistas* in Mexico, *villas miserias* in Argentina, *ranchos* or *barrios* in Venezuela. Morse (1965: 49) notes that a generic name is *población* or *barrio "marginal."* The term connotes many kinds of margin- ality – geographic (peripheral location), functional (deprivation of urban services), sociological, economic and psychological – not all of which need apply in a given case. Morse observes that "the term is slightly ironic in view of the high potential for organization, self-legitimation, and inventive accom- modation to urban life which many 'marginal' communities exhibit" (Morse 1965: 49).

2   This is not to overlook the important ecological studies of Latin American cities carried out before there was an "urban anthropology," e.g., Hansen (1934) in Mérida, Hayner (1945) in Mexico City and (1948) in Oaxaca, Leonard (1948) in La Paz, and Caplow (1949) in Guatemala City.

3 Since this dictum by the Leedes, several good studies attempting to bridge this gap have appeared. See, for example, Brown 1972; Perlman 1976; Lomnitz 1977; and Peter Ward 1976. Ward's article is particularly interesting in that he views low-income housing in Mexico City as an organized series of subsystems, each having distinctive properties of location, structure, and tenure (pp. 330–46).

4 The following is a condensed version of a discussion by Butterworth (1980).

5 For a critique and evaluation in detail of the concept of the culture of poverty the reader is referred to Higgins 1974.

6 Commonly referred to as the "Moynihan Report," the document was published by the U.S. Department of Labor under the title *The Negro Family: the Case for National Action* (1965).

7 Roberts (1978: 137) reports that in Latin America recent estimates suggest that between 20 and 30 percent of the urban population have incomes insufficient for adequate levels of food and shelter. Although conditions may vary from one country to another, Roberts thinks it likely that urban conditions in other undeveloped nations are no better and are probably worse than in Latin America.

8 We use the terms "squatter settlement" and "shantytown" interchangeably (and occasionally "squatment," "self-built settlement," and "owner-built settlement" as well); in general, all are equivalent to the Spanish and Portuguese nomenclature listed in note 1 of this chapter.

9 For informative accounts and case histories of Lima invasions, see Matos Mar (1961) and Mangin's 1963 article and other publications.

10 For recent studies of employment, marginality, and differences between migrants and natives, see Balán (1969) and the various volumes of *Latin American Urban Research*, particularly the bibliographic compilations. Two reviews of recent literature dealing with these topics are worth noting: that of Daniel H. Levine and a companion piece by John Walton, both appearing in Vol. 14 (1979) of the LARR. Berlinck (1975) has written a historical interpretation of marginality and social relations in São Paulo. Portes (1979) analyzes urban poverty and the favelas of Rio de Janeiro during the period 1972–6. In a review of Perlman's work, Portes was critical of her methodological approach and "dead-horse beating" (rejection of the "culture of poverty," etc.), but concluded that her book contains many valuable and interesting contributions.

11 Here we have drawn mainly on the works of Mangin (1968); Cornelius (1975); Perlman (1976); and Goldrich, Pratt, and Schuller (1970), much of whose research provides data concerning political attitudes and behaviors in various squatter settlements within the same city, thus demonstrating the diversities manifested locally in settlements under the same supralocal government.

12 See Portes and Walton (1976: 70) and Perlman (1976). Mangin (1968: 409) also discusses such myths: "They are so pervasive that they often influence the attitudes of the squatters about themselves and about other squatters. They certainly have helped determine governmental policies toward the squatters with the increasing visibility of the settlements since World War II."

13 See Leeds (1973) for his definition of the term "locality." His definition is not specific to squatter settlements but encompasses such settlements.

14 Portes and Walton wrote individual chapters of their volume, which explains the use of the first person singular in this and other quotes. Nevertheless, we cite joint authorship throughout.

15 Inability to implement future goals has been seen as a potential precursor to a change in political attitudes of the settlers. Mangin (1968: 418) noted that "the data do indicate that they have very high aspirations for their children. If mobility is blocked and the children are not able to go on to secondary schools and move up the occupational ladder, from all indications the most likely course of events, then the political climate of *barriadas* could very well change. As of the present, they seem mobilizable only in defense of their homes."
16 See Mangin (1968: 419) and Cornelius (1974: 1132) regarding residents' perceptions that government help is necessary for the achievement of needs satisfaction.
17 See also Peattie (1968: 77), who presents a case description of demand making on behalf of a community in regard to a sewer controversy.
18 Cornelius (1975), Portes and Walton (1976), and Perlman (1976) address the the issue of associations as agents of political socialization.
19 Both Mexico and Brazil have compulsory voting laws, largely unenforced. In effect, voting serves to legitimate the existing government. However, in the Mexico City settlements cited, 44.1 percent of the migrants and 32.8 percent of the urban-born perceived voting in elections to be a civic duty (Cornelius 1975: 85). A large percentage of the favelados studied by Perlman (1976: 176) indicated a high level of support for the system. At the same time, they perceived themselves as powerless to influence the government. In the settlements of Mexico City, 60.5 percent believe that the federal government can be trusted to do what is right, 89.7 percent believe that the PRI (the political party in power) can do the most good for the people, and 50.7 percent that it has made life better for the respondents (Cornelius 1975: 56). The settlements studied by Goldrich and his colleagues (1970: 175–214) appear to be less approving of their government. Only 22 percent of the respondents in Pampa Seca and 18 percent in el Espíritu, both in Lima, felt that in general their system of government and politics was good for the country. They were even more disenchanted with the extent of help given by the officials: 57 percent in Pampa Seca and 51 percent in El Espíritu felt that no help was given by the officials. The respondents from Chile were more supportive of the system of government and politics: 65 percent in Santo Domingo and 53 percent in 3 de Mayo felt it was good for the country, while only 31 percent and 42 percent respectively felt that government officials gave no help. In Lima about half the respondents felt they could "only wait and accept government programs" (Goldrich, Pratt, and Schuller 1970: 103).
20 Safa (1974: 75) notes that "by limiting their participation to voting and other symbolic acts, shantytown residents find it easier to transfer political allegiance should their party fail to win at the polls."

9. International migration

1 Interregional migration may also be defined as migratory movement within a nation from one region to another. Lack of space and adequate data preclude a detailed consideration of this type of migration in this volume. Of the various interregional flows within Latin American countries, those in Brazil have received the greatest attention, mainly because of the availability of data. The most extensive research on interregional migration, as defined in this sense, has been undertaken by Douglas Graham and Sérgio Buarque de Hollanda Filho (Katzman 1977: 93).

2   CELADE has recently published a selected bibliography prepared by Rolando Mellafe on Italian immigration to Argentina, Brazil, and Uruguay (Mellafe 1978).

3   "Economic" and "refugee" migration are not easily distinguishable and many migrations include elements of both. But according to Appleyard (1977: 292), by far the most significant short-term migrations since the end of World War II have been refugee in character, "a fact which reflects both the significance, and the consequences, of changing world economic and political structure and conditions."

4   Economic integration in Latin America began in 1968, when Guatemala, El Salvador, Honduras, Nicaragua, and Costa Rica signed the Multilateral Treaty and later the General Treaty for Central American Economic Integration. The Central American Common Market (CACM) includes some seventeen million persons. Unfortunately, says de Villegas, no social objectives were included in the General Treaty and there is no provison concerning free movement of labor (de Villegas 1977: 60). This would especially affect migrant workers. (The International Labour Office [ILO] defined "migrant worker" as "a person who migrates from one country to another with a view to being employed otherwise than on his own account and includes any person regularly admitted as a migrant worker" [ILO 1975: 46].) The Andean Group, comprising Bolivia, Colombia, Chile, Ecuador, Peru, and Venezuela, was formed in 1969 by the Cartagena Agreement. It is an ambitious formula based on the harmonizing of economic, labor, and social policies and on joint programming. It combines the use of planning with the liberalization–common market machinery (de Villegas 1977: 60). The Migrant Workers International Labour Conference sponsored by ILO recently proposed numerous articles for the protection of migrant workers, especially equality of opportunity and treatment with nationals (ILO 1975). At the Tenth Conference of the American States in 1974, the ILO adopted two resolutions. According to these, "among the principal causes of migration is the unfair distribution of income and the prevailing division of labour. A solution to this situation requires concerted international action to ensure a balanced development among nations." It was also noted that the integration process "cannot become an effective reality unless special attention is devoted to the social and labour problems involved" (ILO 1974; de Villegas 1977: 59).

5   *Migration Today* (1977: 33–6) contains a brief discussion of Chilean immigrants in Bolivia. Bolivia, which for many years exported labor to its southwestern neighbor, is now receiving workers from that country. The journal states that, according to unidentified sources, there are now some 18,800 Chileans in Bolivia. This trend coincides with diplomatic negotiations to secure free access for Bolivia to the Pacific Ocean. The article goes on to say that most of the Chilean immigrants travel as tourists. When their tourist visas expire, some of them go through expensive formalities and manage to have their permits extended; the rest remain illegally.

6   The International Migration Review's special issue, *Caribbean Migration to New York* (vol.13, no.2, 1979). It includes articles about migration from the Dominican Republic, the West Indies, and Haiti; migration of Garifuna (Black Caribs); and a contextual statement about New York City and the new Caribbean immigration.

7   In a series of statutes beginning in 1875, measures were taken to restrict immigration to the United States by means of "quantitative controls." The general law was codified and revised in 1891, 1903, 1907, and 1917. With

each revision the list of excludable people grew. The 1917 act represented the apex of qualitative control; under its terms persons who were feeble-minded, destitute, seriously ill, or morally undesirable were barred from admittance. The basic provisions were incorporated into the present immigration law, although the harshness of its application has been softened (Grebler et al. 1965: D-4). As we shall see, the open-door policy had already been modified in 1882. Three months before the passage of the first general immigration law that year, Congress passed the Chinese Exclusion Act. This act, designed to bar immigration of persons of Chinese ancestry, was the result of racial prejudice and antagonism to coolie laborers who had been imported to the West coast. Three years later, the Alien Contract Labor Law was passed to protect the local labor market by prohibiting the admission of persons who had been brought to this country under a contract to perform services. In 1891 this law was broadened to exclude anyone who came to the United States in response to an advertisement promising employment on arrival. The first deportation law since the Alien Act of 1798 was passed in 1888 to enforce the provisions of this law (Grebler et al. 1965: D-4, D-5).

8   The U.S. Immigration and Naturalization Service (U.S.I.N.S.) defines an immigrant as an alien admitted for permanent residence. A nonimmigrant is an alien admitted with temporary status. Returning resident aliens who have once been counted as immigrants are included with nonimmigrants in the U.S.I.N.S. statistical calculations, although immigration laws define such aliens as immigrants (U.S.I.N.S. Annual Report 1977: 36).

9   For recent information on migration to the United States from other Latin American nations, see Cruz and Castaño 1976; Chaney 1976; Hehl Neiva 1965; U.S. Bureau of the Census 1976; the bibliographies in Interdisciplinary Communications Program 1976; and the issues of International Migration Review.

10   The summary in this section is based largely on Cornelius 1977. Cornelius's monograph draws extensively upon preliminary findings from a three-year (and continuing) study of the causes and consequences of Mexican migration to the United States and to cities within Mexico.

11   The most basic flaw in estimates such as those by Lesko Associates and others is that they either ignore or grossly underestimate the volume of return migration to Mexico. For example, the Lesko procedure assumed that only 2 percent of the illegal migrants entering the United States in a given year did not settle there permanently. But according to Cornelius, all field studies completed to date indicate that the reverse flow of migrants from the United States to Mexico is actually quite large. INS apprehension statistics indicate that the number of Mexican illegals entering the United States is also quite large. The real number of entrants is, of course, considerably larger than the apprehension statistics indicate, because many of those entering illegally manage to evade the INS and eventually return to Mexico undetected. However, a downward correction must also be applied to INS apprehension statistics, because of multiple apprehensions of some illegals within the same year. The apprehension statistics represent events, not numbers of people. It is not uncommon for a single illegal migrant to be apprehended twice or more in a given year. Therefore, the flow of migrants must not be confused with the stock of permanent or long-term resident immigrants, which is likely to be expanding much more slowly than the number of immigrants who simply attempt to enter the United States illegally (Cornelius 1978: 12).

12 Assimilation is a specific kind of social policy. It involves one of the ways a host community may decide to deal with individuals and groups that are alien in cultural, linguistic, and social ways. An assimilation policy may be followed when alien individuals and groups migrate into or are brought within the social-territorial boundaries of a host society (Hunter and Whitten 1976: 46). Acculturation may be defined as one kind of cultural change, specifically the processes and events that come from the conjunction of two or more formerly separate and autonomous cultures. The terms culture contact and transculturation are synonyms for acculteration (Hunter and Whitten: 1).

13 Data in this section are based upon information published by the Mexican-American Study Project of the University of California at Los Angeles. Eleven "Advance Reports" were published and consolidated in the volume by Grebler, Moore, and Guzmán (1970) to which we refer.

14 Ernesto Galarza, writing of the "cultural reactivity" of the Mexican, complains that the intellectual tools available to us are not as sharp as they might be. He observes that terms like "minority," "acculturation," "traits," "primitive cultures," and "self-image" derive from an anthropology that is itself a product of the culture that has overrun the world in the last 300 years, "the culture of the European white man." "Is there," he asks, "by chance, any bias in this of which we should be aware in observing the regional Mexican culture?" (1972: 262). He continues:

> Let me . . . consider the term "acculturation." We are coming to the point where it means a sort of recapping process, a replacement of cultural treads. The implication seems to be that the reconditioning produces something as good as new. I do not believe that this is so. Acculturation, in my view, occurs only once in the life of any individual, during the early years when he is enfolded in the very tissues of the social group into which he is born. Later, he is conquered or he emigrates. Necessity or force compels him to learn different ways. This I would call "remedial acculturation," which I suspect is as inefficient, costly, and ultimately unsatisfactory as remedial reading. [Galarza 1972: 263]

References

Abrams, C. *Man's struggle for shelter in an urbanized world,* Cambridge, Mass., 1964.

"The Uses of Land in Cities," *Scientific American* 213 (1965), 150–60.

Squatter settlements: the problem and the opportunity, Washington, D.C., 1966.

Adams, R. E. W. *Prehistoric Mesoamerica,* Boston 1977.

Adams, R. McC. *The evolution of urban society,* Chicago, 1966.

Adams, R. N. "Introduction to 'social organization,'" in *Contemporary cultures and societies of Latin America,* ed. D. B. Heath & R. N. Adams, New York, 1965.

The second sowing: power and secondary development in Latin America, San Francisco, 1967.

Alba, F. "Mexico's international migration as a manifestation of its development pattern," *International Migration Review* 12 (1978), 502–13.

Alvarez, R. "The psychohistorical and socioeconomic development of the Chicano community in the United States," *Social Science Quarterly* 53 (1973) 920–42.

Amato, P. W. "Elitism and settlement patterns in the Latin American city," *Journal of the American Institute of Planners* 36 (1970), 96–105.

Amis, W. D. and Stern, S. E. "A critical examination of theory and functions of voluntary associations," *Journal of Voluntary Action* 3 (1974), 91–9.

Anderson R. T. "Voluntary associations in Hyderbad," *Anthropological Quarterly* 37 (1964), 175–90.

Anuário Estatístico do Brasil, IBGE, Conselho Nacional de Estatística, Rio de Janeiro, 1954.

Fundaçao Instituto Brasileiro de Geografia e Estatística, Rio de Janeiro, 1977.

Appleyard, R. T. "Major international population movements and policies: an historical review," in *International Population Conference Proceedings,* Liège, Belgium, 1977, pp. 291–305.

Arias B. J. "Internal migration in Guatemala," in *Proceedings of the International Population Conference,* vol. 1, London, 1963.

"Migración interna en Guatemala," in *Principales patrones de migración en Guatemala,* Estudios Centroamericanos no. 3, ed. A. O. Zárate, El Faro, Guatemala, 1967.

Arias, J. and Alcalá, E. "Migración en la Mixteca Baja: informe de un viaje de sondeo," Boletín DEAS 1 (1973), no. 3, México, D.F.

Arizpe, L. "Women in the informal labor sector: the case of Mexico City," *Signs* 3 (1977), 25–37.

Migración etnicismo y cambio económico: un estudio sobre migrantes campesinos a la ciudad de México, Mexico, 1978.

Arriaga, E. E. "Components of city growth in selected Latin American countries," *The Milbank Memorial Fund Quarterly* 46 (1968), no. 2, part 1, 237–52.

Mortality decline and its demographic effects in Latin America, Population Monograph Series no. 6, Berkeley, California, 1970.

Arriaga, E. & Paéz Célis, J. *República de Venezuela: distribución geográfica de la población y migraciones internas,* CELADE Serie C, no. 28, Santiago de Chile, 1972.

Arroyo, L. "Changes in the non-agricultural employment structure of México, 1950–1970," *Aztlán: International Journal of Chicano Studies Research* 6 (1975), 409–32.

Ashton, G. T. "Pluralismo social y cultural en un proyecto habitacional en Colombia," *América Indígena* 34 (1974), 881–904.

Axelrod, M. "Urban structure and social participation," in *Cities and society: the revised reader in sociology,* ed. P. K. Hatt and A. J. Reiss, Jr., Glencoe, Ill., 1957.

Babchuck, N. and Thompson, R. B. "The voluntary association of Negroes," *American Sociological Review* 27 (1962), 647–55.

Baerresen, D. W. "Unemployment and Mexico's border industrialization program," *Inter-American Economic Affairs* 29 (1975), 79–90.

Balán, J. "Migrant–native socioeconomic differences in Latin American cities: a structural analysis," *Latin American Research Review* 4 (1969), 3–29.

"Migración a la ciudad y movilidad social (un caso mexicano)," in *Actas de la Conferencia Regional Latinoamericana de Población,* vol. 1, El Colegio de México, México, D.F., 1972.

and Browning, H. and Jelin, E. *Men in a developing society: geographic and social mobility in Monterrey, Mexico,* Austin, Tex., 1973.

Banco Nacional de Comercio Exterior, S.A., *Mexico 1970: facts, figures and trends,* México, D.F., 1970

Barnes, J. A. *Social networks,* Addison-Wesley Modular Publications in Anthropology, no. 26, Reading, Mass., 1972.

Bastos de Avila, F. "Brazil," in *Economics of international migration,* ed. B. Thomas, London, 1958, 185–93.

Beals, R. L. "Social Stratification in Latin America," in *Contemporary cultures and societies of Latin America,* ed. D. B. Heath and R. N. Adams, New York, 1965.

Benítez Zenteno, R. "La población rural y urbana en México," *Revista Mexicana de Sociología* 24 (1962), 689–703.

Berlinck, M. T. "Marginalidad e social e relações de classes en São Paulo," São Paulo, 1975.

Beyer, G. H., ed. *The urban explosion in Latin America,* Ithaca, N.Y., 1967.

Blanton, R. E. "Anthropological studies of cities," in *Annual Review of Anthropology,* ed. B. J. Siegel, Palo Alto, Cal., 1976.

Bock, E. W. and Iutaka, S. "Rural–urban migration and social mobility: the controversy on Latin America," *Rural Sociology* 34 (1969), 343–55.

Bogue, D. J. "Internal migration," in *The study of population: an inventory and appraisal,* ed. P. M. Hauser and O. D. Duncan, Chicago, 1959c.

"Techniques and hypotheses for the study of differential migration," in *Proceedings of the International Population Conference,* vol. 1, London, 1963.

Boissevain, J. "The place of non-groups in the social sciences," *Man* 3 (1968), 542–56.

Bonilla, F. "Rio's favelas: the rural slum within the city," in *Peasants in cities: readings in the anthropology of urbanization,* ed. W. Mangin, Boston, 1970.

Borah, W. "New Spain's century of depression," *Ibero-Americana* 35 (1951).

Boserup, E. *Women's role in economic development*, London, 1970.

Bott, E. "Urban families: conjugal roles and social networks," in *City ways*, ed. J. Friedl and N. J. Chrisman, New York, 1975.

Bouvier, L. F.; Macisco, J. J., Jr.; and Zárate, A. "Toward a framework for the analysis of differential migration: the case of education," in *Internal migration: the new world and the third world*, ed. A. H. Richmond and D. Kubat, Beverly Hills, Cal., 1974.

Bowser, F. P. "The free person of color in Mexico City and Lima: manumission and opportunity, 1580–1650," in *Race and slavery in the western hemisphere: quantitative studies*, ed. S. L. Engerman and E. D. Genovese, Princeton, N.J., 1975.

Boyce, C. P. *Confronting the problems of low income settlements in Latin America*, Iowa City, Iowa, 1970.

Boyer, R. E., and Davies, K. A. "Urbanization in nineteenth century Latin America: statistics and sources," *Statistical Abstract of Latin America*, July (1973), supplement.

Bradfield, S. "Selectivity in rural–urban migration: the case of Huaylas, Peru," in *Urban anthropology: cross-cultural studies of urbanization*, ed. A. Southall, New York, 1973.

Brading, D. A. *Miners and merchants in Bourbon Mexico, 1763–1810*, London, 1971.

and Wu, C. "Population growth and crisis: León, 1720–1860," *Journal of Latin American Studies* 5 (1973), 1–36.

Brandão Lopes, J. R. "Aspects of the adjustment of rural migrants to urban-industrial conditions in São Paulo, Brazil," in *Urbanization in Latin America*, ed. P. M. Hauser, New York, 1961.

Desenvolvimento e mudança social, São Paulo, Brazil, 1976.

Brandenburg, F. *The making of modern Mexico*, Englewood Cliffs, N.J., 1964.

Briggs, V. M., Jr. "Illegal aliens: the need for a more restrictive border policy," *Social Science Quarterly* 56 (1975a), 477–84.

"Mexican workers in the United States labour market: a contemporary dilemma," *International Labour Review* 112 (1975b), 351–68.

Brown, J. C. *Patterns of intra-urban settlement*, Ithaca, N.Y., 1972.

Brown, S. E. "Love unites them and hunger separates them: poor women in the Dominican Republic," in *Toward an anthropology of women*, ed. R. E. Reiter, New York, 1975.

Browning, H. L. "Urbanization and modernization in Latin America: the demographic perspective," in *The urban explosion in Latin America*, ed. G. H. Beyer, Ithaca, N.Y., 1967.

"Migrant selectivity and the growth of large cities in developing countries," in *Rapid population growth: consequences and implications*, Baltimore, 1971.

"Some consequences of migration on the class structure of communities of origin and of destination in Latin America," in *International Population Conference Proceedings*, vol. 1, Liège, Belgium, 1973.

and Feindt, W. "Selectivity of migrants to a metropolis in a developing country: a Mexican case study," *Demography* 6 (1969), 347–57.

and Feindt, W. "The social and economic context of migration to Monterrey, Mexico," in *Latin American urban research*, vol. 1, ed. F. F. Rabinovitz and F. M. Trueblood, Beverly Hills, Cal. 1971.

Bruner, E. M. "The expression of ethnicity in Indonesia," in *Urban ethnicity*, ed. A. Cohen, London, 1973.

Buechler, H. C. "The ritual dimension of rural–urban networks: the fiesta system in the northern highlands of Bolivia," in *Peasants in cities: readings in the anthropology of urbanization,* ed. W. Mangin, Boston, 1970.

Bustamente, J. A. "Structural and ideological conditions of the Mexican undocumented immigration to the United States," *American Behavioral Scientist* 19 (1976), 364–76.

"Commodity-migrants: structural analysis of Mexican migration to the United States," in *Views across the border: the United States and Mexico,* ed. Stanley R. Ross, Albuquerque, N.M., 1978.

Butterworth, D. S. "A study of the urbanization process among Mixtec migrants from Tilantongo in Mexico City," *América Indígena* 22 (1962), 257–74.

"Factors in out-migration from a rural Mexican community." unpublished Ph.D. thesis, University of Illinois, 1969.

"From royalty to poverty: the decline of a rural Mexican community," *Human Organization* 29 (1970), 5–11.

"Migración rural–urbana en América Latina: el estado de nuestro conocimiento," *América Indígena* 31 (1971), 85–105.

"Two small groups: a comparison of migrants and non-migrants in Mexico City," *Urban Anthropology* 1 (1972), 29–50.

"Squatters or suburbanites? The growth of shantytowns in Oaxaca, Mexico," in *Latin American modernization problems,* ed. R. E. Scott, Urbana, Ill., 1973.

"Rural–urban migration and microdemography: a case study from Mexico," *Urban Anthropology* 4 (1975a), 265–83.

Tilantongo: comunidad mixteca en transición, México, D.F., 1975b.

The people of Buena Ventura: relocation of slum dwellers in post-revolutionary Cuba, Urbana, Ill., 1980.

Cabrera, G. "Selectividad por edad y por sexo de los migrantes en México," in *Conferencia regional latinoamericana de población,* Mexico City, 1972.

Calnek, E. E. "Settlement pattern and chinampa agriculture at Tenochtitlan," *American Antiquity* 37 (1972a), 104–15.

"The internal structure of cities in America. Pre-Columbian cities: the case of Tenochtitlan," in *Actas y memorias del XXXIX Congreso Internacional de Americanistas,* vol. 2, Lima, 1972b.

Camara, F., and Kemper, R. V., eds. *Migration across frontiers: Mexico and the United States,* Albany, N.Y., 1979.

Camargo, J. F. de. *Exodo rural no Brasil: formas, causas e consequências econômicas principais,* Rio de Janeiro, 1960.

Campiglia, N. *La migración a Montevideo,* Montevideo, Uruguay, 1967.

Caplow, T. "The social ecology of Guatemala City." *Social Forces* 28 (1949), 113–33.

Cardona Gutiérrez, R. "Migración, urbanización y marginalidad," in *Seminario nacional sobre urbanización y marginalidad,* Bogotá, 1968.

Carvajal, M. J. and Geithman, D. T. "An economic analysis of migration in Costa Rica," *Economic Development and Culture Change* 23 (1974), 105–22.

Casagrande, J. B.; Thompson, S. I.; and Young, P. D. "Colonization as a research frontier: the Ecuadorian case," in *Process and pattern in culture: essays in honor of Julian H. Steward,* ed. R. Manners, Chicago, 1964.

Casagrande, L. B. "Zacapu: the dynamics of inequality in a Mexican town," unpublished Ph.D. thesis, University of Minnesota, 1979.

Casasco, J. A. "The social function of the slum in Latin America: some positive aspects," *América Latina* 12 (1969), 87–111.

Chance, J. K. "Kinship and urban residence: household and family organization in a suburb of Oaxaca, Mexico," *Journal of the Steward Anthropological Society* 2 (1971), 122–47.

"The colonial Latin American city: preindustrial or capitalist?" *Urban Anthropology* 4 (1975), 211–28.

"The urban Indian in colonial Oaxaca," *American Ethnologist* 3 (1976), 603–32.

Race and class in colonial Oaxaca, Stanford, Cal., 1978.

and Taylor, W. B. "Estate and class in a colonial city: Oaxaca in 1792," *Comparative Studies in Society and History* 19 (1977), 454–87.

"Recent trends in Latin American urban studies: a review article," *Latin American Research Review* 15 (1980), 183–8.

Chaney, E. M. "Colombian migration to the United States (part 2)," in *The dynamics of migration: international migration,* Washington, D.C., 1976.

"The world economy and contemporary migration." *International Migration Review* 13 (1979), 204–12.

Chaplin, D. "Peruvian stratification and mobility – revolutionary and developmental potential", in *Structured social inequality: a reader in comparative social stratification,* ed. C. S. Heller, New York, 1969.

Chen, C. Y. *Movimientos migratorios en Venezuela,* Caracas, 1968.

"Migración interna y desarrollo regional," in *Actas de la conferencia regional Latinoamericana de población,* vol. 1, México, D.F., 1972.

Chilcote, R. H., and Edelstein, J. C., eds. *Latin America: the struggle with dependency and beyond,* New York, 1974.

Childe, V. G. "The urban revolution," *Town Planning Review* 21 (1950), 3–17.

"Chilean immigrants in Bolivia." *Migration Today* 21 (1977), 33–6.

Coale, A. J. "Population growth and economic development: the case of Mexico," *Foreign Affairs* 56 (1978), 415–29.

Cohn, D. L. *The life and times of King Cotton,* New York, 1956.

Connell, J. et al. *Migration from rural areas. The evidence from village studies.* Delhi, 1976.

Conniff, M. L. "Voluntary associations in Rio, 1870–1945: a new approach to urban social dynamics," *Journal of Interamerican Studies and World Affairs* 17 (1975), 64–81.

Conning, A. M. "Rural–urban destinations of migrants and community differentiation in a rural region in Chile," *International Migration Review* 6 (1972), 148–57.

Cornelius, W. A. "Urbanization as an agent in Latin American political instability: the case of Mexico," *The American Political Science Review* 63 (1969), 833–6.

"The political sociology of cityward migration in Latin America: toward empirical theory," in *Latin American urban research,* vol. 1, ed. F. F. Rabinovitz and F. M. Trueblood, Beverly Hills, Cal., 1971.

"Urbanization and political demand making: political participation among the migrant poor in Latin American cities," *The American Political Science Review* 68 (1974), 1125–46.

Politics and the migrant poor in Mexico City, Stanford, Cal., 1975.

"Outmigration from rural Mexican communities," in *The dynamics of migration: international migration,* Washington, D.C., 1976a.

Mexican migration to the United States: the view from rural sending communities, Cambridge, Mass., 1976b.

Illegal migration to the United States: recent research findings, policy implications, and research priorities, Cambridge, Mass., 1977.

Mexican migration to the United States: causes, consequences, and U.S. responses, Cambridge, Mass., 1978.

Corrado, G. "Acerca de las migraciones internas," in *Estudios sociológicos,* vol. 1, México, D.F., 1955.

Costa, M.A., ed. *Migraçoes internas no Brasil,* Rio de Janeiro, 1971.

Cowell, B., Jr. "Cityward migration in the nineteenth century: the case of Recife, Brazil," *Journal of Interamerican Studies and World Affairs* 17 (1975), 43–63.

Craig, R. B. *The bracero program: interest groups and foreign policy,* Austin, Tex., 1971.

Crevenna, T. R., ed. *Materiales para el estudio de la clase media en la América Latina,* 6 vols., Washington, D.C., 1950–1.

Cruz, C. I., and Castaño, J. "Colombian migration to the United States (part 1)," in *The dynamics of migration: international migration,* Washington, D.C., 1976.

Degler, C. N. *Neither black nor white: slavery and race relations in Brazil and the United States,* New York, 1971.

Diégues, M. "Causas y problemas del caso brasileño," *Aportes* 15 (1970), 146–57.

Dillman, C. D. "Commuter workers and free zone industry along the Mexico–U.S. border," *Proceedings of the Association of American Geographers,* n.p., 1970, 48–51.

Dinerman, I. R. "Patterns of adaptation among households of U.S.-bound migrants from Michoacán, Mexico," *International Migration Review* 12 (1978), 485–501.

Dipolo, M. and Suarez, M. "History, patterns, and migration: a case study in the Venezuelan Andes," *Human Organization* 33 (1974), 183–95.

Dobyns, H. F. "Comment on Kerri (1976) article," *Current Anthropology* 17 (1976), 36–7.

Dotson, F. "A note on participation in voluntary associations in a Mexican city," *American Sociological Review* 18 (1953), 80–6.

Doughty, P. L. "El caso de Huaylas: un distrito en la perspectiva nacional," in *Migración e integración en el Perú.* ed. H. F. Dobyns and M. C. Vázquez, Lima, 1963.

Huaylas: an Andean district in search of progress, Ithaca, N.Y., 1968.

"Behind the back of the city: 'provincial' life in Lima, Peru," in *Peasants in cities: readings in the anthropology of urbanization,* ed. W. Mangin, Boston, 1970.

"Peruvian migrant identity in the urban milieu," in *The anthropology of urban environments,* ed. T. Weaver and D. White, Boulder, Col., 1972.

Dovring, F. "El papel de la agricultura dentro de las poblaciones en crecimiento. México, un caso de desarrollo económico reciente," *El Trimestre Económico* 35 (1968), 25–50.

Drake, G. F. "Social class and organizational dynamics: a study of voluntary associations in a Colombian city," *Journal of Voluntary Action Research* 1 (1972), 46–52.

Ducoff, L. J. "Población migratoria en un area metropolitana de un país en proceso de desarrollo: informe preliminar sobre un estudio experimental efectuado en El Salvador," *Estadística; Journal of the Inter-American Institute* 20 (1962), 131–9.

DuToit, B. M. "A decision-making model for the study of migration," in *Migration and urbanization: models and adaptive strategies*, ed. B. M. DuToit and H. I. Safa, The Hague, 1975a.

and Safa, H. I., eds. *Migration and urbanization: models and adaptive strategies*, The Hague, 1975b.

Dwyer, D. J. *People and housing in Third World cities: perspectives on the problem of spontaneous settlements*, London, 1975.

Eames, E. and Goode, J. G. *Anthropology of the city: an introduction to urban anthropology*, Englewood Cliffs, N.J., 1977.

Eder, G. J. "Urban concentration, agriculture, and agrarian reform," *The Annals of the American Academy of Political and Social Science* 360 (1965), 27–47.

El Colegio de México, Centro de Estudios Económicos y Demográficos, *Dinámica de la Población de México*, México, D.F., 1970.

El Rescate, Lima, 1972, p. 1.

Elizaga, J. "Internal migration in Latin America," *Milbank Memorial Fund Quarterly* 43 (1965), 144–61.

"A study on immigrations to Greater Santiago (Chile)," *Demography* 3 (1966), 352–77.

Migraciones a los areas metropolitanas de América Latina, Santiago de Chile, 1970.

"International migration: an overview," *International Migration Review* 6 (1972a), 121–46.

"Migraciones interiores. Migraciones y movilidad social. El progreso de urbanización (Evolución reciente y estado actual de los estudios)," in *Actas de la Conferencia Regional Latinoamericana de Población*, México, D.F., 1972b.

"Migraciones interiores. Evolución y estado actual de los estudios," in *Las migraciones internas*, ed. R. Cardona Gutiérrez, Bogotá, 1972c.

Epstein, D. G. *Brasilia, plan and reality: a study of planned and spontaneous urban development*, Berkeley and Los Angeles, 1973.

Escobar Zulema, J., and Magrassi, E. *Exodo juvenil en Villa María*, Córdova, Spain, 1969.

Evans, J. S., and James, D, "Conditions of employment and income distribution in Mexico as incentives for Mexican migration to the United States: prospects to the end of the century," *International Migration Review* 13 (1979), 4–24.

Fanon, F. *The wretched of the earth*, New York, 1963.

Feindt, W., and Browning, H. L. "Return migration and its significance in an industrial metropolis and an agricultural town in Mexico," *International Migration Review* 6 (1972), 158–65.

Fernandes, F. *The Negro in Brazilian society*, New York, 1969.

Fernandez, R. A. *The United States–Mexico border: A politico-economic profile*, Notre Dame, Ind., 1977.

Fichert, R.; Turner, J.; and Grenell, P. "Increasing autonomy in housing: a review and conclusions," in *Freedom to build*, ed. J. Turner and R. Fichert, New York, 1972.

Financial Trend, November 13–19, 1978; January 15–21, 1979.

Flinn, W. L. "Rural to urban migration: a Colombian case," Madison, Wis., Land Tenure Center Reprint No. 19, 1966.

"Process of migration to a shantytown in Bogotá, Colombia," Madison, Wis., Land Tenure Center Reprint No. 49, 1968.

"Rural and intra-urban migration in Colombia: two case studies in Bogotá," in *Latin American urban research*, vol. 1, ed. F. F. Rabinovitz and F. M. Trueblood, Beverly Hills, Cal., 1971.

and Cartano, D. G. "A comparison of the migration process to an urban barrio and to a rural community: two case studies," *Inter-American Economic Affairs* 24 (1970), 37–48.

and Converse, J. W. "Eight assumptions concerning rural–urban migration in Colombia: A three-shantytowns test," *Land Economics* 46 (1970), 456–66.

Foster, D. W. "*Tequio* in urban Mexico: a case from Oaxaca City," *Journal of the Steward Anthropological Society* 2 (1971), 148–79.

"Survival strategies of low-income households in a Colombian city," unpublished Ph.D. thesis, University of Illinois, 1975.

Foster, G. M. *Culture and conquest: America's Spanish heritage,* Chicago, 1960.

"Peasant character and personality," in *Peasant society: a reader,* ed. J. M. Potter and M. N. Diaz, Boston, 1967.

Applied anthropology, Boston, 1969.

Fox, R. G. *Urban anthropology: cities in their cultural settings,* Englewood Cliffs, N.J., 1977.

Fox, R. W. *Urban population trends in Latin America,* Washington, D.C., 1975.

Frank, A. G. *Capitalism and underdevelopment in Latin America: historical studies of Chile and Brazil,* New York, 1966.

Latin America: underdevelopment or revolution, New York, 1969.

Friedmann, J., and Wulff, R. *The urban transition: comparative studies of newly industrializing societies,* Los Angeles, 1974.

Friedrich, P. "Assumptions underlying Tarascan political homicide," *Psychiatry* 25 (1962), 315–27.

Galarza, E. "Mexicans in the Southwest," in *Plural society in the Southwest,* ed. E. M. Spicer and R. H. Thompson, Albuquerque, N.M., 1972.

and Gallegos, H. and Samora, J. *Mexican-Americans in the Southwest,* Santa Barbara, Cal., 1969.

Gamio, M. *Mexican immigration to the United States,* New York, 1969 (1930).

Garayar, G. "Notas demográficas sobre la migración interna," in *Migración e integración en el Perú,* ed. H. F. Dobyns and M. C. Vázquez, Lima, 1963.

Germani, G. "Inquiry into the social effects of urbanization in a working-class sector of Greater Buenos Aires," in *Urbanization in Latin America,* ed. P. M. Hauser, New York, 1961.

"El proceso de urbanización en la Argentina," *Revista Interamericana de Ciencias Sociales* (2ª época) 2 (1963), 287–45.

"Emigración del campo a la ciudad y sus causas," in *Sociedad, economía y reforma agraria,* ed. H. Gilberti et al., Buenos Aires, 1965.

Sociología de la modernización: psicología y sociología, Buenos Aires, 1969.

"The City as an Integrating Mechanism: The Concept of Social Integration" in *The Urban Explosion in Latin America,* ed. G. H. Beyer, Ithaca, New York, 1967.

"Mass immigration and modernization in Argentina," in *Masses in Latin America,* ed. I. L. Horowitz, New York, 1970.

Gibson, C. *The Aztecs under Spanish rule,* Stanford, Cal., 1964.

Spain in America, New York, 1966.

"Spanish-Indian institutions and colonial urbanism in New Spain," in *El proceso de urbanización en América desde sus orígenes hasta nuestros días,* ed. J. E. Hardoy and R. P. Schaedel, Buenos Aires, 1969.

Gillin, J. P. "Some signposts for policy," in *Social change in Latin America today,* ed. R. N. Adams et al., New York, 1960.

Glazer, N., and Moynihan, D. P. *Beyond the melting pot: the Negroes, Puerto Ricans, Jews, Italians, and Irish of New York City,* Cambridge, Mass., 1963.

Goldrich, D.; Pratt, R. B.; and Schuller, C. R. "The political integration of lower-class urban settlements in Chile and Peru," in *Masses in Latin America*, ed. I. L. Horowitz, New York, 1970.

Goldscheider, C. "An outline of the migration system," in *International union for the scientific study of population*, vol. 4, London, 1971.

González, G. "The migration of Latin American high-level manpower," *International Labour Review* 98 (1968), 551–69.

Gonzalez, N. L. *Black Carib household structure: a study of migration and modernization*, Seattle and London, 1969.

"The city of gentlemen: Santiago de los Caballeros," in *Anthropologists in Cities*, ed. G. M. Foster and R. V. Kemper, Boston, 1974.

González Casanova, P. "Dynamics of the class structure," in *Comparative perspectives on stratification*, ed. J. A. Kahl, Boston, 1968.

González Cosío, A. "Clases y estratos sociales" in *México: cincuenta años de revolución*, vol. 2, Mexico City, 1961.

Goode, J. G., "Latin American urbanism and corporate groups," *Anthropological Quarterly* 43 (1970a), 146–67.

"The response of a traditional elite to modernization: lawyers in Colombia," *Human Organization* 29 (1970b), 70–80.

Gordon, C. W., and Babchuk, N. "A typology of voluntary associations," *American Sociological Review* 24 (1959), 22–9.

"Algunas considerações econômicas para a politíca migratória no meio brasileiro," in *Migraçoes internas no Brasil*, ed. M. A. Costa, Rio de Janeiro, 1971.

Graham, D. "Divergent and convergent regional economic growth and internal migration in Brazil 1940–1960," *Economic Development and Cultural Change* 18 (1970), 362–82.

and Buarque de Hollanda Filho, S. *Migration, regional and urban growth and development in Brazil: a selective analysis of the historical record – 1872–1970*, São Paulo, 1971.

Graves, N. D., and Graves, T. D. "Adaptive strategies in urban situations," in *Annual Review of Anthropology*, vol. 3, ed. B. Siegel, A. Beals, and S. Tyler, Palo Alto, Cal., 1974.

Grebler, L., with contributions by P. M. Newman and R. Wyse, *Mexican-American study project, advance report 2: Mexican immigration to the United States: the record and its implications*, Los Angeles, Cal., 1965.

and, Moore, J. W. and Guzman, R. C. *The Mexican-American people: the nation's second largest minority*, New York, 1970.

Guillet, D. "Migration, agrarian reform, and structural change in rural Peru," *Human Organization* 35 (1976), 295–302.

and Uzzell, D. "Introduction," in *New approaches to the study of migration*, Houston, Tex., 1976.

and Uzzell, D., eds. *New approaches to the study of migration*, Houston, Tex, 1976.

and Whiteford, S. "A comparative view of the role of the fiesta complex in migrant adaptation," *Urban Anthropology* 3 (1974), 222–41.

Gulick, J. "Urban Anthropology," in *Handbook of social and cultural anthropology*, ed. J. J. Honigmann, Chicago, 1973.

Hammel, E. A. "Some characteristics of the rural village and urban slum populations on the coast of Peru," *Southwestern Journal of Anthropology* 20 (1964), 346–58.

Power in Ica: the structural history of a Peruvian community, Boston, 1969.

Hammond, D. "Associations," *McCaleb Module in Anthropology* 14, Reading, Mass., 1972.

Hanke, L. *The imperial city of Potosí,* The Hague, 1956.

Hansen, A. T. "The ecology of a Latin American city," in *Race and culture contacts,* ed. E. B. Reuter, New York, 1934.

Hardoy, J. E. *Pre-Columbian cities,* New York, 1973.

"Two thousand years of Latin American urbanization," in *Urbanization in Latin America – approaches and issues,* ed. J. E. Hardoy, Garden City, N.Y., 1975.

and Langdon, M.E. "Análises estadístico preliminar de la urbanización de América Latina entre 1850 y 1930," *Revista Paraguaya de Sociología* 15 (1978), 115–74.

Harkess, S. J. "The pursuit of an ideal: migration, social class, and women's roles in Bogotá, Colombia," in *Female and male in Latin America,* ed. A. Pescatello, Pittsburgh, Pa., 1973.

Harris, M. "Referential ambiguity in the calculus of Brazilian racial identity," in *Afro-American anthropology,* ed. N. E. Whitten, Jr. and J. F. Szwed, New York, 1970.

Haviland, W. A. "Tikal, Guatemala and Mesoamerican urbanism," *World Archaeology* 2 (1970), 186–98.

Hawthorne, H. B., and Hawthorne, A. E. "Stratification in a Latin American city," *Social Forces* 27 (1948), 19–29.

Hayner, N. S. "Mexico City: its growth and configuration," *American Journal of Sociology* 50 (1945), 295–304.

"Differential social change in a Mexican town," *Social Forces* 26 (1948), 381–90.

Hehl Neiva, A. "International migrations affecting Latin America," *The Milbank Memorial Fund Quarterly* 43 (1965), 119–43.

Hendricks, G. *The Dominican diaspora: from the Dominican Republic to New York City – villagers in transition,* New York, 1974.

Herrick, B. H. *Urban migration and economic development in Chile,* Cambridge, Mass., 1965.

"Urbanization and urban migration in Latin America: an economist's view," in *Latin American urban research,* vol. 1, ed. F. F. Rabinovitz and F. M. Trueblood, Beverly HIlls, Cal., 1971.

Higgins, M. J. "The internal stratification system of a Mexican colonia," *Journal of the Steward Anthropological Society* 3 (1971), 19–38.

"Somos gente humilde: an ethnography of a poor urban colonia," unpublished Ph.D. thesis, University of Illinois, 1974.

Hoenack, J. "Resources and sources: marketing, supply, and their social ties in Río favelas," paper presented at the thirty-seventh Congreso Internacional de Americanistas, Mar del Plata, Argentina, 1966.

Horowitz, I. L. ed. *Masses in Latin America,* New York, 1970.

Hunter, D. E. and Whitten, P. *Encyclopedia of anthropology,* New York, 1976.

Hutchinson, B. "The migrant population of urban Brazil," *América Latina* 6 (1963), 41–71.

Ianni, O. *Crisis in Brazil,* New York, 1970.

Interdisciplinary Communications Programs, *The dynamics of migration: internal migration,* Washington, D.C., 1976.

International Labour Office, *Why labour leaves the land: a comparative study of the movement of labour out of agriculture,* Geneva, 1960.

Migrant workers report 7 (1), International Labour Conference, fifty-ninth session, Geneva, 1974.

Migrant workers report 5 (2), International Labour Conference, sixtieth session, Geneva, 1975.

Migrant workers, International Labour Conference, sixtieth session, report 5, Geneva, 1975.

International Migration Review, "Caribbean migration to New York," vol. 13, 1979.

Isbell, B. J. "The influence of migrants upon traditional social and political concepts: a Peruvian case study," in *Latin American urban research,* vol. 4, ed. W. A. Cornelius and F. M. Trueblood, Beverly Hills, Cal., 1974.

Iturriaga, J. E. *La estructura social y cultural de México,* Mexico City, 1951.

Iutaka, S. "Social mobility and occupation opportunities in urban Brazil," *Human Organization* 25 (1966), 126–30.

"The changing bases of social class in Brazil," in *Modern Brazil: new patterns and development,* ed. J. Saunders, Gainesville, Fl., 1971.

Iyenaga, T., and Sato, K. *Japan and the California problem,* New York and London, 1921.

Jackson, J. A. "Introduction," in *Migration,* ed. J. A. Jackson, Cambridge, Eng., 1969.

Jacobson, D. "Mobility, continuity, and urban social organization," in *City ways,* ed. J. Friedl and N. J. Chrisman, New York, 1975.

Jansen, C. "Some sociological aspects of migration," in *Migration,* ed. J. A. Jackson, Cambridge, Eng., 1969.

Jansen, C., ed. *Readings in the sociology of migration,* London, 1970.

Jelin, E. "Migration and labor force participation of Latin American women: the domestic servants in the cities," *Signs* 3 (1977), 129–41.

Jenkins, J. C. "Push/pull in recent Mexican migration to the U.S.," *International Migration Review* 11 (1977), 178–89.

"The demand for immigrant workers: labor scarcity or social control?" *International Migration Review* 12 (1978), 514–35.

Johnson, J. J. *Political change in Latin America: the emergence of the middle sectors,* Stanford, Cal., 1958.

Jonkind, F. "La supuesta funcionalidad de los clubes regionales en Lima, Perú," *Boletín de Estudios Latinoamericanos* 11 (1971), 1–12.

"A reappraisal of the role of the regional associations in Lima, Peru," *Comparative Studies in Society and History* 16 (1974), 471–82.

Kahl, J. B. "Social stratification and values in metropoli and provinces: Brazil and Mexico," *América Latina* 8 (1965), 23–35.

Katz, F. *The ancient American civilizations,* New York, 1972.

Katzman, M. T. *Cities and frontiers in Brazil: regional dimensions of economic development,* Cambridge, Mass., 1977.

Keatinge, R. W., and Day, K. C. "Chan Chan," *Archaeology* 27 (1974), 228–35.

Keely, C. B. "Counting the uncountable: estimates of undocumented aliens in the United States," *Population and Development Review* 3 (1977), 473–81.

Kemper, R. V. "Family and household organization among Tzintzuntzan migrants in Mexico City," in *Latin American urban research,* vol. 4, ed. W. A. Cornelius and F. M. Trueblood, Beverly Hills, Cal., 1974.

"Social factors in migration: the case of Tzintzuntzeños in Mexico City," in *Migration and urbanization: models and adaptive strategies,* ed. B. M. DuToit and H. I. Safa, The Hague, 1975.

Migration and adaptation: Tzintzuntzan peasants in Mexico City, Beverly Hills, Cal., 1977.

and Foster, G. W. "Urbanization in Mexico: the view from Tzintzuntzan," in *Latin American urban research,* vol. 5, ed. W. A. Cornelius and F. M. Trueblood, Beverly Hills, Cal., 1975.

Kerri, J. N. "An inductive examination of voluntary association functions in a single-enterprise based community," *Journal of Voluntary Action Research* 1 (1972), 43–51.

"Anthropological studies of voluntary associations and voluntary action: a review," *Journal of Voluntary Action Research* 3 (1974), 10–25.

"Studying voluntary associations as adaptive mechanisms: a review of anthropological perspectives," *Current Anthropology* 17 (1976), 23–47.

Kirk, D. "Some reflections on American demography in the nineteen sixties," *Population Index* 26 (1960), 305–10.

Kroeber, A. L. *Anthropology,* New York, 1948.

Kuznets, S. "Introduction," in *Population, redistribution, and economic growth, U.S. 1870–1950,* vol. 3, ed. H. T. Eldridge and D. S. Thomas, Philadelphia, 1964.

Lacroix, M. "Problems of collection and comparison of migration statistics," in *Problems in the collection and comparability of international statistics,* New York, 1949.

Lamphere, L. "Strategies, cooperation and conflict among women in domestic groups," in *Women, culture and society,* ed. M. Z. Rosaldo and L. Lamphere, Stanford, Cal., 1973.

Lanning, E. P. *Peru before the Incas,* Englewood Cliffs, N.J., 1967.

Laquian, A. A. *Slums and squatters in South and Southeast Asia,* Uttar Pradesh, 1971.

Lee, E. "A theory of migration," *Demography* 3 (1966), 47–57.

Leeds, A. "Brazilian career structures and social structure: a case history and model," in *Contemporary cultures and societies of Latin America,* ed. D. B. Heath and R. N. Adams, New York, 1965.

"Future orientations. The investment climate in Río favelas," paper presented at the thirty-seventh Congreso Internacional de Americanistas, Mar del Plata, Argentina. 1966.

"The significant variables determining the character of squatter settlements," *América Latina* 12 (1969), 44–86.

"The concept of the culture of poverty: conceptual, logical, and empirical problems, with perspectives from Brazil and Peru," in *The culture of poverty: a critique,* ed. E. B. Leacock, New York, 1971.

"Housing settlement types, arrangements for living, proletarianization, and the social structure of the city," in *Latin American Urban Research,* vol. 4, ed. W. A. Cornelius and F. M. Trueblood, Beverly Hills, Cal., 1974.

and Leeds, E. "Brazil and the myth of urban rurality: urban experience, work and values in 'squatments' of Rio de Janeiro and Lima," in *City and country in the Third World,* ed. A. J. Field, Cambridge, Mass. 1970.

Leonard, O. E. "La Paz, Bolivia: its population and growth," *American Sociological Review* 13 (1948), 448–54.

Levine, D. H. "Urbanization in Latin America: changing perspectives," *Latin American Research Review* 14 (1979), 170–83.

Lewis, O. *Life in a Mexican village: Tepoztlán restudied,* Urbana, Ill., 1951.

"Urbanization without breakdown: a case study," *Scientific Monthly* 75 (1952), 31–41.

"Tepoztlán restudied: a critique of the folk–urban conceptualization of social change," in *Anthropological essays*, New York, 1953.

"The culture of the vecindad in Mexico City: two case studies," in *Actas del XXXIII Congreso Internacional de Americanistas*, San José, Costa Rica, 1958.

Five families: Mexican case studies in the culture of poverty, New York, 1959.

The children of Sanchez: autobiography of a Mexican family, New York, 1961.

Pedro Martínez: a Mexican peasant and his family, New York, 1964.

La vida: a Puerto Rican family in the culture of poverty – San Juan and New York, New York, 1966.

"Even the saints cry," *Trans-Action* 4 (1966b), 8–23.

with the assistance of Butterworth, D. S. *A study of slum culture: backgrounds for la vida*, New York, 1968.

Lewis, R. A. *Employment, income and the growth of the barriadas in Lima, Peru*, Cornell University Dissertation Series No. 46, Ithaca, N.Y., 1973.

Lipset, S. M., and Solari, A., eds. *Elites in Latin America*, New York, 1967.

Little, K. "The role of the secret society in cultural specialization," *American Anthropologist* 51 (1949), 199–212.

"The organization of voluntary associations in West Africa," *Civilisations* 9 (1959), 283–300.

"The role of voluntary associations in West African urbanization," in *Africa: social problems of change and conflict*, ed. P. van den Berghe, San Francisco, 1964.

West African urbanization: a study of voluntary associations in social change, Cambridge, Eng., 1965.

"Voluntary associations in urban life: a case study of differential adaptation," in *Social organization: essays presented to Raymond Firth*, ed. M. Freedman, London, 1967.

"Urbanization and regional associations: their paradoxical function," in *Urban anthropology: cross-cultural studies of urbanization*, ed. A. Southall, London, 1973.

Lockhart, J. *Spanish Peru, 1532–1560*, Madison, Wis., 1968.

Lomnitz, L. "Reciprocity of favors in the urban middle class of Chile," in *Studies in economic anthropology*, ed. G. Dalton, Washington, D.C., 1971.

"Supervivencia en una barriada en la ciudad de México," *Demografía y Economía* 7 (1973), 58–85.

"The social and economic organization of a Mexican shantytown," in *Latin American urban research*, vol. 4, ed. W. A. Cornelius and F. M. Trueblood, Beverly Hills, Cal., 1974.

Networks and marginality: life in a Mexican shantytown, New York, 1977.

López, J. E. *Tendencias recientes de la población venezolana*, Mérida, Venezuela, 1968.

McAlister, L. N. "Social structure and social change in New Spain," *Hispanic American Historical Review* 43 (1963), 349–70.

Maccoby, M. "Love and authority: a study of Mexican villages," in *Peasant society: a reader*, ed. J. Potter, M. Díaz, and G. M. Foster, Boston, 1967.

McGee, T. G. "Peasantry in the cities: a paradox, a paradox, a most ingenious paradox," *Human Organization* 32 (1973), 135–42.

McGreevey, W. P. "Causas de la migración interna en Colombia," in *Empleo y desempleo en Colombia*, Bogotá, 1968.

Macisco, J. J. "Algunas consideraciones en torno a un marco analítico para la migración rural–urbana," in *Actas de la Conferencia Regional Latinoamericana de Población,* vol. 1, México, D.F., 1972.

McWilliams, C. *Ill fares the land,* Boston, 1942.

Mahar, C. "Squatter settlements in Latin America: the case of Oaxaca, Mexico," unpublished manuscript.

Mangalam, J. J. *Human migration: a guide to migration literature in English 1955–1962,* Lexington, 1968.

and Schwarzweller, H. K. "General theory in the study of migration: current needs and difficulties," *International Migration Review* 3 (1969), 3–18.

Mangin, W. "The role of regional associations in the adaptation of rural population in Peru," *Sociologus* 9 (1959), 23–36.

"Urbanization case history in Peru," *Architectural Design* 38 (1963), 306–70.

"Latin American squatter settlements: a problem and a solution," *Latin American Research Review* 2 (1967), 65–98.

"Poverty and politics in cities of Latin America," in *Power, poverty and urban policy,* ed. W. Bloomberg, Jr. and H. J. Schmandt, Beverly Hills, Cal., 1968.

"Similarities and differences between two types of Peruvian communities," in *Peasants in cities: readings in the anthropology of urbanization,* ed. W. Mangin, Boston, 1970.

"Squatter settlements," in *Biology and culture in modern perspective: readings from* Scientific American, San Francisco, 1972.

and Turner, J. "The barriada movement," *Progressive Architecture* 49 (1968), 154–62.

"Introduction," in *Peasants in cities: readings in the anthropology of urbanization,* ed. W. Mangin, Boston, 1970.

Margulis, M. "Análisis de un proceso migratorio rural–urbano en Argentina," *Aportes* 3 (1967), 73–128.

Migración y marginalidad en la sociedad argentina, Buenos Aires, 1968.

Martine, G. "Volume, characteristics, and consequences of internal migration in Colombia," *Demography* 12 (1975), 193–208.

Martínez, H. "Las migraciones internas en el Perú," *Aportes* 10 (1968), 136–60.

Las migraciones altiplánicas y la colonización del Tambopata, Lima, 1969.

Martínez, J. *Mexican emigration to the U.S. 1910–1930,* Berkeley, Cal., 1971.

Matos Mar, J. "Migration and urbanization – the "barriadas" of Lima: an example of integration into urban life," in *Urbanization in Latin America,* ed. P. M. Hauser, New York, 1961.

Urbanización y barriadas en América del Sur, Lima, 1968.

Mayer, P. *Townsmen or tribesmen. Conservatism and the process of urbanization in a South African city,* Cape Town, 1962.

Medina, C. A. de, *A favela e o demagogo,* São Paulo, 1964.

Mejía, J. V. "Sumario sobre factores sociales en la migración," in *Migración e integración en el Perú,* ed. H. F. Dobyns and M. C. Vázquez, Lima, 1963.

Mellafe, R. *Inmigración italiana a la Argentina, Brasil y Uruguay. Bibliografía selectiva,* Santiago de Chile, 1978.

Melville, M. B. "Mexican women adapt to migration," *International Migration Review* 12 (1978), 225–35.

Métraux, A. "Las migraciones internas de los indios Aymara en el Perú contemporáneo," in *Estudios antropológicos públicados en homenaje al doctor Manuel Gamio,* México, D.F., 1956.

Mexico: DGE, *Sexto censo general de población, 1940,* México, D.F., 1948.
  *Séptimo censo general de poblacion, 1950,*México, D.F., 1953.
  Octavo censo general de población, 1960, México, D.F., 1962.
  Noveno Censo Nacional de Población 1970, México, D.F., 1970.
"Migration around the world: Latin (South) America," *Migration Today,* 19 (1975), 106.
Miller, F. C. *Old villages and a new town,* Menlo Park, Cal., 1973.
Miller, J., and Gakeneimer, R. A., eds. *Latin American urban policies and the social sciences,* Beverly Hills, Cal., 1971.
Millon, R. "Teotihuacan," *Scientific American* 216 (1967), 38–48.
  Urbanization in Teotihuacan, vol. 1, Austin, Tex., 1973.
  "Social relations in ancient Teotihuacan," in *The Valley of Mexico: studies in prehispanic ecology and society,* ed. E. R. Wolf, Albuquerque, N.M., 1976.
Mintz, S. "Men, women, and trade," *Comparative Studies in Society and History* 13 (1971), 247–69.
Molina, J. *Las migraciones internas en el Ecuador,* Quito, 1965.
Moore, J. P. *The cabildo in Peru under the Hapsburgs,* Durham, N. C., 1954.
Moots, B. L. "Migration, community of origin, and status attainment: a comparison of two metropolitan communities in developing societies," *Social Forces* 54 (1976), 816–32.
Morales-Vergara, J. "Evaluation of the magnitude and structure of international migratory movements in Latin America (1958–67)," in *International population conference proceedings,* vol. 4, Liege, Belgium, 1971.
Moreno Toscano, A., and Aguirre Anaya, C. "Migration to Mexico City in the 19th century: research approaches," *Journal of Interamerican Studies and World Affairs* 17 (1975), 27–42.
Mörner, M. *Race mixture in the history of Latin America,* Boston, 1967.
Morris, C. "State settlements in Tawantinsuyu: a strategy of compulsory urbanism," in *Contemporary Archaeology,* ed. M. P. Leone, Carbondale, Ill., 1972.
Morrison, P. A. "The functions and dynamics of the migration process," in *Internal migration: a comparative perspective,* ed. A. A. Brown and E. Neuberger, New York, 1977.
Morse, R. M. "Latin American cities: aspects of structure and function," *Comparative Studies in Society and History* 4 (1962a), 473–93.
  "Some characteristics of Latin American urban history," *American Historical Review* 67 (1962b), 317–38.
  "The heritage of Latin America," in *The founding of new societies,* ed. L. Hartz, New York, 1964.
  "Recent research on Latin American urbanization: a selective survey with commentary," *Latin American Research Review* 1 (1965), 35–74.
  "Trends and issues in Latin American research, 1965–1970 (part I)," *Latin American Research Review* 6 (1971), 3–52.
  "The development of urban systems in the Americas in the nineteenth century," *Journal of Interamerican Studies and World Affairs* 17 (1973), 4–26.
  "A framework for Latin American urban history," in *Urbanization in Latin America: approaches and issues,* ed. J. E. Hardoy, Garden City, New York, 1975.
Morse, R. M. et al. *Las ciudades latinoamericanos. Parte II: desarrollo histórico,* México, D.F., 1973.
Moseley, M. E. "Secrets of Peru's ancient walls," *Natural History* 84 (1975), 34–41.

Muñoz, H., and de Oliveira, O. "Migraciones internas en América Latina: exposición y crítica de algunos análisis," in *Las migraciones internas en América Latina: consideraciones teóricas,* ed. H. Muñoz, O. de Oliveira, P. Singer and C. Stern, Buenos Aires, 1974.

Myers, G. C. "Migration and the labor force," *Monthly Labor Review* 97 (1974), 12–16.

Nagel, J. S. "Mexico's population policy turnabout," *Population Bulletin* 33 (1978).

Nelson, J. M. *Migrants, urban poverty, and instability in developing nations,* Cambridge, Mass., 1969.

New York Times, April 3, 1977; January 9, 1979.

Norbeck, E. "Common-interest associations in rural Japan," in *Japanese culture: its development and characteristics,* ed. R. J. Smith and R. K. Beardsley, Washington, D.C., 1962.

"Associations and democracy in Japan," in *Aspects of social change in modern Japan,* ed. R P. Dore, Princeton, N.J., 1967.

Nuttall, Z., ed. "Royal ordinances concerning the laying out of new towns," *Hispanic American Historical Review* 5 (1922), 249–54.

de Oliveira, O.; Singer, P.; and Stern, C.; eds. *Las migraciones internas en América Latina: consideraciones teóricas,* Buenos Aires, 1974.

de Oliveira, O., and Stern, C., eds. *Migración y desigualdad social en la Ciudad de México,* México, D.F., 1977.

Olson, J. L. "Women and social change in a mexican town," *Journal of Anthropological Research* 33 (1977), 73–88.

Orellana S., C. L. "Mixtec migrants in Mexico City: a case study of urbanization," *Human Organization* 32 (1973), 273–83.

Paddock, J. "Oaxaca in ancient Mesoamerica," in *Ancient Oaxaca,* ed. J. Paddock, Stanford, Cal., 1966.

"Studies on antiviolent and 'normal' communities," *Aggressive Behavior* 1 (1975), 217–33.

Palerm, A. "Notas sobre la clase media en México," *Ciencias Sociales* 18 (1952), 129–35.

Parker, S., and Kleiner, R. J. "The culture of poverty: an adjustive dimension," *American Anthropologist* 72 (1970), 516–27.

Patch, R. *Life in a callejón: a study of urban disorganization,* American Universities Field Staff Reports, West Coast South America Studies no. 6, 1961.

Peattie, L. R. *The view from the barrio,* Ann Arbor, Mich., 1968.

"The concept of 'marginality' as applied to squatter settlements," in *Latin American urban research,* vol. 4, ed. W. A. Cornelius and F. M. Trueblood, Beverly Hills, Cal., 1974.

Pelto, P. J. "Research strategies in the study of complex societies: the Ciudad Industrial project," in *The anthropology of urban environments,* ed. T. Weaver and D. White, Boulder, Col., 1972.

Pendrell, N. *Squatting in Salvador,* unpublished Ph.D. thesis, Columbia University, 1967.

Perlman, J. E. *The myth of marginality: urban poverty and politics in Rio de Janeiro,* Berkeley, Cal., 1976.

Petersen, W. *Population,* 3rd ed., New York, 1975.

Petras, E. M. *Social organization of the urban housing movement in Chile,* Buffalo, N.Y., 1973.

Piddington, R. *An introduction to social anthropology,* London, 1950.

Pierson, D. *A study of racial and cultural adjustment in Bahia, Brazil,* unpublished Ph.D. thesis, University of Chicago, 1939.

Pitt-Rivers, J. "Race in Latin America: the concept of 'raza,' " *Archives Européenes de Sociologie* 14 (1973), 3–31.

Poblete Troncoso, M. "El éxodo rural, sus orígenes, sus repercusiones," *América Latina* 5 (1962), 41–9.

Population Reference Bureau, "Mexico: the problem of people," *Population Bulletin* 20, (1964), 173–203.

Portes, A. "Review of Janice Perlman, *The myth of marginality: urban poverty and politics in Rio de Janeiro,*" Contemporary Sociology: A Journal of Reviews 6 (1977), 745–76.

"Migration and underdevelopment," *Politics and Society* 8 (1978a), 1–48.

"Toward a structural analysis of illegal (undocumented) immigration," *International Migration Review* 12 (1978b), 469–84.

"Política habitacional, pobreza urbana e o estado: as favelas do Rio de Janeiro, 1972–76," *Estudios CEBRAP* 22 (1979), 131–62.

and Ross, A. A. "Modernization for emigration: the medical brain drain from Argentina," *Journal of Interamerican Studies and World Affairs* 18 (1976), 395–422.

and Walton, J. *Urban Latin America: the political condition from above and below,* Austin, Tex., 1976.

Preston, D. A. "Rural emigration in Andean America," *Human Organization* 28 (1969), 279–86.

Price, J. A. "The urbanization of Mexico's border states," n.d.

Ravenstein, E. G. "The laws of migration,' *Journal of the Royal Statistical Society* 48 (1885), 167–227.

"The laws of migration," *Journal of the Royal Statistical Society* 52 (1889), 241–301.

Recaséns Siches, L. "El problema de la adaptación de las gentes de orígen rural que migran en las grandes ciudades o centros industriales," in *Estudios sociológicos,* vol. 1, Mexico City, 1955.

Recchini de Lattes, Z. "Migraciones en Buenos Aires (1895–1960)," in *Actas de la Conferencia Regional Latinoamericana de Población,* vol. 1, México, D.F., 1972.

Redfield, R. "The folk society," *American Journal of Sociology* 52 (1947), 293–308.

The primitive world and its transformations, Ithaca, N.Y., 1953.

and Milton Singer. "The cultural role of cities," *Economic Development and Cultural Change* 3 (1954), 53–77.

Reina, R. E. *Paraná: social boundaries in an Argentine city,* Austin, Tex., 1973.

Reisler, M. *By the sweat of their brow: Mexican immigrant labor in the United States 1900–1940,* Westport, Conn., 1976.

Reyna, J. L.; Villa, M.; and Albrechtsen, K. "Dinámica de la estratificación social de algunas ciudades pequeñas y medianas de México," *Demografía y Economía* 1 (1967), 368–94.

Richmond, A. H. "Sociology of migration in industrial and postindustrial societies," in *Migration,* ed. J. A. Jackson, Cambridge, Eng., 1969.

Rios, J. A. "The cities of colonial Brazil," in *History of Latin American civilization,* vol. 1, ed. L. Hanke, Boston, 1967.

Rivarola, D. M. *Migración paraguaya,* Asunción, Paraguay, 1967.

Roberts, B. R. "The social organization of low-income families," in *Masses in Latin America,* ed. I. L. Horowitz, New York, 1970.

Organizing strangers: poor families in Guatemala City, Austin, Tex., 1973.
"The interrelationships of city and provinces in Peru and Guatemala," in *Latin American urban research,* vol. 4, ed. W. A. Cornelius and F. M. Trueblood, Beverly Hills, Cal., 1974.
Cities of peasants: the political economy of urbanization in the Third World, London, 1978.
Rojas, E., and de la Cruz, J. "Percepción de oportunidades y migraciones internas: revisión de algunos enfoques," *Revista Latinoamericano de Estudios Urbanos Regionales (EURE)* 5 (1978), 49–66.
Rollwagen, J. R. "Mediation and rural–urban migration in Mexico: a proposal and case study," in *Latin American urban research,* vol. 4, ed. W. A. Cornelius and F. M. Trueblood, Beverly Hills, Cal., 1974.
"Introduction: the city as context: a symposium." *Urban Anthropology* 4 (1975), 1–4.
Romanucci-Ross, L. *Conflict, violence, and morality in a Mexican village,* San Diego, Cal., 1973.
Romero, L. K., and Flinn, W. L. "Effects of structural and change variables on the selectivity of migration: the case of a Colombian peasant community," *Inter-American Economic Affairs* 29 (1976), 35–58.
Rose, A. M. *Theory and method in the social sciences,* Minneapolis, Minn., 1954.
Rowe, J. H. "Inca culture at the time of the Spanish conquest," in *Handbook of South American Indians,* vol. 2, ed. J. H. Steward, Washington, D.C., 1946.
"Urban settlements in ancient Peru," *Nawpa Pacha* 1 (1963), 1–28.
Royce, A. P. *Prestigio y afiliación en una comunidad urbana: Juchitán, Oaxaca,* México, D.F., 1975.
Rubbo, A. "The spread of capitalism in rural Colombia: effects on poor women," in *Toward an anthropology of women,* ed. R. Reiter, New York, 1975.
Safa, H. I. *The urban poor of Puerto Rico: a study in development and inequality,* New York, 1974.
Sánchez, L. A. "Introduction," in *The urban explosion in Latin America,* ed. G. H. Beyer, Ithaca, N.Y., 1967.
Scheele, R. L. "The prominent families of Puerto Rico," in *The people of Puerto Rico,* ed. J. H. Steward, Urbana, Ill., 1956.
Schultz, T. P. "Rural–urban migration in Colombia," *Review of Economics and Statistics* 53 (1971), 157–63.
Schwartz, H. *Seasonal farm labor in the United States,* New York, 1945.
Scrimshaw, S. C. "Families to the city: a study of changing values, fertility, and socioeconomic status among urban in-migrants," in *Population and Social Organization,* ed. M. Nag, The Hague, 1975.
Sexton, J. D. *Education and innovation in a Guatemalan community: San Juan la Laguna,* Los Angeles, Cal., 1972.
Shaw, R. P. "Land tenure and the rural exodus in Latin America," *Economic Development and Cultural Change* 23 (1974), 123–32.
Migration theory and fact: a review and bibliography of current literature, Philadelphia, 1975.
de Sierra, G.; Marcotti, D.; and Rojan, C. "Characteristics of international migration in the Southern Cone," *Migration Today* 19 (1975), 55–61.
Silverman, S. F. "Patronage and community–nation relationships in central Italy," *Ethnology* 4 (1965), 172–89.
Simmons, A. B., and Cardona Gutiérrez, R. "La selectividad de la migración en una perspectiva en el tiempo: el caso de Bogotá (Colombia) 1929–1968," in *Las migraciones internas,* ed. R. Cardona Gutiérrez, Bogotá, 1968.

"Rural–urban migration: who comes, who stays, and who returns? The case of Bogotá, Colombia, 1929–1968," *International Migration Review* 6 (1972a), 166–81.

"La selectividad de la migración en una perspectiva histórica (El caso de Bogotá)," in *Actas de la Conferencia Regional Latinoamericana de Población,* vol. 1, México, D.F., 1972b.

Singer, P. "International migration and employment," in *International migration: proceedings of the seminar on demographic research in relation to international migration,* ed. G. Tapinos, Paris, 1974a.

Desenvolvimento econômico e evoluçãlo urbana, São Paolo, 1974b.

Sjoberg, G. "Folk and 'feudal' societies," *American Journal of Sociology* 58 (1952), 231–9.

The preindustrial city: past and present, New York, 1960.

Skeldon, R. "Regional associations and population migration in Peru: an interpretation," *Urban Anthropology* 5 (1976), 233–52.

"Regional associations: a note on opposed interpretations," *Comparative Studies in Society and History* 19 (1977), 506–10.

Sobrequés, S. "La época de los reyes católicos," in *Historia social y económica de España y América,* vol. 2, ed. J. Vicens Vives, Barcelona, 1957.

Solari, A. E. *Sociología rural nacional,* 2nd ed., Montevideo, 1958.

Solaún, M., and Kronus, S. *Discrimination without violence: miscegenation and racial conflict in Latin America,* New York, 1973.

Soustelle, J. *Daily life of the Aztecs,* Stanford, Cal., 1961.

Southall, A. "The density of role-relationships as a universal index of urbanization, in *Urban anthropology: cross-cultural studies of urbanization,* ed. A. Southall, New York, 1973.

Spalding, K. "Social climbers: changing patterns of mobility among the Indians of colonial Peru," *Hispanic American Historical Review* 50 (1970), 645–64.

Spengler, J. J., and Myers, G. C. "Migration and socioeconomic development: today and yesterday," in *Internal migration: a comparative perspective,* ed. A. A. Brown and E. Neuberger, New York, 1977.

Stack, C. B. "Sex roles and survival strategies in an urban black community," in *Women, culture and society,* ed. M. Z. Rosaldo and L. Lamphere, Stanford, Cal., 1974.

Stann, E. J. "Transportation and urbanization in Caracas, 1891–1936," *Journal of Interamerican Studies and World Affairs* 17 (1975), 82–100.

Stavenhagen, R. "Seven fallacies about Latin America," in *Contemporary cultures and societies of Latin America,* 2nd ed., ed. D. B. Heath, New York, 1974.

Stern, C., and Kahl, J. A. "Stratification since the Revolution," in *Comparative perspectives on stratification,* ed. J. A. Kahl, Boston, 1968.

Steward, J. H. *Theory of culture change,* Urbana, Ill., 1963.

Strickon, A. "Class and kinship in Argentina," *Ethnology* 1 (1962), 500–15.

Stuart, J. and Kearney, M. "Migration from the Mixteca of Oaxaca to the Californias: a case study," paper presented in the symposium "Migrations into the Californias: conservatism and change in retrospect and perspective," annual meeting of the American Anthropological Association, Los Angeles, Cal., November, 1978.

"Wage labor migration from San Jerónimo, Oaxaca," unpublished manuscript.

Sunkel, O., and Paz, P. *El subdesarrollo latinoamericano y la teoría del desarrollo,* Mexico City, 1970.

Tannenbaum, F. *Mexico: the struggle for peace and bread,* New York, 1950.

Tapinos, G. *L'économie des migrations internationales*, Paris, 1974.
Taylor, P. S. *Mexican labor in the United States*, 2 vols., New York, 1970 (1930).
Taylor, W. B. *Landlord and peasant in colonial Oaxaca*, Stanford, Cal., 1972.
Testa, J. C. "Las migraciones internas en el contexto del desarrollo social latinoamericano," *Aportes* 15 (1970), 96–109.
Thomas, B., ed. *Economics of international migration*, London, 1958.
Thomas, R. N., ed. *Population dynamics of Latin America: a review and bibliography*, East Lansing, Mich., 1973.
Thompson, R. A. *The winds of tomorrow: social change in a Maya town*, Chicago, 1974.
Todaro, M. P. "A model of labor migration and urban unemployment in less developed countries," *American Economic Review* 59 (1969), 138–48.
Torres Balbás, L. et al. *Resumen histórico del urbanismo en España*, Madrid, 1954.
Tumin, M., and Feldman, A. *Social class and social change in Puerto Rico*, 2nd ed., Indianapolis, Ind., 1971.
Turner, J. "Barriers and channels for housing development in modernizing countries," *Journal of the American Institute of Planners* 33 (1967), 167–81.
"Housing priorities, settlement patterns and urban development in modernizing countries," *The Journal of the American Institute of Planners* 34 (1968), 354–63.
Housing by People: towards autonomy in building environments, New York, 1977.
and Fichter, R., eds. *Freedom to build*, New York, 1972.
Ugalde, A. *The urbanization of a poor neighborhood*, Austin, Tex., 1974.
United Nations Bureau of Social Affairs, *Report on the world social situation*, New York, 1957.
Urbanization in Latin America, New York, 1961.
United Nations Department of Economic and Social Affairs, *Demographic yearbook, 1952*, New York, 1952.
Demographic yearbook, 1963, New York, 1964.
Demographic yearbook, 1973, New York, 1974.
Demographic yearbook, 1974, New York, 1975.
Demographic yearbook, 1976, New York, 1977.
Demographic yearbook, 1977, New York, 1978.
United States Bureau of the Census. *Current population reports. Population characteristics. Persons of Spanish origin in the United States*, Washington, D.C., 1976.
United States Congressional Record, Vol. 109, August 15, 1963, 14389.
United States Department of Labor, Office of Policy Planning and Research, *The Negro family: the case for national action*, Washington, D.C., 1965.
United States Immigration and Naturalization Service. *Annual reports*, Washington, D.C., 1950–79.
Urquidi, V. L. "The underdeveloped city," in *Urbanization in Latin America: approaches and issues*, ed. J. E. Hardoy, Garden City, N.Y., 1975.
Usandizaga, E., and Havens, E. *Tres barrios de invasión: estudio de nivel de vida y actitudes en Barranquilla*, Bogotá, 1966.
Valdivia Ponce, O. *Migración interna a la metrópoli: contraste cultural, conflicto y desadaptación*, Lima, 1970.
Valentine, C. A. "The 'culture of poverty': its scientific significance and its implications for action," in *The culture of poverty: a critique*, ed. E. B. Leacock, New York, 1971.

236   *References*

van den Berghe, P. L., and Primov, G. P. *Inequality in the Peruvian Andes: class and ethnicity in Cuzco,* Columbia, Mo., 1977.
van der Spek, P. "Mexico's booming border zone: a magnet for labor-intensive American plants," *Inter-American Economic Affairs* 29 (1975), 33–47.
van Es, J. C., and Flinn, W. L. "Note on the determinants of satisfaction among urban migrants in Bogotá, Colombia," *Inter-American Economic Affairs* 27 (1973), 15–28.
Vázquez, M. C. "Proceso de migración en la comunidad de Vicos-Ancash," in *Migración en el Perú,* ed. H. F. Dobyns and M. C. Vázquez, Lima, 1963.
Viale, J. O. *Exodos campesinos en la Argentina,* Santa Fe, Argentina, 1960.
de Villegas, M. A. "Migrations and economic integration in Latin America: the Andean group," *International Migration Review* 11 (1977): 59–76.
Wagley, C. "From caste to class in northern Brazil," in *Race and class in rural Brazil,* ed. C. Wagley, New York, 1963.
  "Regionalism and cultural unity in Brazil," in *Contemporary cultures and societies of Latin America,* ed. D. B. Heath and R. N. Adams, New York, 1965.
  An introduction to Brazil, 2nd ed., New York, 1971.
  and Harris, M. "A typology of Latin American subcultures," in *Comtemporary cultures and societies of Latin America,* ed. D. B. Heath and R. N. Adams, New York, 1965.
Walters, R. S. "Laws of science and lawlike statements," in *The encyclopedia of philosophy,* vol. 4, New York, 1967.
Walton, J. "Internal colonialism: problems of definition and measurement," in *Latin American Urban Research,* vol. 5, ed. W. A. Cornelius and F. M. Trueblood, Beverly Hills, Cal., 1975.
Ward, B. "The uses of prosperity," *Saturday Review,* Aug. 29, 1964, pp. 27–9.
Ward, P. M. "The squatter settlement as slum or housing solution: evidence from Mexico City," *Land Economics* 52 (1976), 330–46.
Weaver, T., and Downing, T. E., eds. *Mexican migration,* Tucson, Ariz., 1976.
Weber, M. "Class, status, party," in *From Max Weber: essays in sociology,* ed. H. H. Gerth and C. W. Mills, New York, 1958.
Weil, T. E., et al. *Area handbook for Brazil,* 3rd ed., Washington, D.C., 1975.
Whetten, N. *Rural Mexico,* Chicago, 1948.
Whiteford, A. H. *Two cities of Latin America: a comparative description of social classes,* Garden City, N.Y., 1964.
  An Andean city at mid-century: a traditional urban society, East Lansing, Mich., 1977.
Whiteford, M. B. "Neighbors at a distance: life in a low-income Colombian barrio" in *Latin American Urban Research,* vol. 4, ed. W. A. Cornelius and F. M. Trueblood, Beverly Hills, Cal., 1974.
  "Avoiding obscuring generalizations: difference in migrants and their adaptations to an urban environment," in *New approaches to the study of migration,* ed. D. Guillet and D. Uzzell, Houston, Tex., 1976a.
  The forgotten ones: Colombian countrymen in an urban setting, Gainesville, Fla, 1976b.
Whiteford, S., and Adams, R. N. "Migration, ethnicity, and adaptation: Bolivian migrant workers in northwest Argentina," in *Migration and adaptation: implications for urban policy and development,* ed. B. DuToit and H. I. Safa, The Hague, 1975.
Whitten, N. E., Jr. *Class, kinship, and power in an Ecuadorian town: the Negroes of San Lorenzo,* Stanford, Cal., 1965.

"Strategies of adaptive mobility in the Colombian-Ecuadorian littoral," *American Anthropologist* 71 (1969), 228–42.

Black frontiersmen: a South American case, Cambridge, Mass., 1974.

and Wolfe, A. W. "Network analysis," in *Handbook of social and cultural anthropology*, ed. J. J. Honigmann, Chicago, 1973.

Wiest, R. E. "Wage-labor migration and the household in a Mexican town," *Journal of Anthropological Research* 29 (1973), 180–209.

Wilkening, E. A. et al. "Role of the extended family in migration and adaptation in Brazil," *Journal of Marriage and the Family* 30, (1968), 689–95.

Wilkie, J. "Mexico City as a magnet for Mexico's economically active population, 1930–1965," in *Statistics and National Policy*, ed. J. Wilkie, Los Angeles, Cal., 1974.

ed. *Statistical abstract of Latin America*, vol. 17, Los Angeles, Cal, 1976.

Statistical abstract of Latin America, vol. 19, Los Angeles, Cal., 1978.

Wilkie, J. R., and Wilkie, R. W. "Migration and a rural community in transition: a case study in Argentina," unpublished paper presented at the Conference on the Distribution of Population, Belmont, Md., n.d.

Wilkie, R. W. "Migration and population imbalance in the urban–rural hierarchy of Argentina," in *Environment, society and rural change in Latin America*, ed. D. A. Preston, London (n.d.).

Willems, E. "Urban classes and acculturation in Latin America," in *Urban anthropology: research perspectives and strategies*, ed. E. M. Eddy, Athens, Ga., 1968.

"Social differentiation in colonial Brazil," *Comparative Studies in Society and History* 12 (1970), 31–49.

Latin American culture: an anthropological synthesis, New York, 1975.

Willey, G. R. "Precolumbian urbanism: the central Mexican highlands and the lowland Maya," in *The rise and fall of civilizations*, ed. C. C. Lamberg-Karlovsky and J. A. Sabloff, Menlo Park, Cal., 1974.

Wirth, L. "Urbanism as a way of life," *American Journal of Sociology* 44 (1938), 1–23.

Wolf, E. R. "Aspects of group relations in a complex society: Mexico," *American Anthropologist* 58 (1956), 1065–78.

Sons of the shaking earth, Chicago, 1959.

"Kinship, friendship, and patron–client relations in complex societies," in *The social anthropology of complex societies*, ed. M. Banton, New York, 1966.

and Hansen, E. C. *The human condition in Latin America*, New York, 1972.

Yujnovsky, O. "Urban spatial configuration and land use policies in Latin America," in *Current perspectives in Latin American urban research*, ed. A. Portes and H. L. Browning, Austin, Tex., 1976.

Zangwill, I. *The melting pot*, New York, 1913.

Index

acculturation of migrants, 134, 194–7, 215n
adaptation of migrants, viii; determinants of, 103–7; and ethnicity, 134–5; and kinship, 94–8; of Mexican-Americans, 194–7; and migrant associations, 136–46, *see also* voluntary associations; preadaptation to urban life, 133; and social networks, 98–103
Africa, comparison of to Latin America, 76, 100, 107, 135, 210n
agrarian reform, 78, 80, 88, 203n
agricultural sector: and economic development, 50; mechanization of, 42, 44, 83; and out-migration, 40, 42, 53, 62, 63, 66, 82–3, 85–6; and urban growth, 202, 205n; *see also* land tenure
Argentina: Bolivian migration to, 171–2; class consciousness in, 134; European migration to, 114, 124–5, 136, 171; internal migration in, 45, 46, 82; international migration to, 172, 173; population growth in, 29; population movements in, 44, 207n; reasons for return migration in, 44, 207n; social classes in, 112; social mobility in, 126–7
assimilation of migrants, 194–7, 215n
Aztecs, 1, 5, 6–7

blacks, 12, 14, 15, 21, 25, 55, 63, 127–8, 128–31, 134–5, 150, 180, 196, 211n; *see also* slavery
Bogotá (Colombia), 10, 53, 61, 69, 70, 76, 206n
bracero program, 182–4
"brain drain": *see* out-migration
Brazil: class consciousness in, 134; colonial urban settlement in, 12; European migration to, 125, 170–1; migration in, 41, 42–3, 205n, 207n; population growth in, 29; race relations in, 129, 131; selectivity of migrants in, 206n; social mobility in, 125; social stratification in, 109–10, 121–2
brokerage: and *barriada* associations, 163; cultural and economic, 76; definitions of, 79–81, 82; in Jalisco, Mexico, 80, 81, 86–7; and squatter settlement *caciques*, 163–4; in Vicos, Peru, 79
Buenos Aires (Argentina), 29, 30, 53, 95, 132, 133, 206n

Caciquismo, 46
Cali (Colombia), 68, 69, 134
campesinos: see peasants
capitalism, 8, 27, 28, 110, 149, 173, 199–202, 203n
Caribbean, 96, 213n
Cartagena (Colombia), 10, 15, 129, 130
casta system, 20, 21, 22, 24, 25, 110
Chan-Chan, 4
Chicago school of urban sociology, x, 91–2, 147
Chile: class consciousness in, 134; out-migration in, 41, 65, 70, 205n; political attitudes in, 212n; return migration in, 75; selectivity of migrants in, 48, 206n; social networks in, 122
Chinese Exclusion Act, 178, 179, 214n
Chuschi (Peru), 81, 88
cities: administrative/agricultural, 10–11; coastal, 10; colonial, 9, 10, 26; criteria for, 3; heterogenetic, 8; industrial, 28; orthogenetic, 8; pre-Hispanic, 1–3, 4, 5; preindustrial, 27, 28; primate, 29–30, 204n; regal/ritual, 4, 5; stereotypes of, x
class: *see* social class
Coalición de Pueblos Mixtecos Oaxaqueños, 210n
Colombia: divorce in, 96; ethnic identity in, 134; housing in, 157; migrant selectivity in, 206n; reasons for migration in, 42, 48; return migration in, 76; social mobility in, 125, 131, 132; *la violencia* in, 45; voluntary associations in, 141
colonial period, 2, 8, 9, 12–25
community development projects, 208n
community differentiation, 65
compadrazgo, 88, 155; *see also* kinship and family
conservatism, 89–90
corporate groups, 93–4
Cortés, Fernando, 1, 2, 15
cosmopolitanism, 62, 64
Costa Rica, 41, 205n, 206n, 207n
creoles, 13, 18, 22, 23, 24
cultural mediation: *see* brokerage
"culture of poverty" concept, 148–51, 156, 161, 211n
Cuzco (Peru): as colonial city, 11, 15, 18; as Inca capital, 1, 2, 4–5, 6

239

out-migration (*continued*)
cultural labor, 83; social and political
effects of, 87–90

paleteros, 80, 86–7
Panama City, 10, 207n
panelinhas, 121–2, 128
Paraguay, 45, 207n
patron–client relationships, 14, 80, 124, 126,
141; *see also* brokerage
peasants, 7, 9, 11, 38, 42, 46, 48, 49, 55, 64,
68, 71, 203n
peninsulares, 13, 18, 21, 23; *see also* creoles;
Spaniards
Peru: agrarian reform in, 78, 88; authority
of women in, 55; and dependency concepts, 201; kinship relations in, 97; migrant selectivity in, 206n, 207n; migration in, 45, 205n; squatter settlements
in, 155; voluntary associations in, 88,
138
Peru–Cornell project, 78–9, 208–9n
plantation work, 14, 54, 55
political organization: in Peru, 88; in Tilantongo, 88–90; of urban poor, viii, 151,
152, 155, 158–9, 160–7; of voluntary
associations, 145
Popayán (Colombia): marriage patterns in,
95; migration to, 47, 49, 58, 68, 204n;
politicization in, 166; return migration
to, 73; social status in, 112, 116; *la violencia,* 45; voluntary associations in,
141
Portobello (Panama), 10
Portugal, 9, 12
Potosí (Mexico), 10
Potosí (in Peruvian viceroyalty), 10
pottery making, 52, 86
poverty, 41, 44, 58, 68, 211n; *see also* "culture of poverty"
power structures, 13, 19, 24, 88, 112
preadaptation to urban life, 133
pre-Hispanic civilization, 1–8; *see also* Aztecs; Incas; Mayas; Olmecs
prestige, 13, 19, 20, 25, 88; *see also* social
stratification
psychological and personal factors in migration, 44, 51, 52, 62, 65; *see also* decision making
Puebla (Mexico), 20, 105–6
push–pull model of migration: *see* migration

race mixture, 18, 20–1, 22, 25
race relations, 20, 23, 127–31, 145–6; *see
also* ethnicity
Recife (Brazil), 15, 204n

regional associations: *see* voluntary associations
repartimiento, 14
repatriation campaigns of Mexicans by
United States, 181
return migration: *see* migration
Rio de Janeiro (Brazil): *favelas* in, 147, 152,
153, 159, 165–6, 211n; marriage patterns in, 95; middle class of, 119, 120;
political attitudes in, 212n; population
growth in, 29, 30; voluntary associations in, 204n
ritual and return migration, 88
rural proletariat, 55
rural–urban migration: *see* migration

Salvador (Brazil), 12, 15
San Juan (Puerto Rico), 151, 156, 163
San Salvador (El Salvador), 60, 61, 206n
Santiago (Chile): middle class of, 119; migrant selectivity in, 48, 53, 61, 207n;
migration to, 41, 48, 64, 65–6, 75,
208n; population decline in, 70; population growth in, 30; slums in, 158–9;
squatter settlements in, 147
Santo Domingo, 9, 10
São Paulo (Brazil), 12, 53, 207n
seasonal labor, 67
selectivity of migrants: *see* migrants
sex, selectivity by, 53, 54–8
slavery: of blacks, 14, 18, 20, 25; in Brazil,
110; of Indians, 14
social change, 33, 78–9
social class: antagonism and out-migration,
87; consciousness of, 166–7; and ethnicity, 134–5; lower class, 124, 125, 126,
127–8, 134–5, 136, *see also* "culture of
poverty"; middle class, 118–24, 129,
130; and migration, 131–5; and race,
22–3; and underdevelopment, 200; upper class, 115–18, 124, 125, 126, 130;
see also social stratification
social estate system, 12, 20
social mobility, 24, 27, 34, 54–8, 122–8,
129–31, 134–5, 212n
social networks, 52, 55, 58, 93, 94, 97, 98–
103, 121–2, 136–7
social stratification: colonial, 12, 13, 17, 19–
25; definitions of, 18–19; dual-sector
model of, 111–14, 120; and race relations, 128–31; and squatter settlements,
156; *see also* social classes
social structure of urban areas, 12–32, 61,
65, 91–2, 203n
socioeconomic integration, 82
Spain, 8, 9, 13

Spaniards, 12, 13, 24; *see also* creoles; *peninsulares*
squatter settlements, viii, 91, 99, 140, 147, 151–67, 210n, 211n

Tenochtitlán, 1, 2, 5, 7, 8, 11
Teotihuacán, 5, 6
Tepoztlán (Mexico), 45, 48, 92
Tiahuanaco, 4
Tikal, 5, 6
Tilantongo (Mexico): brokers in, 76–7; effects of out-migration on, 82–3, 86; entrepreneurs in, 81; group organization of migrants from, 210n; and migration, 46–7, 53, 62, 63, 67; politics in, 89–90; retention of property rights in, 78; return migration to, 73–4, 75, 88; urban networks of migrants from, 101; use of life histories in, 73
tourism, 53, 191, 213n
trade, 6, 9, 10, 19, 20, 25, 55, 56
traza: see grid plan
Turner hypothesis of environmental forms, 157–60
Tzintzuntzan (Mexico), 53, 60, 75–6, 86

underdevelopment of Latin American nations, 198–202, 211n
unemployment: *see* occupation
union organization, 123, 141
United States of America: Asian immigrants to, 179; border region of, 188–94; illegal aliens in, 185–8; immigration legislation, 175, 181, 183, 184, 213–14n; Latin American migration to, 85, 173–97, 207n, 208n, 213n, 214n; and Latin American underdevelopment, 199–202; matrifocality in, 96; Mexican commuters to, 189–91; restrictionists, 181–2; as a source of cultural ideals, 116; and squatter settlements, 151
United States Border Industrial Program, 191–4
United States Immigration and Naturalization Service, 214n

urban anthropology: *see* urban studies
urban growth, 30, 67, 199–202, 203n; *see also* demographic statistics
urbanism: definitions of, ix–x, 3; pre-Hispanic, 4–8; stages of, 26; theory of, ix, 92; and voluntary associations, 136; *see also* urbanization
urbanization: definitions of, viii–ix, 34, 204n; and ethnic identity, 135; and fertility, 31–2; of migrants, 70–1, 98; and modernization, 198–9; pre-Hispanic, 2; primary type, 7; and race relations, 130–1, 135; secondary type, 8; theory of, ix; *see also* urbanism
urban planning and policy making, viii, 9, 11, 12, 159–60, 202
"urban revolution," 2, 3
urban studies, viii, x, 41–2, 64, 199, 200–2; methodology of, 62, 66, 73, 115–16; *see also* Peru–Cornell project
Uruguay, 206n, 207n

Venezuela, 31, 44, 69, 206n
Veracruz (Mexico), 1, 10, 15, 67
Vicos hacienda: *see* Peru–Cornell project
violence, 45–6, 47
voluntary associations: of *barriadas,* 163–4; definitions of, 209–10n; of ethnic groups, 134, 137–8; in Guatemala City, 103; in Peru, 88, 100–1, 155; and political organization, 163–4

Women: and birth control, 175–6; as domestic servants, 57–8, 57, table 2; in Guatemala, 77–8; and land tenure in Michoacán, 85; and migrant selectivity, 36, 54–5, 206n, 207n; and migration and fertility, 31–2; and out-migration, 82, 207n; and race mixture, 20, 23; and voluntary assoications, 141, 142–3; and work, 55; *see also* kinship and family; marriage patterns; matrifocality; race mixture

Zacatecas, 10